THE WOOLWORTHS

THE
WOOL

James

McGRAW-HILL
NEW YORK   St. LOUIS
TORONTO

WORTHS

Brough

BOOK COMPANY

SAN FRANCISCO

HAMBURG   MEXICO

1 2 3 4 5 6 7 8 9 D O D O 8 7 6 5 4 3 2

ISBN 0-07-008142-5

LIBRARY OF CONGRESS CATALOGING IN PUBLICATION DATA

Brough, James, 1918-
The Woolworths.
1. Woolworth family.   I. Title.
HF5465.U6W826   381'.45'000922 [B]   81-19389
ISBN 0-07-008142-5   AACR2

Book design by Roberta Rezk

Books by James Brough include:

The Vixens

Consuelo: Portrait of an American Heiress

Miss Lillian Russell

The Ford Dynasty

The Prince and the Lily

An Untold Story (with Elliott Roosevelt)

ঙ] Contents [ও

If a man is wise, he gets
rich an' if he gets rich, he gets
foolish, or his wife does. That's
what keeps the money movin' around.

Finley Peter Dunne
("Mr. Dooley")

1

Once
⊲] Upon a Time [⊳

The location was always downtown, where the shopping crowd strolled the sidewalks and the streetcars clanged. It seemed there wasn't a city without one of those stores with its stacks of rock-bottom bargains piled up behind the plate-glass windows and gilt letters marching across a scarlet front identifying F. W. WOOLWORTH CO.

There was usually a cluster of people peering in through the panes for a preview of current attractions. Inside, neat lines of counters held the everythings of commonplace living. The sweet smell of a mountain of candy blended with the heady tang of *Evening in Paris*; in the sheet music department a phonograph or a piano played *Stormy Weather*.

The crowd sauntered up, down and across the aisles, wandering on past tell-your-weight and read-your-fortune slot machines to the rear of the place, where pots and pans glittered on the racks.

So far, there had been only one visible break with a fifty-year-old tradition. The banner that read "No Article in This Store Over 10 Cents" suddenly disappeared. Overnight, the limit had been hiked to an unprecedented twenty cents. There had been an augury of what was ahead when a few items had begun to be sold piece by piece: a hammer head for a dime, perhaps, and the handle priced at the same figure.

1

But ten cents still bought lead soldiers, a squirt gun or a cowboy wristwatch for Sonny; a paper doll, a movie-star cutout kit or a bag of sweetheart candy for Sis. As birthdays accumulated (cards for all occasions available in Stationery) Sonny could walk out with his first razor blades at a nickel each, Sis with hair curlers, a lipstick or, if she'd been raised a homebody, a spool of sewing thread, any one of them for a dime.

Mom, with a purseful of change, could make a head start on equipping a kitchen, including the curtain rods. Knives, forks, crystal glasses, salt and pepper shakers, containers for coffee and tea, whisks, ladles, potato mashers, cake turners, measuring cups, can openers—no item on the list cost more than ten puny pennies.

The shabbiest came only to look and dream of the day when times must improve because they could scarcely get any worse. The next echelon, a little better placed on the social scale, dipped into their purses for a quarter or two to replace some used-up or worn-out essentials from Housewares or Toiletries; anything beyond that had to wait on an upcoming payday.

Then there were the ladies whose lives had been dented but not disrupted by adversity. Woolworth's was a godsend when a family was forced onto a budget and more and more customers bade a regretful "so long" to the department stores.

Finally, there was the carriage trade, whose Packards and La-Salles were parked along the curb outside. Taking a turn around Woolly's, as some of them were known to call it, remained for them what it had always been: such *fun* and so *convenient*.

Part of a shopper's pleasure lay in discovering the unexpected, some new line introduced because it had dropped within the twenty-cent range now that the austerity of the 1930s was clobbering the manufacturers.

Mr. Woolworth put no trust in paid advertising. No newspaper, magazine or radio station trumpeted the merits of his goods. No-nonsense signs in the windows lured the crowds in: *Water Wavers for Bobbed Hair 10¢ Each . . . Our New Line of White Enamelware Is Now Complete; Our Highest Price 10¢ . . . Visit Our Sanitary Lunch Department; Quality Food; Quick Service; No Portion Over 10¢.*

Exactly who was in charge here? Who commanded the flood tide of stock whose level seemed never to ebb? No floorwalkers patrolled these premises. Responsibility for it all surely didn't rest with skimpily paid salesgirls, uniformed in black, killing idle moments by patting their marcelled waves.

Christmas was the best of times. The whole place became Toyland, with counters piled high with dolls and games, tree ornaments and tinsel, winking lights and gigantic cardboard candy canes, *"Jingle Bells"* ringing out from the music department, electric fans blowing mist off the front windows.

For the millions of customers, Mr. Woolworth represented a kind of all-season Santa Claus. Had he, in fact, been an image of benignity or something different? Whatever he had made of himself, he was no Saint Nicholas. And more than a few people regarded the richest of the Woolworth heirs—plump, pretty, petulant Barbara Hutton—as the most despicable woman in America.

2

❧ A Giant in the Field ❧

He was a man of unbounded appetites—for power, money, social status, women and, most noticeably, for heaped-up plates of the food he had missed as a boy put to work on his father's hardscrabble farm. Now the scales showed his weight creeping up again toward two hundred and fifty pounds, and his jowls overflowed his stiff white collars. But in that age when fat was fashionable, Frank Winfield Woolworth carried less of it on his frame than did William Howard Taft, the current resident of the White House.

Frank, fifty-nine last birthday, was five years older, but in looks the resemblance between the two men was so strong that he liked to emphasize it. Their ponderous mustaches were almost identical. The chief executive wore tall silk hats as a mark of eminence; so did this faithful Republican party follower of his. The first presidential automobile in history was assigned to Will; Frank bought himself a Renault and engaged a chauffeur. When Taft took up the new game called golf and Woolworth equipped himself with a set of clubs, it was impossible to judge who outdid whom as a duffer on the fairway.

The president dozed off in public sometimes, but that was something the dime-store magnate was never seen to do, no matter how low he was feeling in health or spirit. On occasion, however, when tension built within him, he broke into tears. The office in which he sat on this momentous February day of 1912 had been the scene of the last outburst two weeks ago, when he stretched out on the couch with tears streaming down his cheeks, devastated by the thought of losing Jessie May, the youngest of his three daughters, in marriage to a dandified fortune hunter.

But today he was in control of himself and the entire situation. The stage was set for the greatest financial achievement of his thirty-three years in business, the birth of a $65,000,000 corporation that he insisted must carry only his name, omitting reference to any of the other men who would become his partners.

Through the windows, closed tight against the cold this morning, he could look across lower Broadway to New York's City Hall. If he opened them an inch or two, he could hear, above the clatter of wagon wheels on the pavement outside, the din of the construction job under way a stone's throw farther downtown. This was another endeavor he was planning to impress the universe at large. The structural steel of the Woolworth skyscraper was rising simultaneously with the founding of his new company. When he moved into his quarters there, he intended to make them the most spectacular in the western world. "The five-and-ten business," he preached, "is no longer a Cheap John affair. We cater to the masses, but we have gained the respect and trade also of the medium and wealthy classes. We ought to feel proud."

He had eaten his usual multiple-course breakfast and dressed with his usual care in a dark business suit of English cut, its sobriety relieved by the gold of his cufflinks and the diamond stickpin in his tie. Now he sat in command of this meeting of relatives, friends and old colleagues who regarded themselves as his peers, each of them a millionaire self-made from the sale of pots and pans, ribbons and thread, pencils and candy.

He carried in his head the arithmetic of their individual worth. Cousin Seymour Knox owned ninety-eight stores in the United States and Canada, which brought in $13,047,745 a year. Pudgy little Seymour, dressed to the hilt from buttoned-up boots to crisp winged collar, was the smartest of the bunch, in Frank's estimation. His cousin also had an ability Frank himself lacked— knowing how to enjoy himself as a new-rich country squire with a stableful of harness horses.

Then there was Frank's younger brother, Charles Sumner

Woolworth, lean and mournful with a gold watch chain strad-dling his vest. He had been content to follow Frank—never to challenge him. Sum, which was his nickname, ran fifteen stores of his own, selling an annual $1,207,849 worth of merchandise.

Lanky, saturnine Earle Charlton was there, his black hair parted in the middle. He had pioneered the nickel-and-dime trade west of the Rockies to give him a total of thirty-five outlets in the United States, eighteen in Canada, and a gross income of $4,070,683 in the past twelve months.

Fred Kirby, with his boots unpolished, suit unpressed and domed head almost bald, looked as though he was still what they had all once been, a clerk behind a dry-goods counter. Yet he had built a chain of ninety-six stores and sales of $7,253,036.

One face was missing. Old William Moore, who would be seventy-one next August, had not been well enough to travel down from Watertown in Jefferson County, New York, where a sign supplied by Frank identified Moore's modest operation as *Birthplace of 5 and 10¢ Stores*. He had only one other shop, managed by his son Louis in Schenectady. Both places brought in only $149,776 a year, but for sentiment's sake William had to be part of Frank's new empire, with a guaranteed share of the certain profits.

Frank had more stores than all the others could count between them—319 Woolworth locations in thirty-seven of the states and the District of Columbia, plus a dozen more in England. As verified by his accountants, Touche, Niven & Company, his assets stood at exactly $15,962,007.19, compared with a combined $14,802,243.72 for the others. And Frank, who preferred cash to any amount of credit, had a fat $607,214.58 on hand and in the bank, while Seymour could muster a mere $56,310.58. There was to be no further challenge to his cousin, who was master of the house.

The six men had invariably been allies, not rivals. The unwritten rules under which they had cooperated barred competition between them. They pooled their business secrets. By common consent, Frank and his staff did much of the bulk buying for the group. Placing orders for nearly six hundred outlets at a time gave him power to drive harder bargains with suppliers than any one of the six acting alone could have obtained.

Woolworth, a giant in the field of chain stores, viewed that field as a battleground. If the selling of groceries, drug products, clothing and cigars was included, the number of such stores came close to seven thousand. Frank behaved as if sheer size made him as vulnerable as Goliath to David's slingshot.

He suspected his competitors of plotting to unite in a $5,000,000 corporation to steal away his customers. He fancied the ringleader had to be Sebastian Spering Kresge, hated by Frank for his success in putting together a competitive chain and for his sanctimonious principles—Kresge was a generous contributor to the fighting fund of the Anti-Saloon League in its campaign, being waged at present by Mrs. Carrie A. Nation of Kansas with her vengeful hatchet, to wipe out the liquor trade. Frank had no sympathy with that cause: he was a man who enjoyed a few drinks.

He had detected discord developing among the coalition of relatives and comrades. There was danger of their overstepping the boundary lines they had previously agreed to establish between their respective territories. If overtures were made by Kresge's forces, Frank wondered how long his associates might resist.

So last spring he had sent invitations to the five of them, asking them to join him in a secret meeting at the Waldorf-Astoria to explore the possibility of a formal merger. The advantages were obvious. An enormous increase in buying power would enable them to drive manufacturers' and wholesalers' prices even lower. The new empire would be too big for any rival to attack. Profits could be maximized by applying standard procedures to all their stores.

But haggling over pennies was a way of life for them, and they proceeded to argue over figures running into tens of millions. How to divide the stock in order to slice the pie? Who should sit on the board of directors and what titles should they hold? Where to locate the head office when Seymour Knox had settled down in Buffalo, New York; Fred Kirby in Wilkes-Barre, Pennsylvania; Earle Charlton in Fall River, Massachusetts; Sum Woolworth in Scranton, Pennsylvania; and William Moore in Watertown?

The debate, switched to rooms in the Plaza Hotel, had lasted until June. By then, only one stumbling block remained: the question of identification. Every one of them was proud to see his name spread across a storefront and trusted that somehow this could continue.

Frank dug in his heels and cited the arithmetic. They yielded to his pressure, and the sessions were suspended until September, when the finishing touches were applied to the agreement they had hammered out before Frank broke the news on November 2.

"F. W. Woolworth announces that a corporation is about to be formed with a capital stock of $65,000,000, of which $15,000,000 will be preferred stock and $50,000,000 common. . . . The name of the new corporation will be the F. W. Woolworth Company." One detail of his victory went unmentioned: every store would be painted in Woolworth colors, scarlet and gold.

Today, as they gathered in his office, the groundwork was complete. Balance sheets from the accountants and employment contracts drawn by the lawyers were stacked ready for signature. It was a date that earned a place in the record books for another reason. On this Wednesday, February 14, the forty-eighth state, Arizona, finally entered the Union less than two months after the forty-seventh, New Mexico. The West was won, the map was filled, and the frontier stretched to the shores of the Pacific. Woolworth's founders were eager to make the most of their opportunity.

Minutes of the meeting could have been constructed along these lines:

Mr. Woolworth, quoting from a prepared letter he was about to sign, declared, "Gentlemen, I believe the business is still in its infancy and capable under the new organization of great future development."

Mr. Knox agreed, foreseeing expansion in the West, which the group had formerly regarded as Mr. Charlton's exclusive domain.

Mr. Charlton made the lighthearted suggestion that Mr. Knox accompany him on an exploratory visit there, saying, "I know you can't handle an automobile, but there's horseflesh for hire."

Mr. Woolworth, joining in the jest, advised them to be on the alert for earthquakes, citing the destruction by fire of one of Mr. Charlton's stores in San Francisco in 1906.

Mr. Charlton reminded his colleagues that he had reopened at a new location within thirty days of the catastrophe.

Mr. Kirby asked whether Mr. Charlton had detected any falloff in his Canadian business as a result of that country's rejection of President Taft's attempt to reduce United States tariffs on imported goods, which were a mainstay of F. W. Woolworth Co. (The President's desire, known as Reciprocity, was to eliminate or lower almost all duties on farm products and a variety of manufacturers' goods traded between the two countries. But Canadian suspicions that this was a plot for the annexation of Canada led voters there to defeat Reciprocity despite its support by the American Congress.)

Mr. Charlton replied that no adverse effects had been observed, since "a lot of Canucks would prefer to see the Stars and Stripes flying over Ottawa."

Mr. Woolworth accepted Mr. Charlton's opinion because he had many Canadians in his employ at his mill in Fall River, Massachusetts.

Mr. Kirby wondered what news on the subject had been received from her family by Mrs. Frank W. Woolworth, a native of Picton, Ontario.

Mr. Woolworth answered that she had fallen somewhat out of touch, due to health reasons.

Mr. Charles S. Woolworth apologized for again raising the question of the new corporation's status vis-à-vis the antitrust law, whose recent application in the courts had brought about the disruption of the Standard Oil Company and the American Tobacco Company.

Mr. Frank W. Woolworth reassured him that the Sherman Act did not apply. "The trusts force prices up with tariffs and every other trick; we force prices down for everybody's benefit."

Mr. Charles pointed out that President Taft was cracking down with twice as many lawsuits as President Roosevelt had ever filed.

Mr. Frank demanded to know how the new corporation could be considered a monopoly "when our competitors are forever fighting us tooth and nail."

Mr. Charles quoted a paragraph from the prospectus prepared for F. W. Woolworth Co.: "These companies have never in any way been competitors in the sale of goods nor has any of them maintained or operated a store in any city or town in which any other of said companies has maintained or operated a store." Did the choice of language make them liable for investigation under the terms of the Sherman Antitrust Act?

Mr. Frank cut off the discussion by saying he had no objection to signing the prospectus in its present form.

* * *

The mechanics of the merger were straightforward. The combined capital of the six allies constituted the entire capital of the new empire. The percentage of each man's contribution to the pot determined the percentage of his holdings in the new corporation. The arrangement gave Frank more than fifty percent of everything.

But outside investors were excluded, and the founding fathers were hungry for extra cash. Some stock must be offered on Wall Street to create a market. Next Monday, February 19, would see the first block of unseasoned Woolworth securities offered for sale—$7,000,000 worth of the common and $6,000,000 worth of the preferred. The proceeds would be split among the founders on the same percentages as their initial investments. No more stock was to be released for at least a year, but for senior employees they set aside $1,500,000 either in preferred or common; staff members could choose between paying $100 a share for the preferred or $50 for the common.

"I would call that as close to a guaranteed seven percent investment as anybody can find," said Seymour Knox, "when net for the past three years averages almost five times that figure."

Sum, changing the subject, asked his brother if word had come from Jessie May on her honeymoon with James Donahue.

"They should be somewhere halfway across Canada by now. Then they'll spend some time in California, and we'll have her back in New York with us toward the end of March."

"What's her husband plan on doing?" said Charlton.

"He'll probably take her rollerskating, which is how she met him in the first place."

Frank should have felt much happier than he did at the moment. He had accomplished everything he had set out to do. As president and principal stockholder, his dominance of the new venture was complete. Yet instead of being elated, he was listless and morose. The pain in his swollen legs made for fitful sleep. At night he would leave his bed and prowl his imposing house on

Fifth Avenue's Millionaires'Row to seek relief in the sound of music, with which he could fill every room in the place.

Kirby suggested he should take a vacation now that every last detail of the deal was taken care of. "I want to see my building up and open first," replied Frank. "I raised that magnificent building when I was a boy. My folks were poor, as you all know, and we lived in a very small house. Back of our house there were piles of stones, and I started to build a house of my own."

Knox warned him against overstraining himself again. Another voyage to Europe might do him a world of good, perhaps aboard the new Cunarder, the *Titanic*, which would be docking in New York on her maiden voyage toward the end of April.

Somebody had to supervise the construction job to keep the workmen on their toes, Frank said, and he guessed it had to be himself.

But he was paying an architect and a contractor for that, said Kirby, and he quoted from the formal letter Frank had signed as an item on the agenda: "In my judgement, the organization of the company has been so perfected as to render the conduct and further development of the business independent of the individuality of any one person." It was no longer a one-man band.

"That's in reference to the company, not to my building."

Knox knew when to stop arguing. "Have it your own way, Frank. You've always tried to."

A photographer came in and the five men posed by the desk at which Frank was sitting. Three of them—Frank, Sum and Kirby—were once farm boys. Knox had been a dissatisfied schoolmaster, Charlton a traveler in housewares. Together, they had fallen into step with the pace of progress and produced a kind of miracle. The prospectus that was en route to the printer said, "We employ about 20,000 people and cater to about three million customers a day." In the first stores each of them had once opened, their combined seed money had amounted to less than $10,000.

The camera captured no joy on any of their faces. To judge by their expressions, they might have been paying their respects at a wake. Their gatherings had been livelier when they met long ago in a backyard in Brooklyn, where shy Jennie Woolworth served refreshments, then hurried back into her kitchen.

William Moore wrote to Frank from Watertown that week.

"Yesterday I turned over to the new company the keys I have held for more than fifty-five years with feelings of gratitude to you for the honors you have been instrumental in heaping upon me, which I am unable to express in words. . . . When three score years and ten covers your head, I pray you may be as happy as I am."

Woolworth stock had been traded on a "when issued" basis on the New York Curb, predecessor of the American Exchange, from the time Frank's preliminary announcement the previous November. For the February 19 opening, the banks set a price of 101½ on the preferred, 55 on the common. At the close of that day's trading, the prices had soared to 109 and 80¾.

In the course of those few days, Edna, prettiest of the daughters of Frank and Jennie, became pregnant. The child she would bear later that year had much of her grandfather's nature in her. She was willful, extravagant, and she indulged herself heedless of the cost or the consequences. She was christened Barbara Hutton, and in her generation she was the most celebrated spendthrift in the western world.

3

᭡ On Millionaires' Row ᭢

One increasingly conspicuous asset went unmentioned in the application filed on June 26 with the New York Stock Exchange, seeking a listing of Woolworth's common stock. There was no hint of the tallest habitable structure in the world, identified in mammoth lettering as "The Magnificent Woolworth Building," whose steel skeleton pierced the skyline on lower Broadway.

Woolworth had manifested earlier symptoms of what the French diagnosed as *la manie de bâtir,* the mania to build that afflicted Pharaohs and emperors and then became endemic among Frank's generation of American tycoons. His first attack had resulted in the house he currently dwelt in, 990 Fifth Avenue, which with its thirty rooms was one of Manhattan's minor landmarks. His previous home, a rented downtown brownstone, had grown much too cramped and insignificant to suit a man in his circumstances.

In the pecking order of society, the wealthier neighbors had ignored an upstart tradesman's family. With his oldest daughter, Lena, already out of her teens by then and the other two, Jessie and Edna, following close behind her, he had wanted a milieu where they might meet more congenial people and make new friends.

But, above all, the move had been made because of Jennie. He wanted his wife to assume a place in society with him, yet she was

13

increasingly withdrawn, effacing herself while he reveled in possessing more money than he had ever believed possible. One cause for her retreat from his universe emerged in a message he distributed among his senior staff.

"For the first time in twenty years I spent the night before Christmas at home. It's the last time I'll do so. I'd probably be of little service to any store, yet it is pleasanter to be in the fight at the last moment than to wait at home in suspense."

She was driven into retreat by Frank's neglect. He surrounded her with material luxuries, but he withheld companionship, too absorbed in his business to pay more than fleeting attention to her emotional needs. Jennie, in her middle age, was overwhelmed at finding herself so alone.

She had been brought up in poverty, the eldest child among eight sons and daughters of Thomas Creighton, who was a widower. Jennie had substituted as the mother in the household and had continued in the role after she began earning a little money by sewing dresses and mending clothes for a handful of customers in the tiny town on the northern bank of Lake Ontario where most of its people worked in its canning factories.

She was still in her teens when she handed over her housekeeping chores to her younger sisters and ventured south in search of a better-paid living in the United States, an unschooled, pretty blonde with no employable skill except with a needle and thread. She was only twenty when she met and was married to Frank, expecting no more than to play some part in his life, bear his children, and run his household for him, like any other woman of her day who would scarcely have recognized the word "liberation."

The fortune he had made had certainly liberated her from the chores of cooking and cleaning and mothering their daughters. It had also left her without anything else to occupy her time. She had no interest in charitable causes or votes for women. Politics held no more appeal for her than did pouring tea from a silver pot for ladies who looked down on her.

So in her idleness she gained weight and her hands, once roughened by hard work, were as soft as a gentlewoman's. Frank was puzzled by the deterioration he saw in her mind and body. She had stayed cooped up in the house too long. What she needed, he thought, whether it appealed to her or not, was a taste of the fashionable world outside. He was never happier than when he stayed in a grand hotel in London or Paris or Vienna. Until his new Fifth Avenue mansion was built to impress the snobs, he would move the whole family into a suite of rooms in some suitably elegant establishment in Manhattan.

Choosing where to stay was a problem only because the city suddenly had more new hotels than the average citizen could keep track of. The Waldorf, whose thirteen stories overlooked a corner of 34th Street, was the tallest and perhaps the most sumptuous, although Mrs. William Backhouse Astor, the dowager empress of Gotham society, resented it as an unforgivable intrusion into what she wished to retain as her territorial domain. Another Astor, Colonel William, was backing the Astoria, which was to be four floors higher and even flossier when it was erected on an opposite corner.

The red-brick Plaza accorded its guests the most rustic views of Central Park. Devotees of the eleven-story, white stone Holland House at 30th Street regarded it as the most convenient when every room was equipped with what was termed an *annunciator* that, at the turn of a dial, brought a valet, maid, housekeeper, waiter or bellboy tapping on the door.

When the Savoy arose by the southeast entrance to Central Park, the newspapers claimed the Holland House could not hold a candle to the new Savoy with its interiors "fit for an Oriental potentate." The whole structure, said another, was "of Arabian Nights magnificence." The Savoy, Frank concluded, was the spot he had been looking for as a home away from home.

In the salon of a suite embellished with marble and damask, onyx and mahogany, he installed the only musical instrument he could play—a mechanical marvel of the era, a grand piano whose harmonies were determined by perforated fiber rolls revolving on a cylinder when pressure was applied to the pedals. He sat at it by the hour, pumping out recitals of Chopin, Liszt and Beethoven, fascinated by the rippling keys, pausing only to feed in a fresh cylinder from the library of them he was collecting, hands aloft as if he were conducting an orchestra.

Yet for all the splendor of his new quarters and his desire for greater glory, it was impossible for him to give up the patterns of his past. He still sniffed around the city for bargains in factory rejects, job lots and discontinued lines. He boasted to his staff of coming across some thermometers at $7.50 a gross ("although it was awful hard work") and a consignment of chinaware that included chamberpots. "The last item," he declared, "should be a 'corker.'"

He kept a hawk's watch over the cash figures, large or small. When Manhattan banks imposed a collection charge of a tenth of one percent for clearing checks from out of town, he instantly switched accounts to Philadelphia. Staff bonuses for Christmas must not be handed out, he ruled, until December 24 or maybe December 26. "Our object is to secure the services of our clerks at a time of the year when competitors are tempting them with higher wages."

Fear of the competition was always the goad that drove him to grant a boost in wages. "If you get hold of a good girl," he instructed his managers, "pay her a little more to keep her from going to some other store. Some of our stores should not pay less than $3 a week." He insisted that the money be well earned. "The help can do the window washing and cleaning, even varnishing woodwork. When they work late, don't pay them extra but let them come in later the next day."

If Jennie had been left with any kind of job to do, the pace of her decline might have been slowed. But in a hotel she lived in a void with nothing except concern for her daughters to occupy her time. Existence for Jennie was empty without meals to cook, clothes to mend, rooms to clean and a husband to care for. But Frank allowed nobody in his family to work apart from himself, and work for him remained a compulsion.

Her lack of social ambition was bewildering to him. The wives of other wealthy men found a host of activities to keep them busy, with or without a husband at their side. Caroline Astor patronized the opera and entertained the upper crust of society at her weekly dinner parties. Alva Vanderbilt, an Alabama planter's daughter, had outdone Caroline with a series of costume balls. Mrs. Stuyvesant Fish captivated the elite with her banquets, including one at which the favors for the guests turned out to be boxed white mice. With receptions to be organized, soirées to be conducted, couturiers' collections to be inspected, and social calls to complete the afternoons, there was no end of things a woman could find to fill the days.

But Jennie flinched at the prospect of being jeered at for her ignorance and lack of polish. Throughout her stay at the Savoy, she remained secure within her shell, looking forward to the time they would again live in their own home where there would be a kitchen to work in, if Frank ever permitted her to cook.

The mansion at 990 Fifth Avenue was finally ready and the move into it made in 1901. With Woolworth sales the previous year bounding beyond $5,000,000, the cash was there to pay every bill as it was presented—the architect's, the contractor's, the interior decorator's, the art galleries' and the Aeolian-Skinner Organ Company's.

The organ, Frank's greatest pleasure, stood in the drawing room on the second floor, an organ of sufficient capacity to fill, or empty, a church. It was designed along the same lines as a player piano, with rolls turning on a motor-driven cylinder. Frank, maestro of automatic music, "would have made an outstanding orchestra conductor," according to an Aeolian-Skinner spokesman.

The marvelous machine had some built-in features of the owner's devising. In addition to the electric starter button in the console, there was another to douse the normal lighting of the room and a third that produced an instantaneous *son et lumière* performance, causing a series of light bulbs hidden behind a ceiling cornice to glow alternately or in combinations of amber, heliotrope and green throughout the show. His granddaughter Barbara remembered his concerts as a sort of magic act.

Frank's new address put him precisely where he wanted to be, on the most fashionable stretch of dwellings to be found anywhere in a house he reckoned could hold its own among the French chateaux, Italian *palazzos* and Spanish alcazars that studded the street—even with "Carnegie Castle," the baronial bastion of the Scottish-born steel magnate. Wiseacre drivers of the horse-drawn omnibuses that trundled past with their loads of out-of-town tourists began to name Woolworth among the two hundred millionaires who allegedly owned property along the route running north from Washington Square.

The Jay Gould residence at 47th Street, an outmoded brownstone, was nothing spectacular, and neither was Mrs. Robert Goelet's a little farther along. But visitors' eyes started to bulge when their attention was drawn to the somber red-brick structure, resem-

bling a federal armory, that filled the block between 51st and
52nd. Here lived William Henry Vanderbilt, eldest son of the
dead Commodore, while on the opposite corner of 52nd there
gleamed the white marble palace of his younger brother, William
Kissam Vanderbilt, built at the command of his then wife, Alva.

After that, Governor Levi Morton's dwelling was something of
a letdown, but awe was struck again by the architectural fantasies
on view at the crossing of 57th. Behind its wrought-iron railings,
the crenellated mansion of a third Vanderbilt brother, Cornelius,
reached clear up to 58th. South of it was what could easily have
been mistaken for an over-ornamented warehouse of mud-colored
stone—it harbored Collis P. Huntington, another railroad tycoon.
"He started out a poor peddler, sleeping under the stars," the
guide told the rubberneckers. "Then he went into the hardware
trade out in San Francisco. You can see for yourselves where he's
landed today."

Across from the Huntington place stood the Whitney establishment, with the dimensions and appearance of a solidly constructed public school. William C. Whitney, with his street-
railway fortune, had lived in it for years alongside his neighbors,
Perry Belmont, a sportsman who had stolen Alva away from
Willie Vanderbilt, and H. O. Armour, a meat packer. Now the
house belonged to Harry Payne Whitney, William C.'s son, while
the father resided in greater splendor up at 57th, cheek by jowl
with Henry O. Havemeyer, tsar of the sugar trade, whose house
was akin to a museum of fine arts. "I take it most of you have
heard of Rembrandt," the guides would say. "Well, old man Havemeyer bought seven of Rembrandt's masterpieces to hang on
the walls of his drawing room."

The domicile of Commodore Elbridge T. Gerry, a Brahmin
who had never set foot in anything so common as a dime store,
was a rose-pink rococo chateau at 61st that abutted on the Metropolitan Club, founded by J. P. Morgan, whose admission standards excluded the likes of Frank Woolworth. "Go ahead and take
a guess how many people old Elbridge can seat at his dining-room
table," said the guides. "The answer, friends, is well over a hundred. Can you imagine it?"

Mrs. Hamilton Fish lived at No. 810 between 62nd and 63rd,
Mrs. William Backhouse Astor and her son, John Jacob IV, two

blocks farther north in a brand new house copied from French Renaissance originals, a sanctuary from the crass commercialism exemplified by the Waldorf Hotel that was eroding the foundations of society farther downtown.

The city's tax rolls, which Frank had studied, disclosed that No. 833 was home to William Guggenheim, banker and philanthropist; that No. 856 housed Judge Elbert H. Gary, Carnegie's rival in steel; that Thomas Fortune Ryan, promoter of the elevated railroad, occupied No. 858.

The grandest sight of all loomed up at 70th Street: a manor house, of eighteenth-century English style augmented with a flurry of Italian touches, whose owner was Carnegie's partner, Henry Clay Frick, a man of steel in more ways than one. As the guides reported it, "He's the feller that tried to bust the union and got himself half murdered by an anarchist name of Berkman who was supposed to be Emma Goldman's fancy man." The elegant house, the landscaped grounds and Frick's entire art collection, valued in excess of $50,000,000, went on his death to the City of New York.

Frank's pied-à-terre on the northeast corner of 80th Street came almost at the end of the tour—the omnibus drivers turned around after their passengers had a chance to peek at Carnegie Castle at 91st. Seen through a vehicle's windows, the Woolworths' home was anticlimactic, and Frank nursed a notion of building something considerably bigger one day in the future.

The cavernous interior of the house was decorated like a five-star hotel with hand-tooled gesso ceilings and golden wall panels, oriental rugs spread over polished parquet, tapestried armchairs and copies of Louis Seize sofas. The cage in which Jennie confined herself was much bigger and more gilded than anything she had known before. John Woolworth, gnarled with age and endless toil, was invited to make a rare trip down from his farm to take a look at what his son had wrought.

"This must have cost a mint of money, Frank."

"A good deal, Father, but it's worth it."

"Well, Frank, you always did like to lay it on thick."

John, eighty years old in the coming August, seldom strayed from Great Bend, Jefferson County. Sum tried to visit him at least once a year, "but I found it extremely difficult to get away."

Frank's trips up there petered out completely. If he contributed anything to the old man's upkeep, no record was kept of it. John's modest household was run by a housekeeper, aged seventy-three. Elvira Moulton became Mrs. John Woolworth in August, 1906, and a widow five months later.

The organ in his drawing room claimed more of Frank's attention than his father received. The *son et lumière* equipment was soon expanded by the insertion of a translucent panel, lit from behind, into the wall above the console, to give Frank something more arresting than multicolored lamp bulbs under pushbutton control. Now, after he had the room and his audience in darkness and a symphony on cylinders began to roll, a portrait in oils of its composer appeared, dim at first, then growing brighter until it was bathed in light. After-dinner guests were entertained with the faces of Richard Wagner, Ludwig van Beethoven, and the noble brow of Franz Liszt, all of them heroes to Frank.

It may be taken for granted that the pallid face of Felix Mendelssohn emerged on the screen on a spring day in 1904, while his "Wedding March" resounded from the organ under Frank's command. The bride was Lena, his eldest daughter, who would be twenty-six in July; the bridegroom, a personable young attorney, Charles McCann, an alumnus of Fordham Law School. No report of the ceremony appeared in the New York newspapers, either because the event was judged undeserving of mention or because Frank steadfastly declined to pay for a line of advertising anywhere.

The marriage was a triumph for a girl born in poverty on a humble street in Watertown who had never attended finishing school or college or been presented to society. McCann's uncle was a celebrity and a self-made millionaire—Richard Croker, former boss of Tammany and overlord of the city, a man with connections ranging from the blighted slums south of 14th Street to the mansions of Millionaires' Row.

Uncle Richard, older than Frank by nine years, had started even lower down the social scale than the Woolworths; Croker came ashore with his parents after a steerage crossing from Ireland at the age of three. He was a graduate of the notorious Fourth Avenue Tunnel Gang who muscled his way onto the city payroll, was elected an alderman in the reign of Boss William Tweed, and was freed of a murder charge after an election day fracas because the apprehensive jurors could not agree on a verdict.

"In politics," Croker used to say, "the victor gets the spoils." He thought of himself as a businessman in the classical mold: "I work for my own pocket all the time." He dressed like a banker or board chairman, immaculate in suits, hats and topcoats chosen to complement the grey of his beard and bristly crop of hair.

Both Croker and Frank laid stress on the public service aspects of their endeavors, Croker as an expediter who smoothed the path of progress ("A businessman wants to do business with one man, and one who is always there to remember and carry out the business"), Frank as a benefactor of humankind.

"Did it ever occur to you," he asked his underlings one day, "that our business is an indirect charity and of benefit to the people at large? While we are in business for profit, we are also the means of making thousands of people happy. The more stores we create, the more good we do for humanity."

But there the resemblance between the two of them ended, and contact was negligible after Lena became the wife of Charles McCann. Croker, in the mantle of a gentleman, owned one stud farm in Otsego County, New York, and another in England, and his thoroughbreds raced on both sides of the ocean. Frank had not an ounce of the gambling instinct in him, and horses were linked in his mind with farming, which he abhorred.

Croker mixed on equal terms with the mighty—Willie Vanderbilt, J. P. Morgan, William C. Whitney—while Frank had no entrée into such rarefied strata. He had not risked applying to join the exclusive clubs whose members held the financial reins of the United States. The next best thing was to patronize the Waldorf Bar, where Morgan, Croker, Frick, Carnegie, John "Bet a Million" Gates, Judge Gary and William Henry Moore of the biscuit trust congregated for luncheon at a table reserved for their use. (Gary, who lived at 856 Fifth Avenue, was a near neighbor but otherwise completely outside of Frank's orbit.)

Frank found the bar's free lunch, covering a banquet table attended by a platoon of *sous-chefs,* irresistible. Virginia ham, Vermont turkey, bluepoint oysters, scallops, clams, with everything carved or shucked to order and all for the price of a ten-cent beer or two-bit shot of whiskey—it was a great place for a man of insatiable appetite even when he was cold-shouldered by more distinguished patrons.

He was an oddity among the Goliaths of commerce and industry whom he struggled so hard to impress. They were by and large an aggressive, gregarious lot who took almost as much pleasure in hobnobbing with each other as they found in cutting a competitor's throat. They dwelt in a world of their own making, isolated by acquired wealth from mundane reality until it was presented to them as figures on a balance sheet.

Reticent and distrustful of strangers, the pinchbeck trade he was engaged in made Frank a figure apart. It was impossible for him to turn his back on those responsible for his success—his customers. Through recognition of their unexpressed desires he had piled up a fortune that never stopped growing. But the task of recognizing their needs was something that he felt he alone, in the final analysis, was fully qualified to perform. So in spite of its size, the business bore the characteristics of a one-man band. He could not give up mingling with the working classes the way his fellow tycoons did.

4

৵] All at Sea [৯

Along with most of the plutocrats whose style he aimed to emulate, he liked to sail the sea, specifically the Atlantic Ocean, and not in a yacht of his own, like J. P. Morgan in the *Corsair*, but aboard a luxury liner.

He enjoyed the leisurely rituals of a first-class passenger's life from the moment he awoke in an upper-deck stateroom to synchronize his gold watch with the ship's time of day, adding an hour on the eastward crossing, subtracting an hour on the westward. His personal steward would run the bath for him, fresh water or salt in accordance with his wishes, and lay out the outfit to be worn for a gargantuan breakfast in the dining salon, the suit pressed and the shoes polished overnight in a cubbyhole down the corridor.

With the meal, usually eaten at the captain's table, over, Frank would take a brief constitutional around the boat deck, weather permitting, before another steward installed him in a teak deckchair and wrapped him in a plaid blanket to await the serving of a cup of hot bouillon at eleven o'clock, followed ninety minutes later by a descent below to tackle a luncheon of unlimited courses.

A nap on the bed, tucked in by a steward or stewardess, helped fill the afternoon before the time came for his steward to assist him in dressing—black tie, tuxedo, diamond cufflinks, patent

23

leather shoes—for drinks and then dinner to the music of the uniformed band.

After that came another short stroll on the promenade deck, with a Havana cigar to puff; a flutter at the card tables or on the ship's pool, won each day by the passenger who made the most accurate guess of the distance covered in twenty-four hours' sailing; an armchair seat at an evening concert; a buffet supper; and finally a night of rare, unbroken sleep, lulled by the sound of the sea against the hull.

Frank the voyager was scarcely recognizable as Woolworth the dime-store tsar. He was at ease with himself, relieved for a while of the crushing burden of responsibility self-imposed, happy to joke with other men on the passenger list and ogle pretty women. An ocean crossing for the sake of his health was the standard prescription of his doctors. More often than not, he sailed without Jennie.

After the $65,000,000 merger was finalized in 1912, his fits of exhausted sobbing continued. He was losing weight so fast that his clothes began to hang loose on his frame. The question of a trip on the *Titanic* was settled when the Cunarder went to the bottom with the loss of 1,513 lives after running at full speed into an iceberg. By then, he had been ordered to bed by his physicians with a warning that, if he stuck to his present course, he probably had no more than two years of life ahead of him.

He left for Europe in the middle of May. His daughter Edna, not yet visibly pregnant, went with him, along with her husband, Franklyn Hutton, a valet, and two nurses. Jennie was excluded; the doctors, it was claimed, "wanted no one along who would give the invalid too much sympathy." His office staff was ordered to screen every item of mail before it was forwarded, since letters from his old associates set him off weeping again.

He endured a succession of long and disagreeable days during the summer. He yearned for precise details of how the new corporation was shaping up and how work on his skyscraper was progressing. But back in New York his colleagues kept their letters to him brief and to the point, avoiding any word of problems to upset him.

The latest sea voyage had done nothing to restore his health. The Panhard limousine he kept garaged in Paris had met him at the dock to carry him to Carlsbad. At that royal spa in Bohemia he would take the cure promised by daily doses of the salty water gushing from hot mineral springs.

He arrived there early in the season, when the normal population, about the same number as the Woolworth Building would accommodate when it was completed, was tripled by the influx of vacationers and sufferers from rheumatism, upset livers, venereal diseases and an excess of uric acid. Frank's troubles were ascribed to uric acid, though "nervous disability" was another of his doctors' diagnoses.

For six weeks he submitted to diet and exercise. He drank pints of the steaming, crystal-clear water that bubbled up from the rocks and was bathed in gallons of it, while his daughter and son-in-law, Edna and Franklyn Hutton, idled away the days by inspecting the shops, listening to band concerts and walking the manicured paths that led up through the pine woods to the Aberg, the Dreikreuzberg and the König Otto Hohe.

Insomnia still plagued him, and his cheeks grew gaunter. The resemblance to William Howard Taft was lost. The face Frank saw reflected in a mirror was more like that of his Grandfather Jasper, on whose farm he had been born.

He was left alone with the valet and nurses when the Huttons went off to Paris, expecting to return after a short stay there. But French doctors warned Edna that her baby might be born prematurely. Instead of rejoining Frank, she and Franklyn booked immediate passage for New York to ensure the child American citizenship. Her father had never spared time to form strong bonds of affection between himself and his daughters. He had been generous with his gifts of money, frugal in expressions of love. He could get along without Edna.

There was virtually nothing for him to do then to while away the long days except to mull over the distant years when the greatest hardship he had known was frustrating poverty.

5

◁] No Place Like Home [▷

He had been a Tuesday's child, born on April 13, 1854, in the clapboard cottage his father rented on the farm he managed for Grandfather Jasper at Rodman in Jefferson County, New York, and he had been christened in the nearest Methodist church, where his parents, John and Fanny Woolworth, sang together in the choir on Sundays.

"He was a country boy who had strong genes and vigor which I inherited, thank God," said Barbara Hutton at a time when she was busy spending her inheritance. But Frank's strength was a tale concocted to impress. He was thin, frail and solemn in his schooldays. What was strong in him was determination.

Working the land had been a family tradition ever since the founder of the American side of it, Richard Wooley, who changed his name later on, landed in the new world in 1653. John had been raised to follow the plow like his father, though methods of work were changing fast, with old-fashioned hand tools outmoded by horse-drawn machines like Cyrus McCormick's reapers.

Fanny Woolworth bore Frank's brother, her second and last child, on August 1, 1856, and named him Charles Sumner in admiration for the abolitionist from Massachusetts, struck down by a Dixie congressman for denouncing slavery in a speech to the Senate.

"My mother and father," Frank remembered, "worked very

hard to make ends meet. My father would think nothing of getting up at four in the morning and work till eight at night in the
summertime at hard manual labor. Everything that came into
farm labor I had experience in, and my mother would break me
into housework, too. I got both ends of the stick."

When Grandfather Jasper reached his seventieth birthday, he
concluded he'd had enough farming to last him the rest of his
days. His sale of the place forced his son to look for somewhere
else to live. John bought one hundred and three acres of land and
the cottage that went with it a mile beyond the village of Great
Bend that stood within a horseshoe curve of the Black River on its
course down from the Adirondacks, across Jefferson County, into
Sackets Harbor on Lake Ontario, twenty miles below the Thousand Islands and the Canadian border. Great Bend boasted the re-
finements of a general store-cum-post office, a single-room
fieldstone schoolhouse, a Methodist as well as a Baptist church,
and a population of 125 necessarily hardy people.

With a $1,600 mortgage at seven percent and interest pay-
ments of $56 to be scraped up in cash twice a year, John
Woolworth was compelled to work himself and his sons harder
than ever. Firewood for sale, a potato crop and a herd of cows
made up the only sources of income.

The two boys were roused out of bed at five o'clock to trudge
to the barn and help with the milking. Shoveling manure was
their job, too, along with pitching hay up into the loft every summer and tossing it down for winter feed. Felling trees and splitting
logs was their father's chore, but he had a poor head for business.
The wood he hauled to market over the eleven miles of dirt road
that led to Watertown was likely as not to be green and unseasoned. After a day of waiting for customers, he'd have to sell at
knockdown prices.

A budget as tight as piano wire allowed each boy one pair of
boots a year. In spring and summer, boots were reserved for the
Sunday morning walk to church. On a daily basis, they were worn
only for winter plowing and harrowing. Fanny Woolworth, who
looked for a moral in everything, taught her sons that "you have
to work for everything you get in this world."

When frost came early in the fall and they were sent out to
herd the cattle in for milking, they would pause for a moment to

warm their bare feet in the grass where the cows had been lying. Winter brought the task of gathering spaded-up potatoes from the chilled fields with numbed fingers. Snow, always heavy in the lee of the lake, was an annual curse, not a pleasure. Storms might strike any time from November until May, blanketing the path between cottage and barn that the boys had to keep shoveled clear.

They walked to and from the Great Bend schoolhouse whose teacher, in a custom of the times and place, took turns boarding as a nonpaying guest in the homes of her students. Mrs. Emma Otis lived on in Frank's memory. She had found his mother so good a cook that she was delighted to be asked to stay on past her pre-arranged departure date. She had spoken well of him. "Frankie is a bright pupil and never gives me the least trouble. He's inclined to be sober minded, not at all prankish, and he always has his lessons ready."

He had found some relief from drudgery in the old upright piano with its attached pair of brass candleholders that had pride of place in the parlor. He couldn't read a note of music or carry a tune, but Fanny taught him to pick out melodies on its yellowed keys. No doubt about it, he had been a mother's boy, much closer in spirit to her than to his father—a milksop and mollycoddle in local estimation.

Something besides music began to stir his imagination. It was an easy walk from Great Bend to the deserted mansion that Napoleon Bonaparte's elder brother Joseph built for his mistress, Anne Savage, when he fled to the United States after the emperor's final surrender. Mild-mannered, supine Joseph, for fifteen years king of Spain, clung to luxury and the glory of the Bonaparte name, though he declined an offer by Spanish revolutionaries to install him on the throne of Mexico.

The doorposts of the abandoned house were carved with the Corsican's crest. Nearby there was Joseph's hunting lodge, where an imported Venetian gondola had been stored to take him fishing in the Indian River. Joseph had been dead for twenty years, but the boy marveled at old men's tales about him.

Confederate cannon began bombarding Fort Sumter on the eve of his ninth birthday. Yet in the next four years only two events in the world beyond Jefferson County impressed themselves on his memory. He remembered his joy over Lee's surrender at

Appomattox, his horror at the news of Lincoln's death. Though John Woolworth had been a founder of the Republican party in northern New York State and Fanny was an outspoken abolitionist, John stayed clear of the Union Army and put in service as a school trustee.

Frank recalled a drive he took with Sum and their father into Watertown in the fall of '62. The brothers were shopping for a gift for their mother's thirty-third birthday, which would not come around until April, but with snow on the way, this might be their last chance to get into town before spring. They sidled into a dry-goods store on Public Square, which was choked with wagons on market days, when most of the town's ten thousand citizens were out to trade gossip, barter and buy. The boys gawked at the displays in the glass-fronted cabinets and at the rolls of fabric stacked on the shelves, watched by a wary sales clerk.

They decided on a set of imitation tortoise-shell combs that they thought would look pretty in her jet black hair. The price was fifty cents; a nickel was all they could raise between them. The clerk waved them out the door. Sitting on a curbstone to wait for their father to dispose of his cordwood, Frank outlined an ambition to Sum: "One day I'm going to have a store, and nothing will ever cost more than five pennies, and everybody can touch anything they like."

A shopping expedition in those days was as formalized as dancing the quadrille. Customers entering a dry-goods store saw stretches of empty counters, with clerks stationed behind them as stiffly as troops on a parade ground. Handling the merchandise was not allowed in case it became soiled and unsalable except at reduced prices. So it was stored on shelves and in boxes behind the counters, out of reach by anybody but the clerks.

Perhaps the customer wanted a few yards of calico. Off a shelf came a roll of it, spread for inspection by the clerk as he glanced at the tag, usually encoded with two prices, one to be quoted at the start of the haggling, the other to be settled for if the haggling persisted. If the customer shied away from buying anything at all, the clerk's duty was to pester her until she did. The keeper of a general store employed a trick of another sort: a brand-new broom propped against the cash register, its price to be included in any unwary shopper's bill.

In village stores, barter flourished. Phineas T. Barnum landed his first job in one of them before he went on to make and lose fortunes as a showman with his conviction that "the American people like to be humbugged." As he recalled: "Ours was a cash, credit and barter store; and I drove many a sharp trade with old women who paid for their purchases in butter, eggs, beeswax, feathers and rags, and with men who exchanged for our commodities: hats, axe-helves, oars, corn, buckwheat, hickory nuts and other commodities."

"There is something to be learned," he concluded, "even in a country store. We are apt to believe that sharp trades, especially dishonest tricks and unprincipled deceptions, are confined entirely to the city, and that the unsophisticated men and women of the country do everything on the square. I believe this to be measurably true, but know there are many exceptions to this rule. Many is the time I cut open bundles of rags, brought to the store by country women in exchange for goods and declared to be all linen and cotton, that contained quantities of worthless trash in the interior, and sometimes stones, gravel, ashes, etc."

But to Frank work in any kind of store was an enviable job. A sales clerk stayed warm and clean, out of touch with cows and potatoes. He invented a new game to play with Sum. He raided the drawers and cupboards of his mother's kitchen, then spread out on the scrubbed plank table her supply of knives and forks, skillets and saucepans for make-believe sale to his brother and a host of imagined customers.

Here and there in the universe unknown to him, the traditions of storekeeping were being overturned. In Paris, Aristide Boucicaut, a former counter clerk, had dumbfounded his competitors by storing everything for sale within his patrons' reach, marking every item with legible, nonnegotiable prices. His customers were free to wander as they wished and encouraged to return anything for a refund if they were dissatisfied with it. His Bon Marché had made him rich. When he died in 1877, his widow Marguerite, who had borne no children, sold shares to the staff, and as the business expanded faster than before, other entrepreneurs from the United States and elsewhere stopped by to study the techniques applied in the world's first department store.

At the other end of the scale, Yankee peddlers came knocking on Fanny Woolworth's kitchen door, making their rounds as they had from the time the land was secured at last from British Red-coats and Iroquois braves. It was a happy moment for Frank if he happened to be home when a peddler showed up to break the monotony.

There was a streak of artistry in Frank that his schoolmates de-rided. The kitchen stuff he played with was laid out in careful patterns. To encourage him in his music, Fanny gave him a flute, though he had no more luck with it than with the piano. He re-warded her by sawing enough wood to erect a picket fence outside the cottage, which she had always wanted in order to pretty up the yard.

By then, the Confederacy lay in ruin, pillaged by carpet-baggers, its economy destroyed. In Northern cities, the easy profits picked up in wartime were harder to come by, but an emerging generation of merchant princes realized what had to be done. They had made fortunes by selling uniforms and boots to the Un-ion armies and from legions of civilian customers with inflated currency to dispose of. American storekeepers scented an era of af-fluence and national esteem opening for them, as long as they at-tracted new armies of shoppers and paid close attention to the overheads.

Rowland Hussey Macy had an eye for the charms of the ladies in front of his counters in Manhattan but not the the straits of the girls who worked behind them. Cutting their pay from $2 to $1.50 a week, he explained that he could no longer afford "high war wages." At the same time, he acquired a second store at the rear of the first on West 14th Street, to be botched together in an "L" whose floor levels were permanently out of alignment.

On the front of the premises he set his distinguishing mark: a red star copied from the tattoo on his hand, which was a memento of days spent before the mast after he shipped out of Nantucket aboard a whaler at the age of fifteen. The little needle and thread shop in Boston that was his first venture into dry goods had been a disaster. "I have worked two years for nothing," groaned the Quaker who had learned how to cuss. "Damn, damn, damn, damn."

Five more efforts had ended in failure before he set up shop on 14th Street three years before the Confederate States named Jef-ferson Davis their provisional president. The former cabin boy was then thirty-six, with a stomach ulcer aggravating a fiery temper. Cash on the barrelhead was his watchword: "We buy exclusively for cash, and we sell exclusively for cash." The war and ownership of what could plausibly be claimed to be America's original department store combined to make him a millionaire.

The war and its aftermath turned another dry-goods man into a national celebrity. Alexander Turney Stewart had been educated for the ministry at Dublin's Trinity College before he took ship from Belfast to New York and worked there as a twenty-year-old schoolteacher. A friend borrowed money from him to help in the opening of a store. When it faltered, Stewart commandeered the remaining stock in settlement of the debt. On a hasty return trip to Belfast, he bought $3,000 worth of Irish lace to add a touch of class to the inventory and within a matter of days was advertising, "A. T. Stewart offers for sale a general assortment of Fresh Dry Goods at 283 Broadway." The distinction between "dry" and "wet" had its origins in the general, all-purpose store, where kegs of rum and hogsheads of hard cider stood against one wall, containers of more durable wares against another.

Stewart expanded his venture step by step, moving from one site to an ever larger site on lower Broadway until he had enough money to erect what New Yorkers called his Marble Palace—the "marble" was a deft paint job applied over cast iron. Its half-dozen stories and fifteen plate-glass windows extended along the sidewalk for the full block between Reade and Chambers streets, a building unique in itself that needed no name or sign on its walls. Long after monthly sales topped $250,000, the proprietor persisted in teaching his two hundred clerks the twin arts of wooing customers and wrapping packages in a manner that minimized the use of paper and string.

Apart from old William Backhouse Astor, nobody in New York City was wealthier than this morose, arrogant ex-schoolteacher whose voice squeaked like chalk on a blackboard. The bulk of his income, like Astor's, came from real estate rather than from the ladies who streamed into the most talked-about store in town to shop for Lyons silks, French laces, Brussels carpets, Paris gowns, and cashmere shawls tagged as high as $2,000.

He sent cargoes of food to famine-ridden Ireland and donated massive sums to Northern charities during the war, though Mrs.

Lincoln chose to shop at his competitors, Arnold Constable & Company, another establishment with a façade of alleged marble. Society shunned Stewart as a money-grubbing tradesman and decided he was one of the meanest men who ever lived. However, Ulysses Grant, installed in the White House, picked him to be his treasury secretary on account of favors he had rendered to the Union cause. The invitation had to be withdrawn because the president had overlooked a statute excluding from that office anyone engaged in the import business.

Stewart consoled himself by constructing on the corner of Fifth Avenue and 34th Street a vast, pillared mansion of genuine marble, a residence more expensive and more pretentious than any other in the city. He and his wife dwelt there alone, childless and condemned by the elite for his extravagance.

* * *

Without Fanny's intervention, Frank's schooling would have been over at sixteen. His father wanted him at work full time on the farm; she thought he deserved an opportunity, however brief, to better himself. She scrabbled to rake up the tuition fee to pay for a few months of commercial courses in Watertown. He was everlastingly grateful. "The education I got in two terms in a business college," he used to declare, "did me more good than any classical education I might have got."

But the interlude seemed to have been time wasted. Nobody around wanted to hire a lad with a smattering of bookkeeping and not much else. He had no choice but to go back to tending cows and hoeing potatoes.

* * *

The notion of selling goods of every description under a single roof was a concept that dated back to the covered markets of feudal Europe. A charter for one in Italy was granted in 493 A.D. In America, the little general store, where colonists shopped for whatever they couldn't make or grow for themselves, was a kind of prototype for what was to follow in the second half of the nineteenth century, but between those times storekeeping in the United States fell back into a pattern of fragmentation.

As hamlets grew into villages and villages into towns and cities, most shops sold a single kind of merchandise—the grocer, foodstuffs; the chandler, candles. A draper sold cloth as a retailer, a mercer as a wholesaler. Glovers, hatters, tailors, shoemakers, hardware merchants and druggists followed their trades independently. The general store appeared to be en route to extinction.

Then the idea of establishing something akin to it, but on a more grandiose scale, began to take hold soon after Boucicaut's Bon Marché had shown how it could be done. Instead of merchandise being piled up higgledy-piggledy, it would be grouped in categories in separate departments, each carried on the ledgers as a discrete operation.

The Quaker partnership of Strawbridge & Clothier started to experiment in Philadelphia, the Hecht Company in Washington, D.C. The three Stern brothers—Louis, Isaac and Bernard—left Buffalo for New York City to open their doors on Sixth Avenue with a range of prices as wide as a piano keyboard. "While we want to serve the masses," Louis explained, "we can't afford to overlook the classes."

Seven hundred miles west of Manhattan there was evidence of what a member of the most distrusted class of peddlers could achieve once he settled down. Adam Gimbel, Jewish immigrant from Bavaria, had unloaded his pack for the last time. He established a frontier trading post with some of the marks of a general store on the banks of the Wabash River at Vincennes, Indiana, and announced his creed: "Fairness and Equality of All Patrons, whether they be Residents of the City, Plainsmen, Traders, or Indians." His heirs were planning to press ahead first into Milwaukee and then into New York.

At the end of the spectrum farthest away from A. T. Stewart's $2,000 shawls, a customer with only a penny to spend could walk out of a *real* bargain store with twenty-four sheets of notepaper, a cake of soap, twenty-five marbles, a dozen pencils, two fishing lines, two balls of twine, one handkerchief or two hundred yards of cotton thread.

* * *

Frank's first organized bid for freedom from the farm came in the early spring of 1875, the year in which he would reach twenty-one. Snow covered the ground as he hitched up the mare to his father's cutter for the four-mile drive to Carthage, where a population of 1,500 supported a meat market, a furniture store and an undertaker's parlor. Gawky, chilled and unsure of himself, he

called on all three, seeking a salesman's job. All three turned him
away.

His next ambition was to work on the railroads that stretched
across the plains and over the mountains, bringing hope—or in-
creased frustration—to young men eager to slip out of bondage.
Trains could take him clear through to California now that the
Union Pacific, extending from Omaha, had linked up with the
Central Pacific, laying track eastward from San Francisco.

The Rome, Watertown & Ogdensburg Railroad served Jefferson County. The call of steam whistles in the night tempted
Frank. What should he apply for—ticket puncher, candy butcher,
telegraph operator or a locomotive engineer in control of a machine that could bear him away twenty times faster than any
horse? He took to doing chores for the neighbors until he had $50
in stake money for a getaway.

It was a railroad man who hired him, but in an unexpected
role. As a sideline, Dan McNeill, station agent at Great Bend,
owned a small grocery at the rear of the depot shed. He listened to
Frank's tales of discontent, then told him he could serve behind
the counter. "Only for the experience, mind you; I can't afford
wages."

The new, unpaid assistant was soon under pressure to quit.
Uncle Albon McBrier, Fanny's brother, had need for an extra
hand on his farm. Frank would do nicely, at $18 a month, with
bed and board thrown in. His father, said Uncle Albon, could get
along without him now that Sum, seventeen next birthday, was
old enough to fill his brother's boots.

Fanny was against it. Frank was none too strong, and he
oughtn't to work too hard. John agreed to mull over Albon's proposition. Meantime, Frank could hang on at McNeill's grocery.

He spelled out the situation to McNeill, who made him a
promise: "I'll see if there's anything might be done for you next
time I'm in Watertown." He delivered on his pledge a day or so
later. "I heard of an opening at Augsbury and Moore's. I know
Augsbury. I'll give you a letter to him."

Alexander Augsbury and his junior partner, William Harvey
Moore, were in the dry-goods trade, owners of the Corner Store,
which occupied part of the ground floor of a four-decker building
that also housed the Western Union office on Public Square.

Frank remembered every detail of the day he ventured in on a March morning in 1873.

Augsbury, he was told, was at home, nursing a cold. Frank asked where he lived and went straight to the house, a skinny, tow-haired hobbledehoy in handed-down clothes, with a wool scarf of his mother's making wound around his neck. There was ice on the streets, but excitement kept him warm.

"Hello, bub," said Augsbury. "What do you want—a job?"

Yes, sir; he did. The inquisition began. "Do you drink? Do you smoke? What do you do that's bad?"

"Nothing, sir. I go to church every Sunday, and I don't live in a locality where they do bad things."

"You're too green; you've had no experience."

Disappointment was so plain on Frank's face that Augsbury thought again. He would be in the store that afternoon. Meantime, the would-be recruit should talk with William Moore.

The pungent smell of the shelvesful of yard goods—bleached linen, printed cotton, tweeds and worsteds—tantalized Frank. But Moore, seated in his long-tailed coat with satin lapels behind a desk on a platform that commanded a view of every counter, was discouraging.

Finally, after both partners had crossexamined him, they agreed to try him out. "I imagine," Frank remembered, "I was about the greenest fellow who ever came off a farm. They did not try to hide their opinion that I probably had no ability at all."

"What are you going to pay me?" he asked them.

"You don't expect any pay, do you?" Moore snapped.

"I don't see how I'm going to live without pay."

"That doesn't interest me. You should work a whole year for nothing as a schooling. You have to pay tuition when you go to school. We won't ask you any tuition fee." Moore, a dozen years older than this new apprentice, ran a finger over his pomaded mustache. "You will have to do all the mean work—deliver packages, wash windows, get in early and sweep the floor, do all the cleaning. It will be the hardest work you ever did in your life."

Frank was not deterred. He was eager; he was humble. Whatever was asked of him he would do, because Mr. Moore obviously had no idea of the rigors of work on a farm. "How long shall I have to work for nothing?"

"At least six months."

He calculated that his $50 would cover the room he would need in Watertown for only half that stretch of time. Perhaps after three months he would have proved he was worth a few dollars in wages. The one-sided deal was struck. He could start in at the Corner Store next Monday morning.

He had a favor to ask. "Would you mind if I'm a bit late. My father will be bringing in a load of potatoes, and if I ride with him it will save me thirty-three cents in train fare."

This, too, was agreed to.

His farewell to the farm was a scene worthy of Currier and Ives. Dawn lingered an hour away. Snow banked higher than the picket fence glistened in the light of Sum's lantern. Frank stored a bundle of clothing on top of the barrels of potatoes, then slid onto the seat beside their father. Fanny flicked her tears away, certain that her elder son would not live here again. John Woolworth cracked his whip over the rumps of the horses. Fanny waved until the sleigh runners squeaked around the first turn in the rutted road.

It was after ten o'clock when they reached Watertown. Frank threw aside the shaggy buffalo robe that had covered their legs and sprinted across Public Square. Mr. Augsbury and Mr. Moore were waiting for him just inside the door.

"Bub, don't they wear any collars in your neighborhood?" asked Mr. Augsbury.

"No, sir."

"No neckties, either?"

"No, sir."

"Is this old flannel shirt the best you have to wear?"

"Yes, sir."

"Well, you'd better go out and get a white shirt and a collar and tie."

How long would the $50 last if it had to be spent at this ruinous pace?

6

The Rube
Behind the Counter

He was certain that everybody on the payroll as well as the two bosses looked down on him as a boob, a turniphead, a rube with straw in his hair. He was lucky, he thought, to last out the first day after he had rigged himself out as Augsbury had ordered.

"Nobody told me what to do," Frank recalled. "I hung around, feeling foolish. The clerks stared at me and jeered at me."

Noon arrived, and the rest of them went out to eat, leaving him to fill in for them, alone but for William Moore. An old graybeard from one of the outlying villages walked in to buy a spool of thread. Frank hurried over to his boss to ask where thread was stored.

"In front of your nose," said Moore, bent over a ledger. There was an undercounter drawer crammed with spools.

"I want number forty," the old man said. Frank hadn't known until then that thread was numbered. A second trip to Moore brought the master himself over to fish out a number forty.

"How much?" asked the farmer. Eight cents. Frank was handed a ten-cent paper note, in common use during postbellum days. "Mr. Moore, where do I get change?"

"Come over to the desk and make out a ticket."

The unpaid recruit to the trade pored over the pad of printed slips and was stumped again. "Mr. Moore, I don't believe I know how to make it out."

"Give it to me. I will show you."

An unanswered question still hung in the air. "Where do I get change?" Moore's patience was under strain. "The cash register's right there. Can't you see it?"

Another customer of the same rustic breed followed close behind the first, asking for a pair of mittens. "Have we got any mittens, Mr. Moore?"

"Hanging in front of you, young man."

After trying on a variety of them for fit, the customer was ready to ask the inevitable riddle: "How much?"

"I don't know. Mr. Moore, if you please—" Patience evaporated. "Look at the ticket," barked the boss. "Can't you see the ticket on there?"

Twenty-five cents. Frank could handle the sale when the owner of a new pair of mittens produced a dollar bill. "I finished the transaction without bothering Mr. Moore again. I was keeping my eyes open as best I could."

People who fancied they knew Frank concluded that he would never amount to much. Here he was, twenty-one years old and doing about as much as he was fit for, running errands and polishing cuspidors. He plodded the streets as if he were behind a horse-drawn harrow, grave-faced, shy, with no apparent spark of ambition in him.

His savings were ebbing away at the rate of $4 a week paid to his landlady for meals and a bed. Dating a girl and treating her to a soda would be a wicked waste, so he steered clear of women. Living in monkish celibacy, he found music a consolation. But the flute was more than he could manage. He bought a cheap violin, and his fellow boarders regretted it; the practicing he did most evenings had been easier to put up with before he took up the fiddle.

He discovered another outlet for the frustration that plagued him. When Moore instructed him to trim the front window of the store, Frank spent hours trying out combinations of bolts of cloth and stockroom samples until he had come up with a display he judged was as pretty as a picture. Moore inspected it in silence; praise for the help was rare. But the new assistant was commissioned to tackle all future window dressing. Frank decided that one day William Moore deserved to be repaid for his kindness.

Ed Barrett also went onto the gratitude list. The head clerk at the Corner Store made "a tremendous salary" by Frank's reckoning—$13 a week. "It was through his kindness that I had nerve enough to stay in that store long enough to learn the retail dry goods business."

Then there was apple-cheeked Mrs. Coons, who served the women and girls who came in to buy items never even to be named in the presence of the opposite sex. She mothered Frank and even offered him a dollar or two from her pay. After thirteen weeks, he was scraping bottom when Moore figured he was worth $3.50 every payday. At the end of six months, he was raised half a dollar more, with an extra fifty cents added at the start of his second year.

He lived as frugally as a hibernating squirrel, foregoing the pleasure to be had with a woman or the taste of a good dinner. He was growing up a loner, uneasy in company, unappealing to strangers. Later, he would preach the virtue of self-denial. "Nobody ever got on who was in bondage to the body. You can't build a business on thoughts of having a good time."

He had worked for eighteen months before his pay was hiked to $6, a dollar for every working day that lasted from seven in the morning until nine at night. "I felt," he remembered, "that I was indeed on the highway to success."

In the fall of 1875, Ed Barrett staggered him with the news that he was quitting Watertown to head west with his friend Golding, chief salesman at Bushnell's, which was a competitor of the Corner Store on Public Square. They were off to Port Huron, Michigan, said Barrett, to launch a "99 Cent Bazaar," which was something new in storekeeping, with prices as standardized as the goods on sale.

Frank disallowed his chances of succeeding Barrett. But Arthur Bushnell would need a man to fill Golding's place. Frank presented himself for appraisal.

"What are you asking?" said Arthur Bushnell.

"I think I'm worth ten dollars, sir."

It had taken him nearly three years to acquire the courage to set such value on himself. He was no more amazed that it paid off than William Moore, who constrained himself from making a matching offer.

The room in the boardinghouse was empty most of the time now. Frank was required to bed down on an iron cot in Bushnell's basement with a pistol under his pillow to protect the store from thieves. He had the companionship of seventeen-year-old Harry Moody, who slept in a cot beside his. Harry, too, won a place on the roster of people to be kept in mind for reward if an opportunity arose.

Bushnell, a traditionalist, refused to let Frank fuss with prettifying windows. What he demanded in a clerk was hotshot salesmanship, in which this new hand was glaringly deficient. On an inescapable morning, the boss summoned him to the cellar. "I've got boys earning six dollars a week who sell more stuff than you. I have to cut you to eight dollars."

"This was a terrible blow," Frank remembered, "and under it my health gave way." He lasted until February. Then the doctor he consulted warned him he must quit and go home to his parents to rest, for the highway he was traveling led to self-destruction. Bushnell, blind to the cause of his clerk's slow decline, assured Frank that since he would be back in harness within a week or two, his replacement would be taken on only as a pinchhitter.

Frank was put to bed, dog-tired and dejected, by his mother. He was incapable of work for the next eighteen months. "I became convinced I was not fitted for mercantile life."

Running the house and working in the barn and fields were as much as Fanny could handle; she could not nurse her son without outside help. So she invited a girl who had done some dressmaking and mending for her to move in with the Woolworths to take over the task of attending to the invalid in return for a bed to sleep in and three meals a day.

For Jennie Creighton it was a step up in the world. She would not be alone or go hungry again, as she had when she was eking out a living as a seamstress in a rented room in Watertown.

The blue-eyed Canadian girl had an air of impenetrable innocence. Sharing in a family's life would help fill the gap in her own—she missed her father and the eight brothers and sisters she had left behind in Ontario, though letters were exchanged between them every week or so.

She was as virginal as the young man she was hired to care for. She had taken over the household at home when her mother died, and now she mothered Frank. Nursing him back to health brought hitherto unknown intimacies—the touch of a girl's hands, her presence at his bedside, the scent of her skin and her always neat clothing.

Ignoring the demands of sexuality was no longer possible for him, yet he hesitated to declare his feelings for her. Perhaps she would have to make the first move to let him know that compassion for him in his long illness had changed into something more powerful. The conversation between a simple-hearted girl and a confused man who rated himself a failure can be reconstructed like this:

"Frank, things don't seem the same as they used to be. Anyway, that's how it appears to me."

He would have leaped to the wrong conclusion. "What's gone amiss? You're not thinking of taking off, are you?"

"No. Nothing like that. That's the last thing I'd choose to do."

"Well, what then?"

"It's just that I've got different feelings about you than when I moved in."

"You mean you can put up with me easier now?"

"I mean I have to think about leaving. It won't be long before you're back to work, and there'll be no need for me."

"But you're like one of the family, like a sister."

"Not really. I don't think about you like a sister does."

He was invariably slow to understand emotion in himself or anyone else, but gradually the point was made: she saw herself as his future wife. "But I've got no money and no prospects of making any, either. There's nothing I can do but go back to farming, so help me."

"I can help you. I don't mind how hard I have to work. And happiness means a lot more than money when you come to think about it."

Finally he proposed to her. They were married, with his parents' blessing, in the parlor of the farmhouse on June 11, 1876.

Jefferson County was home to any number of McBriers, most branches of the family more prosperous than the Woolworths. Fanny's father Henry owned six acres and a little house in Great Bend that he was willing to let Frank take over without a nickel in cash changing hands. His grandson signed a note for $300; a bank mortgage covered the rest of the price.

"I was twenty-four years old," Frank reminisced, "and back almost where I had started three years before. About the only difference was that now I owed quite a bit of money for my farm and had a household to support."

Methodists didn't countenance cursing. "Great Scot!" was the limit he allowed himself, even on the day he planted one of his fields with potatoes. A flock of chickens, he hoped, would bring in money for eggs and provide food for the table. Chicken in any guise, boiled, broiled, fried or fricasseed was intolerable to him after he had spread his name across a chain of dime stores.

After twelve infernal months of it, a letter from William Moore invited Frank back to work in the Corner Store. Augsbury had sold out; the signs over the door and on the windows now read "Moore & Smith." They both seemed happy to have Frank on the payroll at an unprecedented $10 a week. If there was any debate about what was to happen to Jennie, the chickens and the potato crop, it was soon settled. He would board at his old lodging and visit her every alternate Saturday night and stay through Sunday. With no complaining about it, she would spend the rest of the time alone, taking care of the farm as best she could.

It was a short-lived arrangement; after a fleeting weekend in October, Jennie was pregnant. She kept up the work that had to be done for as long as she had the strength to cope with it—weeding and watering, digging the soil, loading the crops into sacks and toting them into storage, mixing feed, collecting the eggs, wringing the necks of the hens destined for the butcher's shop. Then the day came when she was compelled to let him know she could not continue handling it alone.

She put aside the old dress, coarse apron and heavy boots of everyday wear and prettified herself in a homemade gown ready for Frank's arrival. Her roughened hands lay in her lap as she spoke. "Frank, I hope it won't cause too much trouble to make things different, but it's getting to be too much for me, and I don't want our baby to suffer as a consequence."

"We'd have a bit more laid aside if you could hang on a bit longer."

"I wish I could, Frank, but I don't think I can."

"So what do you have in mind?"

"I ought to be able to earn something at my old trade, except we don't have a sewing machine."

"Nor the means of buying one. Besides, where would you find enough customers in these parts?"

"We could sell off the chickens and use some of that money. And then we could rent the farm and move back into town. It would save you paying for that room, and we'd be together again."

It was one of the few times she was given her way. The chickens were not sold but swapped in exchange for a second-hand Singer. A tenant took over from Jennie, and she and Frank carted their sticks of furniture to 236 Franklin Street, Watertown, the home of a painter and decorator where she had had a room before. It would be too crowded when the baby came, so they took over quarters in an extension no bigger than a shed that had been added to the left side of the house. On Saturday nights, she made an extra dollar or two, serving alongside Frank at Moore & Smith's.

Far off in the future, Constance Woolworth McMullan, a granddaughter of Frank and Jennie, played with the thought of restoring the place as a memorial to her celebrated grandfather. She concluded that it was too woebegone to be worth preserving. The house and its clapboard wing were razed in accordance with her instruction to a wrecking company.

Something more permanent than snow overshadowed the winter of 1877–78 for Frank and Jennie. A livery-stable team and sleigh got them to Great Bend in time to see his mother die. The only woman Jennie could rely on having with her when her baby came would be a midwife. But she would not allow herself to fret about that. She turned instead to making the clothes that would be needed. Mr. Moore might be willing to give Frank a day or two off when her time came. She prayed that if that happened he would not find his wages docked as the price of having him with her at her confinement.

In every state and territory of the Union, the head count of Americans was increasing, with the total soon to exceed fifty million. In the first five years after Lee's surrender at Appomattox, more cotton spindles had been put into operation, more iron furnaces built, more iron smelted, more iron bars rolled, more factories started, more houses and stores erected than in any equal span of time in the country's history. Yet business at Moore & Smith's was slow now. Money in circulation throughout the nation, $20.57 a head in 1865, was down to $15.58 and still declining. The winds of recession were cold. The two partners examined their books and came to a routine decision: wages must be cut to reduce expenses and maintain profits. A few weeks before Jennie's baby was born, Frank's pay was pared to $8.50.

The memory of how harsh had been the struggle to make ends meet was erased from his memory. It was less painful to recall the birth of the *idea,* not of their first child. He gave credit for his experiment with a five-cent counter where he felt it was due: not to any inspiration of his own but to Mr. Golding, former salesman at Bushnell's who stopped by the Corner Store on a trip east from Michigan.

"He asked Mr. Moore, in a conversation which I overheard, if he ever had a five-cent counter. Mr. Moore replied that he had never heard of such a thing, and Mr. Golding stated that he had tried a five-cent counter and it proved to be a big success."

Helena Maud Woolworth was born in the bedroom of the Franklin Street flat on July 17, 1878. In August, William Moore made a buying trip to New York and called on a firm of jobbers that Golding had recommended. Spelman Brothers carried a whole line of merchandise priced to retail at a nickel. It filled a demand, unheard of in Watertown, that had sprung up years ago, though in some cities five-cent counters had turned out to be something of a nine-day wonder, abandoned after a month or two when customers' interest and the proprietor's profits sagged together.

Moore left an order of less than $100 with Spelman's for pens, safety pins, button hooks, tin pans, washbasins, thimbles, soap and stationery, to be delivered to coincide with the Jefferson County fair. "I helped to display these goods on a counter in the center of the store in Watertown," Woolworth reported. "That was the beginning of my experience in the five and ten cent business."

He summoned the latest $2-a-week stockroom boy, Fred Kirby, to set two long tables end to end and hang a crudely lettered cardboard sign from a rafter overhead: ANY ARTICLE ON THIS COUNTER FIVE CENTS. Moore padded the collection with some antiquated items that had been gathering dust on the shelves.

The crowd cramming the square for the opening of the fair

kept the screen door swinging to and fro all day. Dusk came, and everything was gone. "The goods," Frank boasted, "vanished like snow in April." He took off for the Western Union office on the next floor with a telegram from Moore, a rush order to Spelman Brothers for another $75 worth of goods.

John Woolworth was making out poorly with no wife to care for him. A housekeeper might be the answer if money could be raised to pay her. Frank's solution was to look for work for his brother to do so that Sum could free himself from farming and also pay a share of housekeeping expenses. Frank arranged for Moore to cast an eye over Sum.

"Do you suppose you could go around to the houses in the city, ring the doorbells, and pass out handbills?" the younger Woolworth was asked.

"I reckon I could."

"Well, how much do you want for that sort of job?"

"Oh, I guess three or four dollars a week."

"I'll give you three dollars," said Moore, and Sum, aged twenty-two, was hired. He realized afterward that he had been a deeper shade of green than his brother in the matter of bargaining. "Mr. Moore came back like a flash, naming the lower figure. It taught me never to mention the lowest price first—to decide in advance and state a figure that was ample but fair."

If it was true that he cottoned onto that principle of negotiating in a single sitting, he was smarter than Frank, who had ten more years ahead of him before he mastered the craft. With Sum chipping in, they doled out $50 a year to their father. Jennie struggled to put aside a like amount in deference to her husband's creed: "I am a great believer in thrift."

Five-cent fever was spreading again. Other storekeepers succumbed and turned to the Corner Store for their supplies. Farmers cashed in on the craze and set up trestle tables in their barns, with signs tacked onto roadside telegraph poles to attract customers. Moore & Smith's served as middleman and ran a wholesaling business. "Maybe," Moore reflected, "a man might operate a store where nothing sold for more than a nickel."

Day after day, Frank saw the tide surge. "It fired me with a desire to go into the game myself."

He sounded out Moore: how much capital would it take? The answer: $300 to $350.

"Father would have backed me if he'd had the money. He was a generous man, whose money got away from him much more easily than it came back."

He tried out Uncle Albon. "He said I was very foolish to think of such a thing, and that if I knew which side my bread was buttered, I'd hang onto my $8.50 job."

So, filled with misgiving, he tracked back to Moore. Could he possibly let him have, say, $300 worth of items on credit? Woolworth was still no great shakes as a salesman, but he was honest; once he started anything, he stuck with it. Moore agreed to accept as security a note countersigned by John Woolworth.

His son had to control himself and not allow excitement to cloud his judgment, but he was used to doing that. He must remember whatever he could of the commerce school courses in making up budgets and balancing books. It was imperative to think as a businessman, a proprietor, a boss instead of a hired hand. He might make mistakes, though none could be more calamitous than his experience at Bushnell's. If things went wrong, he would pull out and try again.

The first step was to discover the best spot for the gamble. Not Watertown, because the field there was overplowed. Great Bend was too small, and the same held true of Carthage. He must cast around until his untested instinct told him this was the right place. Jennie would have her sewing and seven-month-old Helena—Lena to her parents—to keep her busy while he was away.

He selected from the Corner Store's warehouse the gimcrack Yankee notions on which he was staking his future, wrapped them, had them crated. A freak storm had shrouded Watertown with snow on Thursday, the ominous thirteenth of January 1879, when he left home to tramp to the depot. "Everything looked chancy to me, and not a single person to encourage me in my new venture," he wrote years later. No encouragement even from Jennie? If that was true, then one inference was that she was content with their married life together and saw no cause to change it. She would have preferred to have Frank at home with her rather than see him setting off chasing rainbows. A different interpretation of his words was that, while she supported his decision, he found her loyalty so automatic that it was not worth mentioning. Instead, he recorded an encounter he had on the street with another sales clerk, on his way to work at Moore & Smith's.

"Hello, Frank. Where are you going? I see you've got a bag there," Dan Roberts said.

"I am going out to get my fortune, going off on a train to start a five-cent store."

"I wish you success. Pretty cold weather to start out, isn't it?"

Somewhere along the eighty miles to Syracuse the train buried itself in a snowbank and arrived hours late. Frank scoured the streets of a city that was bursting at its seams as the population grew. The one man he knew here was George Chambers, who had shut down his cigar store in Watertown to try his hand in the five-cent fad. Chambers convinced his visitor that there was no room for him as a competitor in town, so Frank headed for Weedsport for a free supper and bed at an aunt's.

The next morning, he went to Rochester in another vain search for a suitable location. He spent Friday night and Saturday back at his aunt's. "She did not try to encourage me," he said, sorrowing for himself, "and I commenced to lose heart."

He stayed on through Sunday, to make an early start on Monday for Auburn. Nothing within his range was available for rent. Finally, in Utica, he found what he was looking for in a tiny vacant store on Bleecker Street. Look before you leap—that was Woolworth lore. "Not being satisfied, however, I went to Rome so as to be sure I was on the right track." He dismissed the quaint old city on the Mohawk River as being "very dead." He would settle for Utica. The size was right, according to what he'd gleaned: about 33,000 people, including a large proportion of Welsh. In any case, he had little choice. His travel money was all but spent; he couldn't afford to go much farther.

The Bleecker Street hole in the wall was on the ground floor of a building owned by two bankers. "One of them had a little faith in me, the other had none, and I had great difficulty renting the store for one month at $30. They wanted the money in advance, and of course I didn't have it, and I told them I would pay them at the end of the month. After a lot of dickering, one of the bankers decided to take the risk, and I showed him the bill for how much merchandise I had coming, and everything was all right to start."

At that moment, he felt panic rather than triumph. "I lacked courage. I would have given all the old boots I ever had in life to be back in my old position, as I never had much experience in the cold, cruel world before. All I had to do was send a telegram to Watertown to have the goods shipped, and they would be there in two or three days, but I hesitated. I walked up and down the street, went past the telegraph office two or three times."

The profit to be made on many a nickel item was less than a penny. Unless he could turn the stock over at a fast pace, he was doomed. Then he'd be burdened with repaying his debt to Moore out of a clerk's wages, which would condemn him and Jennie to poverty for years to come. What would she say to that? It was the least of his worries.

He entered the office, filled in a yellow blank, then left it folded inside a coat pocket. At last, he strode in, handed the form in, "and from that time on I seemed to have renewed life." Only one message went out on the line to Watertown. "I didn't wire my wife because I wanted to tell her myself." Just when the opportunity might arise was unforeseeable. He could not possibly leave Utica until there was cash in the till.

"I wanted to open on the following Saturday, and for some reason all of our stores have opened on Saturday ever since, with very few exceptions. I employed a young man and a young lady to help me open up the goods and display them, and got a carpenter to put up a temporary counter."

Cost of pine boards and carpentry: $8. Lamp and can for the kerosene: $5.60. Red cloth to cover counter's front: 53¢. Freight charges from Watertown: $7.43. Desk and stool: $2.20. Cash box: 50¢. Daybook, accounts book and ledger: 80¢. Wrapping paper: $1.64. Feather duster: 15¢. Sign lettered with the legend THE GREAT FIVE CENT STORE: $3. He was almost ready for the grand opening, in perfect time for Washington's birthday.

He checked, rechecked and checked again Moore & Smith's invoice for $315.41 as he entered every item, at its wholesale price for a gross, in the records he kept all his life: drinking cups, $3.50; cookie cutters, $3; purses, $5.25; tack hammers, $4.85; candlesticks, $4.50; pie plates, $5.75; tin spoons, $4; baseballs, $4.75; jewelry, $5; writing books, $5; lather brushes, $5.50; police whistles, $5; and so on down the list. Handkerchiefs at 50¢ a dozen and thread at 39¢ in the same quantity were included toward the end of the tally.

His biggest potential moneymakers were soup skimmers—he'd clear nearly 3¢ apiece on them. On the other hand, boot polish, for instance, came in at a fraction more than 4¢ wholesale, leaving him less than a penny profit on every tin. Rent, wages, wood for the stove, oil for the lamp, food to keep him going, a boardinghouse bed—it might be less hazardous to dance on a tightrope or take off in a barrel over Niagara Falls.

The two thousand handbills he ordered from a printer cost $7.50, but he was of two minds about distributing them. The deadline he had set seemed out of reach. Behind the sheets of brown paper tacked over the windows for privacy's sake, the floor was littered with discarded wrappings and wood chips, the stock piled up in no kind of order on shelves and counter. "For fear the customers would get there before the store was ready for business, we sent the first circulars out to New Hartford, a place about two or three miles outside of the city." He was stalling.

George Washington was ruefully eliminated and plans pushed forward to Monday. At six o'clock on Saturday night, the proprietor was fretting about the mess everything was in when someone rapped on the locked door. The woman out there on the sidewalk carried one of his announcements in a mittened hand. "But the store isn't open for business, madam. If you will come back—"

"All I want's a fire shovel."

Instinct took over. "Just step inside, and I'll wrap it for you."

He remembered, "I was looking for money. The first sale that was ever made in any of our stores was made right there and then." The wholesale price of a shovel was the same as that of boot polish. Net take: nine-tenths of a cent. He regretted afterward that he hadn't jotted down her name as a footnote to his personal history.

He was spurred into revising the timetable once again, scurrying around to tidy up the place by eight o'clock as more people gathered outside. Excitement was tempered by a sense of being cheated. "We found the boys we had hired to distribute the circulars had put about a hundred in each doorway in order to get their money and then play the rest of the time." Another strand of his character was being woven on the loom.

Customers streamed in as soon as he turned the key in the door and kept him and his temporary staff of two, Mr. Edwins and

Miss Stubbins, busy for the next three hours. A midnight count showed $9.40 in the cash box, mostly so-called "shin plasters"—paper money in denominations of two, three, five, ten and twenty-five cents that had been issued during the war and continued in circulation.

He had learned enough in commerce classes to make him leery of recording such a minute sum in his ledger. "I made out no sales report because I did not care to have anything put on the books as small as that." His creditors might ask to see the figures, and there was barely enough loose change to produce a rattle.

Monday was better—$52.20, inscribed with a flourish in a ledger column. Tuesday: down to a dismal $17.66. Wednesday and Thursday: $26.00 and $36.65. A falloff on Friday: $33.90. Saturday: an exhilarating $80.03 for a week's score of $246.74.

He splurged a dime on a canvas money sack, opened a bank account, and mailed off $100 to Moore. In the middle of March, Frank walked in on Jennie to make amends for being away almost one full month.

She would have greeted him calmly, knowing displays of emotion disturbed him. He allowed that he had missed her and her cooking. He had brought her a present: the fur wrap seemed an enormous extravagance when he said he limited his spending on himself to $5 a week.

The only jewelry she wore was a plain wedding band. Her strong fingers were often clasped together as if in an effort to restrain them from going to work again. He assured her the gift had been a bargain. "A fur piece like that retails for as much as sixty dollars. I paid forty-five." There would be good times for both of them, he promised, now that the snowball was starting to roll.

What she looked forward to, she said, was having the little family settled down together again. It was a bit too early for that, he replied.

He checked on Sum's progress at the Corner Store and heard only praise for him. The two partners found a five-cent counter served a dual purpose, converting obsolete goods into ready cash, and drawing customers who could be sold on buying higher-priced merchandise. The formula worked so well that Moore & Smith now operated branch stores in outlying villages, unloading shopworn stock at knockdown prices. Sum, pushing ahead as hard as his brother, had been promoted to manager of the outlet in Morristown, on the banks of the St. Lawrence. Morristown was too minute to win classification even as a village, but directly across from it stood the bustling port city of Brockville, Ontario, from which steamers set out every day. William Moore was relying on Canadian customers to boost his profits.

Sum set out with a batch of handbills and hired a boatman to row him across the river. The two of them walked through Brockville, passing out the announcements of the bargains waiting in Morristown. Local merchants called in the police. Sum endured half a day under scrutiny in a cell. It ended with his handbills confiscated and the two intruders shipped out in the rowboat. But the mission was accomplished. "A considerable part of our success," he thought in retrospect, "was due to the trade we had from Canada." When Frank listened to the tale, he calculated he might find good use some day for his brother's ability, loyalty and any cash he had on hand.

When would that day arrive? How long would the Great 5 Cent Store last on Bleecker Street? Would the people of Utica soon have bought all the nickel items they needed? He had no idea of the answers. If the present venture collapsed, he was ready to continue along the road in the style of a fly-by-night peddler. Perhaps this kind of puny store never could become a permanent fixture in any location. If that was correct, he would simply keep bailing himself out, pack up and move on.

The equipment he'd require for another attempt was minimal: packing cases to serve as counters, draped with a few yards of cotton cloth in his favorite turkey red; tin pans to hold his wares; a hanging lamp; a cardboard sign, the cash box and accounts books. Any seedy little shop on a busy street would meet the need, provided the landlord could be talked into renting it to him month by month. So long as he kept his credit sound with Moore, he could go on trying, hit or miss, selling his stock as fast as possible at every stop, then pulling up stakes when trade fell off.

The first omens appeared in April; he dispensed with the last of his hired help and worked alone. Sales one day in May dipped to $2.50, and the rest of the month was not much better. Time was up. He was satisfied with his decision not to uproot Jennie from Watertown. He shut down before creditors closed in on him and shipped the remains of his stock back to Moore & Smith's.

"I got cold feet," he confessed to Jennie. After three months of struggle, he had sold out for a profit of $150, which was $20 more than he could have earned in his best days as a clerk. He found encouragement in that. He could take heart, too, in the thought of what Adam Gimbel had accomplished when he settled in Vincennes. And in Chicago another German-born ex-peddler, Henry Siegel, had emerged as a full-fledged merchant prince, teaching his secrets to future princelings.

Frank withdrew $30 from his bank account to stake himself, a wanderer without a pack, to another scouting trip.

7

A Chain of
⌁ Circumstance ⌁

He had ten dollars and loose change left in his pockets after the string of railroad tickets had been bought that would take him to and back from southeastern Pennsylvania, with one change of trains to make between Grand Central Terminal and Pennsylvania Station in New York City and then another to carry him the final sixty-five miles west from Pennsylvania. Jennie had brushed his drab Sunday suit, which was as worn as his valise, and packed food to last him through the day.

A friend had recommended a trip to Lancaster, the thriving city on Conestoga Creek, with its mix of Quakers and thrifty Dutch who, God willing, might be attracted by the bargains Frank had to offer. The same should hold true, he hoped, for the farmers in the countryside around, from communities like Paradise, fifteen miles away, and the place with a name it seemed shameful to pronounce—Intercourse.

Evening was darkening the fields of tobacco, wheat and corn alongside the tracks before the journey was over. As soon as he walked out from the depot, he felt a tingle of excitement. "The sidewalks were jammed with people, the stores were filled with customers, lights were blazing, and there was an amazing air of business and prosperity." He sensed it right away: "Lancaster was the place for me."

He toured the downtown streets until he was hungry, ate a cheap supper, then paid fifty cents for a night's lodging in a com-

54

mercial hotel—"a vile old one it was, too." Next morning, he skipped breakfast to press the search. The quaint little shop at 170 North Queen Street was no bigger than fourteen feet wide by thirty-five deep, but he liked the look of it. He struck a bargain with the landlord and caught the next train bound for Philadelphia, heading for Utica to make his last payment on the rent there and tidy up his affairs, "almost stranded financially, but with my hopes renewed and my purpose strong."

Home again in Watertown, he begged Moore to increase his line of credit by another $300; Moore & Smith's was still the only wholesale house he had the courage to approach. He delighted Jennie by inviting her to bring eleven-month-old Lena and go back with him to Lancaster.

Setting up shop a second time went more smoothly now that he knew some of the pitfalls. Three days of work put everything into shape for a Saturday grand opening. He rounded up a scratch team to help serve the crowd he expected, and he roped Jennie in for counter duty, too.

"I knew that the city was in the midst of a farming community"—and Frank considered himself an expert on farmers' idiosyncrasies. "I knew of the so-called plain people who wore Quakers' garb or the black of the Shakers. I knew that they lived simply, made close bargains, and slowly grew rich. They knew the value of a nickel." So did Frank, who prayed he might follow them on the road to prosperity.

On Sunday, June 22, he mailed a postcard to his father: "I opened my store here for trade yesterday and did not advertise any. No one knew there was a 5¢ store in this city until Friday night and we managed to sell yesterday in one day $127.65, which is the most I ever sold in one day; we sold $80 in the evening alone. I had 7 clerks and they had to work, you bet. We could have sold $200 if this store had been larger. Jennie helped me last night. We got here Tuesday P.M. Did you get my machine all right? I want you to write and let me know all about it as soon as you get this. I think some of starting a branch store in Harrisburg, Pa., and putting Sumner in it if Moore & Smith will spare him."

With more gusto than affection, he signed off with a business-like "F. W. Woolworth." A magisterial tone emerged in "I want you to write" and in his designs for his brother's future. The machine he referred to may have been a simple cash calculator.

Two months later, his plans for Harrisburg were realized. He paid $5 in advance rent on two hundred square feet of floor space there and imported Sum to manage it at a salary of $7. The "Great 5 Cent Store" sign was only fractionally smaller than the shop itself. Moore & Smith supplied the stock. The first selling day put $85.41 in the new cash box.

In Lancaster, thirty-five miles away, the proprietor controlled both enterprises from his perch on a platform at the rear of the store, guarding the cash and supervising the three girls who received $1.50 from him every Friday, minus the price of anything they broke. Each sale was entered on a slip for totaling and analyzing every night. Tinware, toys, washbasins, towels, handkerchiefs and ribbons sold best. Packages were wrapped in surplus newspapers bought at the *Intelligencer-Journal's* back door—two cents a pound instead of wrapping paper at eight cents—and hoisted onto his shoulders to be borne away. It was the only money of his the *Journal* ever saw; he didn't believe in squandering income on advertising.

Any lease for a period of more than a month was rejected; he was still fearful of failure over a longer term. When the Harrisburg landlord demanded a few more dollars eight months later, Frank shied off. Maybe it would be a mistake to imagine five-cent bargains would continue to sell. The brothers took inventory. They had made a profit of $800. The wisest course would be to call it a day and look elsewhere for safer ground.

York, Pennsylvania, which for the better part of a year had been the nation's capital at the time of the Continental Congress, was Sum's next stop, with an extra dollar a week added to his pay for encouragement. He was given a chilly welcome in the city where Ben Franklin's printing press, preserved from destruction in Philadelphia, issued $10,000,000 of Continental money. Woolworth's first week's sales of $222.52 sagged and continued to sag until on a day three months later no more than $3.05 was entered in the books.

"We sold about $1,000 worth of goods," Sum reported. "Our net profit was exactly $36." He locked the door and went to work in Lancaster headquarters. "But we had no thought of resting on our oars." Jennie over that summer's weekends lost her husband again when he took to the road with his brother.

One excursion landed them in Scranton, a city unlike anything either of them had come across so far. Industry, not farming, made Scranton prosper. Selling to the English and Welsh, the Germans, Poles and Russians who labored in anthracite mines and factories, mills and blast furnaces would be a new challenge. The amount of space available at 125 Penn Avenue overwhelmed the brothers the first time they inspected it. Unless it was bisected with a partition, their stock would look pathetically paltry.

A nickel was a fixed star in Frank's firmament. He resisted Sum's arguments that it set too strict a limit on what they could sell. Suppose, Sum said, they were to introduce a second line of items priced at a dime. That would broaden their base and enable them to stay rooted.

Frank ultimately agreed, but with reservations and a certain nostalgia. "As soon as we added 10¢ goods to the line, we took away part of the 5¢ store's charm, the charm of finding only one price on a counter and only one price in a store. But as long as we kept the 5¢ goods on one side of the store and the 10¢ goods on the other, the charm was not entirely lost."

The signpainter's handiwork for the November 6 debut was new: "5 & 10 Cent Store." The relic of Utica days, "The Great 5 Cent Store," was preserved for the sidewalk show of pots, pans and washboards due to be set up, when the weather turned warmer, on planks laid over sawhorses on each side of the doorway. Most of the stock had covered many a mile's journey, freighted from York to Lancaster and now out to Scranton, to be augmented with some new additions from Moore & Smith's warehouse.

Sales seesawed, up one week and down the next, but Christmas proved lively. More than $200 was taken in on December 24, leaving the brothers with enough to buffer the blow when an icy January day depressed the gross to $5.95. They went window-shopping to check on other shopkeepers' prices, then shaved theirs to create what the trade knew as "loss leaders," designed to beguile a customer into buying an item on which they cleared nothing, hoping she or he would buy other things to give them a modest profit.

Their competitors were taught, in Sum's words, that "there was another fish in their pond," and they resented the invasion.

"The Corsican Brothers" was one of the politer descriptions of the Woolworths. With Bonaparte lingering in his thoughts, Frank enjoyed that label.

He was bringing in good money at both locations, pondering over the reason for success now while he had come to grief in the past. "Some of my first stores failed because I hadn't studied the situation thoroughly. I placed them in the wrong part of town. There's a right place. Find it."

He was satisfied with his fixed-price policy. "Everybody likes to make a good bargain. Let them. Small profits on an article will become big profits if you sell enough of the articles."

Insisting like Rowland Macy on spot cash all the way down the line was another principle to stick to, though people often asked Frank for credit even when the bill was in dimes. Some of his competitors extended credit; he never would. "I believe in doing business by and with cash," he declared. He had been such a green hand when he opened in Utica that he hadn't known how to make out a bank check, which was an advantage of a kind. "Large credit is a temptation to careless buying."

So far as his nature allowed him certainty about anything, he felt sure that letting his customers paw over the stock was essential to his success. People weren't used to being trusted like this, and there would be some shoplifters among them, but it was a risk he had to take. They came, they examined the merchandise, they were tempted into buying, usually into buying more than they had been looking for. He concocted a standard invitation for his salesgirls to relay to everyone who came in: "Look around while you're here and see what we're selling for only five cents."

He began to understand why both his stores prospered. They were permanent fixtures, not something as transient as a gypsy camp. A satisfied customer came back for more—and spread the word among friends about the kind of buys to be found at Woolworth's.

The first seven days in Lancaster brought in more than enough money to pay for his entire stock as it stood on opening day. He had been compelled to hustle around the jobbers of Philadelphia to keep his counters filled. In the process, he discovered there were many more items to be offered for a nickel than Moore & Smith ever carried.

After six months in Lancaster, he paid off every debt and had cash left over. There must be a way, he reasoned, to put the excess money to work to speed up his progress. Other men made easy millions on Wall Street; it was time for him to try a flutter. The railroad stock he bought caused him nothing but regret. The market was constantly churned by high-rolling speculators like Jay Gould, Jim Fisk, and the Vanderbilts. Frank was a novice in an era of brass-knuckle finance. He found he was giving more attention to the seesawing quotations listed in the morning newspapers than to the running of his business. He unloaded his few shares at a loss and swore off future dabbling in anything but sure-fire securities like mortgages and Treasury bonds.

It was impossible to tell whether Frank ran the stores or the stores ran Frank. To find the new items needed to expand his sales, he had to travel farther and farther afield in search of suppliers, always paying cash to shave a sliver off their prices, seldom learning anything except by the process of trial and error, as Meyer & Schoenaman, Philadelphia importers, found when he went in to buy some toys.

"About the first thing they did was to drag out a lot of colored glass ornaments the like of which I had never seen before. 'What are those things?' I asked. They explained that these goods were, oh, such fine sellers, but I laughed. 'You can't sell me any foolish things like that,' I said. 'I don't believe they would sell and most of them would be smashed before there was a chance to sell them.'

"They explained that the profit was big enough to offset the breakage, but I was incredulous. It was hard to understand what the people would want of those colored glass things. We argued back and forth a long time, and finally the house made me the proposition that it would guarantee the sale, at retail, of twenty-five dollars worth of the Christmas tree ornaments.

"The goods arrived a few days before Christmas and, with a great deal of indifference, I put them on my counters. In two days they were all gone, and I woke up. But it was too late to order any more, and I had to turn away a big demand. The next Christmas season, I was on hand early with what I considered a large order, but it was not large enough. They proved to be the best sellers in my store for the holidays."

Tree ornaments always turned a handsome profit, but Christmas was never a time of sentiment for him. Eleven years later, when the count of Woolworth's stores reached twenty-eight with sales exceeding $1,000,000 a year, he addressed a lecture to his managers.

"Give your store a holiday appearance. Hang up the Christmas ornaments. Perhaps have a tree in the window. Make the store look different. This is our harvest time. Make it pay. This is also a good time to work off 'stickers' or unsalable goods, for they will sell during the excitement when you could not give them away other times. Mend all broken toys and dolls every day.

"Also watch your clerks and customers to see they do not steal. When the store is crowded, don't allow any boys or girls in the store at all, unless they are with their parents, as most of them come in on purpose to steal.

"The cashier also needs your watchful eye, as it has been the experience of at least one store every year to lose large amounts through the cashier's dishonesty. Remember, the cashier has the best chance of all to steal."

Doubts about the honesty of patrons and staff lay dormant in the early Lancaster years. On Sunday afternoons, he had his salesgirls over for tea at the small red-brick house he rented on Lemon Street. One of Jennie's sisters, Sidney, came down from Ontario, to stay on and lend a hand with the housework. By the close of 1880, he decided he had earned a vacation, the first he or Jennie had ever known. "I was worth $2,000, which looked bigger to me then than $20,000,000 would now," he remembered. He had grown a mustache to add an air of authority.

For their holiday in Watertown, he bought her a new outfit and he sported a new derby hat as he walked her around the square. ("Well, Frank, you always did like to lay it on thick," his father would tell him.) Yet there was more to it than showing off: with an eye on the future, he was scouting for trustworthy people who would respect what a country boob could make of himself if he tried hard enough.

At Moore & Smith's he shook hands, man to man, with his old boss, then received a kiss from Mrs. Coons. He was intrigued to find that Fred Kirby, the stockroom boy, had been upgraded to bookkeeper at $8 a week; since his formal education had ended at fourteen, the promotion owed something to his attending Mr. Moore's Sunday-school classes.

Fred was another graduate of the farm and a close friend of Sum, who had told the background story to his brother. Kirby was a *sticker* who walked the six miles between his job and the family farmhouse in every kind of weather. He watched every penny he spent and paid room and board to his mother, Angeline—"one of the nicest women I ever knew," Sum said. It was a vital contribution when a potato crop sold for fifty cents a bushel and hay for $8 a ton. Fred's adventuring had been done vicariously, listening to the tales of his father, William, schooled in England, an old Forty-Niner who had trekked to California to dig for gold. He had made and lost a fortune before he buried himself in farming.

Frank was prepared to start another store somewhere with Fred as his partner if he could chip in a share of the capital. But Kirby was only nineteen, too young to leave home, in his mother's opinion, and his father's ups and downs had made him leery about taking risks.

Dan Roberts, clerking at the Corner Store, took his turn at shaking Frank's hand, reminding him of the icy morning of his departure for Utica when Frank had forecast he was going out to get rich. Dan's family had farmed land in Jefferson County since 1804, but his father, Charles, had broken away after the death of his first wife. At his grocery on Court Street, he employed the three sons of his second marriage. Dan and Fred Kirby hung around together, though Dan aimed at being something a cut above a clerk—a buyer, maybe, or a traveling salesman. Frank made a mental note: Dan was a man worth keeping tabs on.

There was a slew of them in the fraternity of counter hands who worked around Public Square. At the noontime break, they traded gossip about the foibles of their bosses and the eccentricities of the customers. On Sundays, they strolled here with their sweethearts, window-shopping, boy and girl firing each other's imagination with daydreams. America, they thought, was the best possible country in the whole universe for doing that. The secret was perseverance, whether a man made his killing in railroads like Vanderbilt or in real estate like the Astors. You might find your million in spinning wool and cotton as Robert Lowell had in the mill town named for him in Massachusetts. Or in steel like Andrew Carnegie there in Homestead, Pennsylvania. ("Have you ever bumped into him, Frank?" No, he had not.) On summer evenings, the young ones continued their dreaming to the lilt of music from the white-domed bandstand that stood at the center of the scene.

Distance was the intimidating obstacle. The world where wealth waited for a fellow with spunk enough to grab it lay a long way from Watertown. City boys, accordingly, had the edge over country boys. You'd be a fool to believe that city streets were gold paved, but chances of finding a nugget or two as you hustled along them were a lot brighter than on Public Square. His companions judged Frank had done right: if you had hopes of picking up a fortune, you had to go out to get it.

He took Jennie over to Bushnell's to meet his young friend who had once slept on a neighboring cot in the cellar. Harry Moody was twenty-two now, a hard worker soon to become head salesman. His education had been even skimpier than Fred Kirby's—finished when he was an eleven-year-old compelled to help support his mother, Ellen, whose farmer-husband, Anson, was mortally wounded in the fighting at Fair Oaks in '62. Harry's health was as precarious as Frank's. He, too, had fallen sick and spent a year as an invalid on his grandfather's farm in Pulaski before being taken on at Bushnell's.

Frank scented ambition in him, and Harry was eager to leave Watertown. But he felt too safe in his present job to yield to the urge to explore. Besides, he had no stake money.

The "temporary" assistant hired by Arthur Bushnell to replace Frank during his illness was still on the payroll, looking forward to becoming cashier. It was a limited goal for twenty-four-year-old Carson Peck with two years at St. Lawrence University in Canton, New York, behind him and ancestors he traced back to *Mayflower* days. He was held in check not by poor health but by a need for security. He was an orphan, raised on a farm by his uncle, Abner Peck, Jefferson County sheriff, and Abner's wife Laura. Carson had trodden a path similar to Frank's, up every morning at five-thirty to milk the cows before he ate breakfast.

He had qualities Frank was looking for: a sturdy backbone, foresight, integrity. Maybe a place could be made for him if the five-and-tens lived up to their promise. Carson was courting another store clerk, Clara Sargent, aiming to be married next year. That might hasten the day when he decided to better himself.

Mr. and Mrs. Woolworth went on their way. A school friend of his, Clinton Case, worked at Campbell & Moulton's, a third retailer of dry goods on Public Square. Clinton, twenty-five, and Frank, twenty-eight, had grown up together in the hamlet of Champion, where Clinton's parents were pioneer settlers. That was one link between the two boys. Another was young Mrs. Case, born Mary Louise Johnson, who had taught school in Rome, New York, before she and Clinton were married last year from the home of her aunt, Mrs. Elisha Moore, in old Trinity Church by Bishop Brewer. The newlyweds lived on Franklin Street, a few steps from Frank and Jennie's old address. Elisha Moore's brother-in-law was William, of Moore & Smith's. The way Frank saw it, Clinton was the next best thing to a cousin. He could rely on Clinton to be fair and square with him.

Then there were visits to blood relatives to be made. He drove with Jennie to Champion. In the house of Uncle Elijah and Aunt Mary Woolworth their son, little Cousin Fred, babbled about working in a store when he grew up, and he would not be nine until New Year's Day.

Uncle Albon and Aunt Calista McBrier had to be called on in DeKalb to let the old skinflint see how his nephew was prospering in spite of Albon's refusal to involve himself in five-cent foolishness. The McBrier's son, sedate Edwin, seemed to have no more interest in storekeeping than his father. As soon as he graduated from high school, Edwin planned on being a teacher.

There was a trip to see Aunt Jane Emily and Uncle James Knox, who worked a small farm in Russell—Jane Emily was a younger sister of Fanny Woolworth's. Frank had only fleeting contact with their eldest child, Seymour, when he attended the village school that was housed in an old stone arsenal originally built to store muskets, shot and powder to fight off raiding Indians. Seymour had been a student teacher for a single semester before he heard about Frank's accomplishments in Lancaster. If his cousin, who was not unduly endowed with brains, could make a good living as a storekeeper, Seymour figured he could do at least as well. He had left home last April, a week or so short of his nineteenth birthday. Now he had a job behind a men's clothing counter in Grand Lodge, Michigan. Aunt Jane Emily promised to mention Frank in her next letter to her son.

By the time he and Jennie started back for Lancaster, Frank had a clear idea of the men he wanted to hire if the time came when he could afford it. William Moore stood at the top of the list. Carson Peck and Fred Kirby both had a place on it, along with Dan Roberts, Harry Moody and a trio of cousins, Seymour, Edwin and little Fred Woolworth. Sooner or later, every one of them would take off to seek a fortune as if in answer to a tune played by Frank like the Pied Piper of Hamlin.

They were astonishingly alike in many ways: farm boys, limited in their education; strangers to the arts and any kind of luxury; early risers; sticklers for detail and attention to routine; men of his own breed. He felt at ease with them because he could trust them, as they trusted him. They would never think of trying to bamboozle or sneer at him, which was more than might be said of a lot of outsiders.

It was an age of faith in man-made miracles, in the betterment of life by the power of invention. Inventors were a species of national hero, the greatest of them a former newsboy on the Grand Trunk Railway who was now known as the Wizard. Thomas Edison's first patent, for recording votes by electricity, was a dozen years old. His latest, for "a phonograph or speaking machine," produced tinny sound from a hand-cranked cylinder and sold in the shops for $18. Though most inventions were group efforts, the public fancied the inventor labored alone, inspired by God. In Edison's case, this was close to the truth: the Patent Office could trace nothing remotely like a phonograph.

Frank came to be looked upon as an inventor of sorts. Some histories would credit him with creating a new method of selling, opening up stores close to a customer's doorstep, as opposed to the department stores, whose patrons had to be lured into setting out from home on a day's shopping.

But Woolworth never claimed to have invented anything. His talent lay in adapting ideas, not innovating them. Success, he realized, must be a joint effort, drawing friends and relatives into something akin to a farmers' cooperative. His personal capital added up to a few thousand dollars, and he refused to borrow more. He had satisfied himself that, given the right conditions, a five-and-ten could turn a profit. Since income from a single store would never make him rich, he must open another and another until he operated a chain of them, in the style of the Great Atlantic & Pacific Tea Company.

That prototype of American chain stores had settled on a name for itself a year before Frank and Jennie's vacation trip to Watertown. The Great American Tea Company was the label first adopted by the firm of George F. Gilman and George Huntington Hartford. Now it was the Great Atlantic & Pacific Tea Company, Gilman had gone into retirement in Bridgeport, Connecticut, and Hartford had sole charge of its outlets, each of them painted the same bright red and gold that Frank copied for his own ventures.

Hartford had been the innovator from the start, when he was working in Gilman's hide and leather shop in New York City. A canny Maine Yankee, Hartford calculated that tea, not yet replaced by coffee as the country's favorite brew, was wildly overpriced when it sold at a dollar a pound. By importing chestfuls of the leaf direct from the Orient, the partners could eliminate middlemen's charges and bring down the price to an unheard-of thirty cents.

They advertised their vow "to do away with various profits, and brokerages, cartages, storages, cooperage and waste, with the exception of a small commission paid for purchasing to our correspondents in Japan and China, one cartage, and a small profit to ourselves which, on our large sales, will amply repay us."

At the outset, they stationed themselves on the New York piers and peddled tea as soon as it was hoisted from a clipper ship's hold. Then they opened a shop at 31 Vesey Street. With a mastery of ballyhoo that Frank wished he might emulate, Hartford adorned its front with a mammoth capital "T" spelled out in gaslight. Lamps of red, white and blue flared in the windows. Band concerts drew in the crowds every Saturday night, to select tea from rows of bins lacquered in red and gold, while the cashiers sat in Chinese-style pagodas and a green macaw cackled on its perch on the ground floor.

Atlantic & Pacific red was the color of the wagon hitched to a team of greys that paraded through the streets to drum up more business, with $20,000 pledged to anyone who could guess the exact weight of the turnout. Hartford gave away lesser prizes—kitchenware, dishes and oleographs of bouncing babies—by the carload. When he and Gilman felt themselves on firm ground, they introduced a variety of kitchen foodstuffs, bought whenever possible without recourse to jobbers or brokers. Coffee, soap, condensed milk and baking powder were a few of the new items stacked on the shelves.

The hammering of the golden spike at Promontory, Utah, to mark completion of the transcontinental railroad in 1869 was the catalyst in Hartford's thinking. Now that steel track stretched from coast to coast, so might his grocery stores. At present, after twenty-one years, he had one hundred stores in operation, ranging south to Baltimore, north to Boston and west to St. Paul, Minnesota.

Other chains of stores were being assembled while Frank had gone no farther than Lancaster and Scranton. The Jones brothers of Brooklyn, taking off on the heels of the Atlantic & Pacific, started a tea company of their own, later to be known as Grand Union. A Cincinnati grocery clerk, Bernard Kroger, got off the mark with a venture whose title, Great Western Tea Company, was more imposing than its size; it had a long way to go before it became the Kroger Company, with peak sales of $286,000,000 a year.

The country was growing so fast it took a man's breath away. If he had a few dollars laid by, this was the time to invest them, so he could watch his money blossom along with everything else. It paid to be prudent, though, when anyone with his head level on his shoulders knew there were sharks in the sea who'd strip a man of his last nickel if he let them. The best place for spare cash was in the hands of someone dependable, like a member of the family. With this line of reasoning, an uncle of Frank's, Henry Wesley McBrier of Cedar Springs, Michigan, sought a slice of the five-and-ten business.

Until he retired, he had been a merchant himself. What he wanted now was a dime store, with one of his Woolworth nephews managing it. He outlined his proposal in a letter not to Frank but to Sum, promising to pay his expenses if he'd come west to confer with him.

Sum returned from Cedar Springs eager to join forces with Uncle Wes. Frank, equally eager to hold onto a capable manager, put up an alternative proposition: if his brother would stay on with him, he'd sell Sum a half interest in the Scranton store. That impressed Sum as the safer course to follow. A new sign, "Woolworth Bro's," went up when the deal was closed on January 9, 1881, but it was February 14 before Frank turned over the books, perhaps an indication that he regretted his decision.

Two years afterward, Sum bought Frank out completely, paying half the value of the stock plus $1,000 for "good will," a fair price for a business whose sales were already running ahead of Lancaster's. Sum's ambitions did not always coincide with Frank's. "I well remember the first night after I bought Frank's interest," he recalled, "how as I turned the key in the front door when locking up for the night, I said to myself, 'This business is all mine, and it is paid for, and I do not owe anybody a dollar.' "

In the four years that had passed since Frank took the plunge in Utica, the chain of pure gold he envisioned was reduced to a single link.

8

The Lesson
᛫] of B. Typhosus [ᛕ

Frank was thirty-one years old and he felt he was slowing down in what he sensed to be a race against the clock. He calculated his worth at precisely $9,129.13. He had to hurry to improve on that, drive himself harder, concentrate on business, though it entailed neglect of his wife and daughter.

Sum was introducing higher-priced items in his Scranton store. Frank decided to try the same maneuver. Sales had improved after he'd raised his limit from a nickel to a dime. Raise it to a quarter, and profits might jump again.

Space at 170 North Queen Street was already tight, so he rented a nearby shop for the experiment. Five months later, he acknowledged it had failed. "To my surprise, the sales did not increase, and it made trouble with the customers. I had a sign up outside, '5 and 10¢ Store,' and when they came in and found goods at the higher prices, they were disgusted." Yet he clung to the thought of quarters as well as dimes and nickels being rung up on the cash register. Twenty-five cent tags would be reintroduced later, with the same dismal result.

He drew heavily on his bank account to make his first sortie into a major city. The five-and-ten he opened on North Second Street, Philadelphia, was a loser from the start; within three months he gave up the lease, reduced once more to being a one-store operator, frustrated by the need for a greater variety of things to sell and for the buying power generated only by ownership of a string of shops.

"People," he reflected, "violate their own experience. Occasionally they do what they know they shouldn't. I find myself tempted to do once again things I have already learned not to do."

If he had listened to Jennie, he might have quit struggling and taught himself to accept that he had traveled as far as he was intended by God to go along the road to fortune. It was a mystery to her why he tortured himself by taking on more than he could handle without risk to his health. Why not settle down to enjoy what they already had?

Everything he had attempted to date had been financed from his savings, which gave him all the profits and burdened him with all the problems. He brooded over a scheme to bring in partners willing to match him dollar for dollar, manage a store, and take home half the profits. He would supply every item of stock, demand a daily accounting from them, and pay them six or seven dollars a week for expenses. That way, he could stay in the catbird seat.

There was a crucial flaw in the plan. Nobody he knew except William Moore, who was too big a fish for him to tackle, combined the necessary experience with the kind of money Frank was looking for. No friend of his in Watertown earned more than eleven dollars a week.

Out of the blue came a letter from Cousin Seymour Knox, written at his mother's urging. He was eager, he said, to team up with Frank, and he had some savings he was willing to invest. Frank's reply invited him to make his first trip to New York City for a two-man look at the town, including the wholesale firms Frank dealt with. The hotel he chose for the two of them, the huge white-marble St. Nicholas at Broadway and Broome Street, had caught his eye every time he passed by it; $1,000,000 had been spent on its furnishings; it accommodated eight hundred guests; central heating pumped hot air into all its rooms. Its parlors, lobbies and ground-floor library overflowed with awe-stricken out-of-towners who rated the place on a par with Grand Central Station.

It was probably none of these attractions that drew Frank to the place; it was the women of the town who loitered by the entrance doors, irresistible to a man who was continually away from home, "cruisers" in the terminology of the time. They patrolled Broadway from Canal Street to Madison Square from midafternoon until early morning, twirling their parasols when the weather was warm, swinging fur muffs when the days turned cold.

Frank reported that his cousin "was very much delighted and excited over the traffic and noise and confusion," but the words applied more aptly to himself. This first stay in a cosmopolitan hotel, where money could buy anything, left an indelible impression. Hotel living meant the luxuries of good meals, soft beds and available women.

Seymour was being courted by his cousin, and Seymour was playing skittish. When Frank took him to Lancaster to give him a glimpse of "a real five-and-ten cent store," he "seemed to be very enthused," but he was in no hurry to answer Frank's question: how much cash did he have to put up?

The answer was pried out at last: $600. That was both surprising and disappointing. The Knox family had always seemed so superior to the Woolworths that he'd thought there would be more. A half share in a new store was going to cost Seymour around $1,000, but that hurdle could wait until they got to it. The immediate need was to find a promising site.

Frank relied on instinct, though it had deceived him often enough before. He believed he was developing a feel for the right street in the right town in much the same way as a trawler captain senses where the fish are schooling.

Reading, Pennsylvania, forty miles away, struck him as a likely spot. The factory city with its work force of industrious Dutch had seen dime stores come and go, but the field was empty at present. He was staggered by the rent a landlord demanded for 720 square feet of floor space. Paying $900 a year would leave no margin for error. Seymour must make a go of it from the day the doors were opened.

"At that time," Frank recalled, "it seemed rather a tremendous big plunge for us. However, I had a little nerve left." He also had confidence in his cousin, "a bright, intelligent, go-ahead young man." Frank signed the lease.

Now the problem of financing had to be confronted. He had

$1,000 ready as his end of the deal; Seymour was $400 short. One cousin threw an extra loop around the other by lending him the $400, on the strict understanding that it was to be repaid as fast as possible out of Seymour's share of the net profits.

More than three-quarters of their combined capital was gone by the time Frank had shopped around New York City to fill the counters at 530 Penn Street; he had never before laid out so much money on a buying trip. Doubts about his cousin's ability started to nag him. Seymour's experience had been limited to selling men's suits and shirts at much higher prices. His only firsthand contact came when he helped uncrate the goods delivered for the ritualistic Saturday opening.

That night at eleven-thirty when he tallied the take, his spirits rose again. "I have never sold so many goods on an opening day," he exclaimed to Seymour: $210 was piled up in the till. He stayed on in their rented room overnight, to go home to Jennie on Sunday morning. He left with a parting caution for his overconfident cousin: "Telegraph me at once if you get into trouble."

Seymour's S.O.S. was delivered in Lancaster before noon on Monday. The Reading store was undermanned, with too few clerks to wait on the crowds that circulated through the aisles. Frank caught the next train out.

His concept of how a manager should behave was already crystallized in his mind. A manager must act with dignity, making it clear that he was a cut above his staff in manner, dress and expertise, since help must be hired cheap. "I was dumbfounded to find Mr. Knox behind the tinware counter with his coat and vest off, wrapping up tinware and taking in money as fast as possible."

He drew Seymour aside and recited the rules to him. A manager's role was to patrol the floor as a greeter and to *supervise* his staff. It was unbecoming for him to wait on customers, tie up packages or, worst yet, work in shirtsleeves. Seymour admitted the error of his ways. "Mr. Knox was always a very ambitious man," Frank remembered, "and if you told him once he was getting in wrong, he would never do it again."

Seymour urged his cousin to tone up the stock by adding some twenty-five-cent lines. Frank resisted, relating his sad tale of what had happened in Lancaster. Seymour, the more forceful of the pair, held firm to his opinion. When space next door on Penn

Street fell empty, Seymour talked Frank into diving again into a treacherous sea. Not a dollar from Seymour was added to the extra $1,000 put up to launch the two-bit store, "F. W. Woolworth & Co.," in which Knox was installed as manager, to draw a percentage of its income.

Stocking the place cost Frank a total of $1,900; on the day of its mid-October debut, $127 was rung up on the register. He reexamined the books on December 27. It had been another Christmas he would have preferred to avoid. In two and a half months, the store had cleared precisely $110. Chalking up yet another misfire, he vowed never to swerve again from the true faith: if his fortune was to be made, it must come from nickels and dimes.

He found a crumb of comfort when he had finished his year-end accounts and compared his situation with his cousin's. The previous year Frank had $13,416 to his name. On December 31, 1884, the figure had risen to $16,417.20. Seymour's brief spell as partner-manager had earned him $898.78 after he had paid off his debt. "I was a very rich man compared with Mr. Knox," Frank exulted, "but he made more money in the first three-and-a-half months he was in the five-and-ten business than he had made in all his life before, therefore he was perfectly satisfied." The arithmetic was correct; the reading of Seymour's sentiments was not. To satisfy himself, he had to prove he was Frank's equal.

Jennie had borne a second daughter in 1883. Edna was one year old when her father expanded the pattern of his traveling to snap up more than the job lots, canceled orders and discontinued lines he bought at a discount for cash. He was on the lookout now for promising localities as well as for compliant young men to recruit as his working partners. Moral fiber was a mandatory requirement; if they found themselves to be the only males on duty in a store, he did not want them to "take advantage" of the girls they hired to labor six days a week for $1.50.

Both inside and outside his family of relatives there were volunteers eager to put up their savings to enter the game. The looms, lathes, kilns, presses and stamping machinery of northern industry were pouring out a spate of goods at prices so low they fell below the profit requirements of a high-class department store whose overheads had to cover the cost of providing elegance in the form of ornamental fountains, comfortable "retiring rooms" for weary women shoppers, and free delivery. Frank's kind of store was a by-product of the factories, its development forced by the pressure of the flood of merchandise like water bursting through the rubber of a clogged garden hose.

Sum was on a tack similar to his brother's and doing about as well at it in Scranton. He moved his store from Penn Avenue to roomier quarters on Lackawanna Avenue, reserving the second floor there for items more expensive than Yankee notions. He, too, went hunting for a partner. His choice was his old Watertown workmate, Fred Kirby, currently earning $11 a week as the Corner Store's bookkeeper.

Sum saw opportunity shining through the murky skies of Wilkes-Barre. Would Fred like to share the risk and the potential profits of a venture there? If he could match Sum's $600 with an equal sum of his own, they would try together.

Fred closed out his savings account and borrowed $100 from friends and family. In eight years of clerking, he had $500 stashed away. "I could not have saved this money," he said, "without denying myself many a pleasure that I would have liked."

In the five-and-ten that carried a "Woolworth & Kirby" sign, his office was a discarded crate. First day sales: $26.32. Sum was happy to sell out and be replaced as a partner by sixty-year-old William Kirby, the old Forty-Niner, who found the pickings slimmer than they had ever been in California.

Long afterward, Fred and Sum, both multimillionaires, spared themselves nostalgia about the past. "It was tough sledding," said Kirby. "We had to cut corners pretty close," Sum agreed.

Cutting corners did not save Moore & Smith's from ruin after more than half a century on Public Square. Perry Smith pulled out and moved to New Jersey. William Moore went into bankruptcy, and the stock was sold under an auctioneer's hammer.

A strange kind of sentimentality ran strong in Frank. In a list he drew up of his early ventures, he assigned number one to Great Bend, where he had worked only briefly and without pay for Dan McNeill, the station agent-storekeeper. The value Frank set on friendship—at least equal to his regard for Jennie and their daughters—compelled him to bail out William Moore with a loan of $2,000 and so convert the Corner Store into something akin to a Woolworth's branch. Moore was set up as sole proprietor of a new five-and-ten on the original premises. Frank did all of Moore's buying at wholesale and charged nothing for the service.

His search for new partners met with mixed results. In Harrisburg, where a landlord's greed had once driven him into retreat, he enlisted little H. H. Hesslet, a local businessman, to join him in a sortie under the banner of "Woolworth & Hesslet." The memory of defeat in Utica still rankled, but the time had not come yet for a renewed effort there.

An introduction by Sum led his brother into harness in Trenton, New Jersey, with a New York glove salesman, Oscar Woodworth; the store they opened soon became the biggest money-spinner in the steadily growing group. Cousin Seymour, resentful of being overshadowed by Oscar, had a proposal to put up to Frank. Knox would find a buyer for his half-interest in the Reading operation and team up with Woolworth to seek fatter profits in some bigger city.

The reunited cousins settled on Newark, New Jersey. Rent, $1,200 a year. Value of stock on opening day in May, $4,675. Sales that same day, $161. Seymour's dejection deepened in December when the shutters went up for the last time. Frank felt he had once again been deluded by another man's enthusiasm. "If I give our men a piece of my mind once in a while," he decided, "it isn't because I feel superior to them. It's because we all need it."

Some areas of Pennsylvania had not yet been exposed to his lines of merchandise, and he knew what Pennsylvanians looked for on his counters. Erie, with its host of factory hands and a population that was doubling its size every decade, struck him as a possibility. He steeled himself to lease more space than he had ever taken on before and shipped in $2,500 worth of stock, which looked so lost that he hired a carpenter to close off sixty feet of a store as big as a barn.

The fresh coat of scarlet paint on its front was still wet when Frank and Seymour checked into a cheap hotel room, again to share a bed for the sake of economy. Sleep was fitful for both of them on the eve of the opening. Starting up a store evoked the same sense of hazardous excitement that a producer felt at a Broadway premiere: the first day's take might determine its life or death. Their working future depended on tomorrow's results.

In the morning, shaving at the chipped washbowl was performed with unusual care; the proprietors of a new business must

bear a look of well-groomed prosperity. From his travel-worn valise, Frank took out a clean white shirt, starched and ironed by
Jennie. He brushed the lint from the overused dark suit that had
been folded over the back of a hardwood chair. He and his cousin
were now in uniform for victory or disaster.

On their way to the dining room, Seymour found a letter from
home waiting in the pigeonhole behind the front desk. He opened
it at the restaurant table, and tears trickled down his chubby
cheeks. Frank interrupted his munching on a preliminary hunk of
buttered toast. What was amiss?

Seymour silently handed him the page that Frank's Aunt Jane
Emily had written to her son. "You must not lose heart. I have
been cutting down on household expenses and thus have accumulated quite a lot which I want you to have." Enclosed was a
money order for $40.

"Well, every little bit helps," Frank said.

They spent the morning at the store, arranging and rearrang-
ing the stock and counting customers. Only twenty-five came in.
After that, Frank needed more than a quick sandwich for lunch;
food, he was discovering, was an antidote for tension.

He led Seymour on a hunt for an eating place whose servings
promised to be hearty if the menu on view in the window could
be trusted. Neither man had acquired the ease in unfamiliar surroundings that a well-stuffed wallet bestows. They edged into the
lobby, respectfully removing derby hats from their pomaded
heads, then followed a waiter to a table for two. One plate was
picked clean by Frank, the other picked at by Seymour, who for
the moment had lost his appetite.

"We ought to be getting back," he said.

Frank was in no hurry. "Let's take a walk somewhere."

"You don't want to face it, do you? Neither do I."

"No need to get into that. Let's just bide our time."

They found a bench in a park along the lakeshore, putting off
a confrontation with the cashbox that would determine whether
their partnership, already dented, would be destroyed. When they
finally rounded the corner of the street where Woolworth & Kirby
was in labor, they broke into a trot. A throng of people was pushing in through the doors and jamming the aisles inside. Erie was
safe. The only drawback Frank could see was the fact that profits
here must be shared with Seymour, as losses had been in Reading

and Newark. He wished there were a way of reverting to the days when he hadn't to share anything with anybody.

For the present, he stuck to the partner-manager formula, setting up in Elmira, New York, with Earl Northrup and making a deal in Easton, Pennsylvania, with a Mr. Getman, who put his son in to run the store. "We are all one big family," Frank liked to say, "and our interests are mutual." With a hint of cynicism, his cousin Edwin McBrier, a latter-day historian of the company, judged that to be "a fine sentiment which he doubtless thought he sincerely entertained."

There was no change in Frank's position as kingpin. In essence, he was chief executive officer of a $10,000-a-year operation that returned one tenth of that sum in profit. He called for daily trading reports from each of his partners and supplied everything that was piled on the counters.

Jennie saw less of him than of some of her relatives. A husband whose creeping advance toward success was dependent on paring costs to the bone did not toss money around. The Woolworths owned no horse or carriage. She had no domestic help apart from that of her sister Sidney until another young sister, Mary Ann, came down from Canada to join in. Jennie's last child was born in 1886 and christened Jessie. Like her sisters, she had more of her mother's looks than Frank's.

The baby was three months old when he concluded he must shift his base to New York City, where the bulk of his buying was done. The move would make it easier to deal directly with distributors and, now that he was accumulating capital, even with manufacturers themselves if they agreed to work at his prices.

He combed the streets around lower Broadway, hub of the commercial district, until he came across a salesman for a Philadelphia line of tinware who was willing to rent him desk space for $25 a month in a sunless loft at 104 Chambers Street. Frank marked it as his headquarters by having the door painted with a framed "W." Across the East River in Brooklyn, linked to Manhattan by a three-year-old bridge that was rated an engineering marvel, he took a house for his family at 365A Quincy Street. He rode to and fro on the cable cars with a briefcase clutched under his arm and most of his business otherwise carried in his head.

He remembered making do without a stenographer or any other help for more than two years. "I did all the work myself, bought the supplies and arranged for the shipping of all the goods for my stores. No one ever had more to learn than I, and as I look back on my business experience, it seems to me that sometimes I was mighty slow in learning my lessons."

Besides making up the orders, paying the bills and keeping the books, he began to circulate a daily letter to his managers as a means of welding the scattered stores into a semblance of an organization. Eleven more links were added to the chain, some exclusively his own, some with partners.

Space became so cluttered that he leased another loft at 321 Broadway—office in front, storeroom at the rear. He slogged on alone for one more year before he doled out $6 a week to hire his first assistant, sixteen-year-old Alvin Edgar Ivie. Five days later, the office was moved into the cast-iron building that bore the name of the merchant prince who had erected it, A. T. Stewart, on the corner of Broadway and Chambers Street. It would be Frank's business address until he financed a structure of his own that created as much hullabaloo as had the dedication of the Brooklyn Bridge.

By the time Alvin entered the scene, Frank had survived a challenge from Cousin Seymour. The man Knox wanted as an ally was pious Cousin Edwin McBrier, recreant schoolmaster, now stationed in Elmira as general agent for an Albany publishing house.

Elmira's new five-and-ten, plain evidence of Cousin Frank's steady progress, fascinated Edwin. He spent evenings hanging around the place to get acquainted with its manager, Earl Northrup, and learn something about the trade. The subject came up when Edwin paid a visit to Seymour, Frank's commander in Erie.

Seymour enlisted Edwin in a plan to organize a business of their own outside the range of Frank's control. They drew up a formal alliance and Seymour cast around in New York State, applying Frank's yardsticks: was the street well traveled, the rental low, the population expanding, the competition minimal?

The terraced city of Lockport, bisected by the old Erie Canal and spanned by the steel of the New York Central Railroad, attracted Seymour. He leased space at 83 Main Street before he wrote to Frank, his unsuspecting partner in the Erie operation, to inform him of the emergence of Knox & McBrier.

If Seymour were allowed to get away with this maneuver, ev-

ery other partner-manager might take off after him and Frank's
slowly assembled enterprise would soon crumble. A telegram summoned Seymour for a confrontation in the Broadway office. Frank
railed at him, trying to split him away from Edwin. Knox stood
his ground. "If you claim the right to expand your business without me, I have the same freedom—without you."

Neither of them reported how long their clash lasted or how
many more encounters it took to resolve the quarrel. The outcome, Cousin Edwin wrote blandly at a later date, "had a distinct
influence in changing Mr. Woolworth's policy." Frank bulldogged
Seymour into making him a partner in the Lockport launching
and paid nothing for the privilege. He would handle all the buying and the bookkeeping, too. Seymour would provide half the
capital—nothing else. Edwin would furnish the other half of the
funding and manage the store, whose name would be Woolworth
& McBrier. Half the profits were earmarked for Edwin, one quarter for Frank, the remaining quarter for tricky Cousin Seymour,
whom Frank had deftly euchred and humbled.

The farmer's boy had overcome his callowness and self-doubt.
The pursuit of success had toughened his morale. Family and
friends had to reckon with a man whose character had changed.
Haggling in the arena of the marketplace as a condition of his survival had taught him how to fight. He liked to pretend he was still
an innocent greenhorn in the world of commerce, but this was a
sham. Victory over his cousins confirmed his thinking about what
the next step should be.

In Edwin's emotionless words, "Instead of continuing to establish partnerships, he gradually bought out the interests of his partners, placing managers in charge. These managers made no
capital investment in the business. They were engaged on the
basis of a participation in the profits; and this participation was
usually considerably smaller than the fifty percent basis of the net
profits which had formerly been the arrangement with the partners. One man, Frank W. Woolworth, *owned* [Edwin's italics] the
business; all the managers were employees."

One of the last investors to be let in before the door was
slammed shut came from the Watertown platoon. After thirteen
years at Bushnell's, Carson Peck was married now and eager for a
chance to get ahead. When Frank prepared to try again in Utica,
Carson volunteered to join forces with him. He borrowed his half

of the capital required to raise the Woolworth colors at 153 Genesee Street and set about working at the same breakneck speed as Frank to pay off the loan. As an official history of the modern company put it, "a glow of satisfaction came to Woolworth"; Carson was living up to expectations.

Frank and Alvin, a God-fearing youth, still comprised the only staff at New York headquarters. Alvin confided that "Mr. Woolworth seemed able to keep going all the time. He made decisions quickly, then stuck by them. But he was always ready to take time out for a joke, and if you did your work, he took you right to his heart."

But tackling every bit of correspondence in his scrawled longhand and writing a "general letter" six days a week for duplication on a turn-screw press was too much for the captain to cope with. He engaged spritely Miss Tallman to take dictation. The typewriter, as she was labeled in the vocabulary of the day, soon needed help of her own, and another stenographer was added to the staff.

After a while, Frank felt he should submit his books to a professional audit. The result was told as one of his favorite anecdotes.

The accountants asked to see his work force. Alvin, Miss Tallman, and one or two other girls were assembled on parade. "You don't mean to say you do business that runs into millions of dollars with this handful of people?" the senior examiner exclaimed.

"Yes, sir. This is my business force."

"Show us your bills receivable."

"I have none."

"Bills payable?"

"None. No bills payable or receivable."

"Good Lord! What kind of business is this? Let us see your January receipts."

It took three pairs of hands to carry in a packing case full of paper. "We'll have the other boxes brought in within a few minutes," said Frank.

The CPA dismissed the thought. "Never mind." At the end of the day, as the door closed behind him, he muttered to his deputy, "There must be something wrong with a business of that size that doesn't owe *anything*."

New five-and-tens covered the eastern states. After Utica came

Poughkeepsie, New York, and a manager whose appointment sent ripples through the organization: perky little Mary Ann Creighton, with her headful of pretty bubble curls, was Frank's sister-in-law.

The chain gained one more link in Wilmington, Delaware, and a partner in Baron W. Gage, a local entrepreneur. Then on into Allentown, Pennsylvania, and to run the store there, Woolworth reached back to Franklin Street, his old address in Watertown.

Clinton Case and his wife Mary lived there these days while he stayed with his job at Campbell & Moulton's and she taught in the Lamon Street school. Clinton at thirty-three felt he was wasting away in Jefferson County and immediately accepted the invitation to be partner-manager in Allentown. He scored so well that he was slated for further promotion.

In Buffalo, Frank and Seymour called a truce and entered into a fresh partnership. In Syracuse, Frank picked one more woman as a manager, enticing Mrs. Coons away from Watertown, where she had mothered him at Moore & Smith's. For the job in New Haven, Connecticut, he turned again to Jennie's family and chose her brother Allen.

The era of trial and error was over. The lesson had been learned, and it could be formulated in a simple sentence: mass sales build mass buying power. And the tide was with him. Soaring output from the factories was being matched by a sharp drop in wholesale prices, cut by more than half during the three decades after the end of the Civil War. Frank found more and more products falling within his reach.

He continued to bombard his people with commands. "To push trade in a dull season," said one directive, "keep your goods in as attractive shape as possible and trim your windows twice a week with big leaders with prices attached on each article and if necessary sell a few leaders for 10 cents. Among good leaders I can mention such things as two-quart glass pitchers that cost $1 a dozen and about 2 dozen in a barrel. They will cost you about $1.35 to lay down in your store. A lamp with burner and chimney to sell complete is also a good leader and costs about $1.15 (*per dozen*) laid down. . . .

"Another thing you must watch close in dull season is your expense account. Be sure and not have more clerks than you can possibly use and don't turn all the gas burners on every night. The same applies to coal. Watch your freight bills. Some of you have got the habit of placing goods that cost $5, $5.50 or $6 per gross on the 5-cent counter without looking at the articles to see if you can get 10 cents for it or not. Because the goods were bought cheap is no reason they should always be sold cheap. Put leaders in the front. That is our mode of advertising."

He realized that he himself was a mediocre salesman, and his partners put up no argument about that. He had no false hope that a girl paid $1.50 a week would be any more effective than he was. His solution was to reduce them to wrapping packages and making change. Salesmanship was unnecessary; his merchandise must sell itself. Customers were won by displaying everything within reach of their hands. Every item must evoke an impulse to acquire it. Concentrated buying power kept his price tags low. Generated in high voltage, its force was infinitely stronger than any sales promotions an individual store could devise.

He looked upon himself not as a buyer searching for what satisfied his own tastes but as an agent acting for his clients. Every product had to pass the same test: would it appeal to the average customer? He was armed by the prosaism of his own standards, a commonplace man who sensed the wants of commonplace people. His managers must devote themselves to managing. The power and responsibility of buying must be his alone.

The stream of battle orders continued unabated. "I wish to impress every manager to put the neatest, cleanest and most attractive girls behind your candy counter, as it surely helps to increase the sales. The manager gives a weak excuse when he says cats drink out of the fire pails. Always keep them full. The bad condition of the jewelry case should never be tolerated in any store. And signs at the back of the counter should be kept nice and straight."

He studied the incoming mail while the envelopes were still unopened. "We received the following letters this morning with postage due. From Bethlehem 2 cts due, Paterson 4 cts due, and Utica sent in a letter with a 5 cent stamp on. Please study up postal laws again, and weigh your letters. If you have anything to pay on our letters, let us know."

The one-man band could not play on forever. Strain and over-work pared his weight down to one-hundred-thirty-five pounds, and his clothes drooped on his bony frame. He was working by gaslight with Alvin one December night when he complained that he was in pain. Next morning, Alvin waited in vain for his boss's arrival. In the afternoon, a postcard was delivered from Jennie: "Mr. Woolworth has been sick and asks you to come here and bring the mail."

Typhoid fever, an implacable leveler in the Victorian age, rec-ognized no distinction between rich and poor, proprietor or em-ployee. The bacteria of B. *typhosus* bred in water. When epidemics flared, anyone who took an unboiled sip of it risked infection, and a city might then count its toll by the thousands—one outbreak in Philadelphia caught 14,082 victims. Men suffered considerably more than women and remained susceptible to the disease that bore a variety of names—slow fever, gastric fever and nervous fever were some of them—for a lengthier span of years.

In the house on Quincy Street, Frank's temperature was stead-ily rising. He was restless, languid and uneasy, the flush on his cheeks growing darker as the day wore on. There was no cure, no remedy, no medicines to be given him apart from those to lessen the ache in his head and groin.

"Let me know what you'd like to eat," Jennie would say, "and I'll run down and get it for you."

"I can't keep anything on my stomach."

"Can I give you another sponge bath?"

"Do anything you like so long as it gets me on my feet again."

"You mustn't fret, Frank."

"That's easy for you to say."

She applied cool water to his burning body at intervals throughout each day, hiding her concern over the rose-colored spotting that came and went on his chest and back. He accepted her attention as her wifely duty, but his interest was centered on his own condition and on Ivie's arrivals with the office mail and the latest batches of orders.

"What time is Alvin due today?"

"He'll be here this morning. He came last evening, but you weren't quite yourself then. The doctor says we have to expect the fever to go up at night."

"Why didn't you tell me he was here?"

"It wouldn't have done you any good. You were so busy talking to yourself you wouldn't have known what he was saying."

"Do you mean I was out of my head?"

"Yes, you were, Frank. And it wasn't the first time that's happened this week."

Anyone as sick as Frank was an immediate source of danger to those in contact with them. By the end of the third week, his tongue was so dry and brown he could barely speak. This was the time of greatest peril. Death could come from a number of causes—exhaustion, inflammation of the brain, heart failure, internal bleeding. There was nothing Jennie could do to help except soothe him with tepid water.

Once he had survived the climax, his convalescence followed the classic pattern, spells of recovery alternating with relapse. In clearer moments, an image rooted in childhood returned repeatedly to his mind. A business was like a snowball. One man could easily push it along for a while as it grew, but the snowball he pictured became so big that help was needed to roll it. And if you didn't keep it rolling, it would melt away sooner or later.

He was bedridden for nine weeks. It was February before the office staff saw him again, frail, trembling, convinced by illness that he had to amend his ways. His task now was to organize and deputize. If he persisted in going it alone, the business would continue at a standstill, which in the end would lead to its oblivion.

"I contented myself with the important matters," he remembered, "planning for expansion and the general oversight of the business, placing responsibility for execution of details upon my associates." He spelled out the lesson for himself. "As soon as a business grows beyond one's ability to attend to all the details himself, he must trust to organization and cooperation to carry it forward."

Before the year was over, he had allowed his colleagues a glimpse of another dream. In his convalescence, he had pored over census figures and statistics measuring the recent surge in immigration: a paltry 8,385 aliens admitted into the country in 1820 had reached a peak of 5,246,613 in the decade starting in 1880.

On October 11, 1889, he wrote: "I have had under consideration for some time the formation of a stock company. . . . There are 35 cities east of the Rocky Mountains that have a population of over 50,000 people in which we do not have stores. There are a large number of cities between 20,000 and 50,000 in which we do not have stores in which our business would be sure of success. . . . My idea would be, after the company was organized, to open up stores in these cities, perhaps ten or twelve a year."

Scouts would look for the most likely places, rent space, order the stock from New York. Then another advance guard would take over to uncrate the goods, engage the help, and stay on in charge of the debut before a permanent manager was appointed. So much for new stores.

"Now my idea would be to have a man make it a business to visit the stores, continually, and give them points on all new goods, new prices, new ways to display things that come up."

A supervisor installed at headquarters would handle group finances and oversee the staff there. Frank even pictured himself relieved of buying responsibility, which would call for training a team to take over from him. "For the first year, we would all have goods shipped direct to stores, but after that we might carry stock in a warehouse in New York of some of the small goods that we could buy to good advantage in large quantities."

This was the plan he outlined. Twenty-three years elapsed before it was realized. For the present, the major task was to ease the burden on his shoulders.

Alvin Ivie was among the tiny circle of men Frank depended on. Ivie became a jack-of-all-trades, laying out the fixtures and masterminding the opening of new outlets, beginning in Manchester, New Hampshire.

The same fidelity qualified Carson Peck, whom Frank called on in Utica. Out of earshot of the clerks, who were not to be trusted, he took him for a stroll on Genesee Street. "I have watched your work here, and I have liked it. I want you to come down to New York to help me."

Would that mean Carson had to give up his investment and go onto straight salary? Yes and no. Frank would buy out his interest, but Carson as his right-hand man would share in the chain's overall profits. One more precedent was set, the deal was struck, and on New Year's Eve 1889, Carson said farewell to his staff and went home to help his wife with the packing.

In New York, Frank chafed over the delay in assembling the year-end trading figures. The Saturday, January 4, bulletin chided his managers:

"You must now prepare yourselves for a good talking to. I have been obliged to get a new Typewriter and she is not as much accustomed to your writing as I and Miss Tallman the Lady I had before and I wish you would make a special effort when you make out orders to have them only one item on a line, only one firm on a page, and write on only one side of the sheet and use the cost marks to designate the cost of the goods and above all things write them plain so a person can read them and each word in full without abbreviations. After you have made out your orders give them to one of your girls to look over and see if they can read and understand them and that will be proof enough. . . .

"I expect Mr. Peck here tomorrow and he will be ready to commence work in the New York office next week. The clerks in Trenton and Syracuse stores have the 'Grippe' and they all seem to be afflicted more or less. Only two stores have sent in inventory yet. Remember all bills bearing date of December, 1889, go under last year's report and should be added to your inventory no matter if the goods did not arrive until after January 1."

The distinction was more important than a matter of routine bookkeeping. Pursuing his aim to own everything, Frank on December 31 had again severed his ties with Seymour, reducing to ten the number of links in the wholly-owned Woolworth chain. The Erie and Buffalo operations were now Seymour's exclusively. Ownership in Lockport reverted to Seymour and Cousin Edwin McBrier, since Frank had nothing invested there.

With his wagon hitched to his own star, Seymour set out to compete with Frank. From Buffalo headquarters, S. H. Knox & Company stores were strewn across New England and as far west as Detroit until the total reached 112 and Seymour was a millionaire. Edwin took off in a different direction. Leaving a younger brother, Mason, in charge at Lockport, McBrier sailed for China as a bachelor missionary of the Methodist Episcopal Church.

The tally of every last cent showed that in 1889 Woolworth stores had grossed $246,782, with their net worth calculated at $68,376, compared with a fragile $1,517 a decade earlier. He celebrated by going shopping for a house, to own rather than rent, in

Brooklyn. Jefferson Avenue may have appealed to him because it carried the same name as the corner of the earth from which he had sprung. No. 209 stood within a fenced-in backyard in a row of identical brownstones of middle-class respectability. He left early each morning to commute by cable car to Broadway and was seldom home before nightfall. He had come a long way from the farm in Jefferson County, yet he felt he had barely started along the road. Ambition, feeding on itself, did not include much in the way of life with his family.

9

A Sampling of Grandeur

The years in Brooklyn were probably the most contented Jennie ever knew. She finally had a home to settle down in, with enough money to furnish it in the solid comfort that had so far been missing. All her material needs appeared to have been satisfied. Lena, blonde hair frizzed with curling irons, attended public school. Edna would soon be tagging along after her. Jessie was no longer a baby, and she had her sisters for playmates. The three girls' stock of pretty dresses testified to their mother's skill with a sewing machine and an ironing board.

If Jennie had any problem, it was concern for Frank. She was used to his absences, so she accepted the inevitability of that, and she was grateful for the jobs he had given her brother Allen and sister Mary. She wished he would take better care of his health, but there was no point in harping on about it when he was not in the habit of listening to her. She had no friends outside her family and the people he employed, but she did her best as hostess whenever he brought them to the house to be entertained.

One such weekend was reported in a playful account for his managers: "The Lady Members of the WOOLWORTH SYNDICATE, Mrs. Coons and Miss Creighton, are in New York having a grand time. They have not been in the lockup yet, but they were locked out of my house last Saturday midnight and finally got us woke up after they had aroused all the neighbors."

He organized the first "Grand Five and Ten Reunion," as he

called it, to mark his recovery from typhoid fever. Sum came from Scranton and William Moore from Watertown. Seymour was there, jacket buttons strained by his increasing girth, together with Fred Kirby, clean shaven where the rest wore whiskers. Most of the men sported derby hats, but Frank, face still as pale as his silk cravat, donned a topper, and Mary Creighton had a confection of velvet ribbon pinned to her curls. There were second helpings all round, refills for the glasses, and a cigar for every man. When they posed against the backyard fence for the photographer, Mary grabbed a seat next to Frank, with a hint of flirtation in her smile. Half the party was unambiguously tipsy by then, and the style had been set for similar get-togethers held in the years ahead. No surviving photograph captures any sign of Jennie.

Frank had begun prodding American factory management to produce a variety of items specifically for the syndicate. Candy was a case in point. On Wooster Street, west of Broadway, he came across a little shop, "D. Arnould—Confectioner," where women worked in a backroom kitchen turning out chocolates, marshmallows, caramels, fondants, butterscotch, nougat, licorice and fudge for sale at the going rate of anything between twenty-five cents and a dollar a pound.

He introduced himself to the proprietor and explained that he was on the lookout for candy to retail at no more than a nickel for four ounces. "I can't possibly pay higher than that."

"I'll think it over and see what I can do," said Arnould. "Come back tomorrow."

He had a whole list of sticky delights waiting the next day when Frank arrived. A hundred pounds of assorted treats was ordered for every Woolworth store. How could the stuff be put on display? Frank hunted for glass trays and measuring scales, then dashed off a bulletin to all managers, alerting them to expect imminent delivery of a brand new line of merchandise.

They protested in chorus. Candy was perishable. Nobody would dream of buying it in a five-and-ten. And if anybody did, the margin of profit would be as thin as tissue paper. Frank overruled them, and they had to taste humble pie. Every candy counter had been cleaned out by the end of the first day it went on sale, and Arnould's confectionary business finished up as a factory that stretched along Canal Street.

At 280 Broadway, Carson Peck took on an extra assignment. Candy would fall within his province, which already included ordering enamel and tinware, wooden goods, twine, wrapping paper, Fourth of July specials and novelties imported from Japan. Peck, conscientious to the end, sampled every shipment of sweetmeats before they were divided among the stores.

Frank felt such confidence in his deputy that he soon planned to take off aboard the *City of Paris* for his first crossing to Europe in the company of B. F. Hunt, a buyer for an import firm with whom Woolworth had struck up a friendship.

He had shopped in advance for the gear he imagined he would need for a February sailing: a rubber raincoat, two pairs of Arctic overshoes, flannel underwear, a lap robe, a steamer cap. He bought a leather trunk, a valise, some bars of scented soap, a Kodak camera. A supply of medicine to calm his stomach was packed by Jennie. He tucked in a gift he'd received from Mary Creighton, his favorite sister-in-law, and on a single sheet of paper wrote a simple will, leaving Jennie everything he owned, while she wrote her own will with the same intention.

He would never have dared to go alone, but the man who had sold him on the idea was traveling with him. Toys were cheaper in Europe than in the United States, said Hunt, who knew the ropes and spoke some German, too.

His base of operations would be in Bremen, the commercial center of northwest Germany through which cargoes of woolens, linens, glassware and toys were funneled for shipping overseas. He wanted to travel on the cheap, which meant sharing a cabin with Hunt, and he underlined the fact in his parting instructions to his staff: "Postage on letters to Bremen is five cents per half ounce, so you must use thin paper and envelopes to save expense." And a final admonition: "I notice some of the bank accounts are getting low. Now you must be very careful and not order more goods than you can pay for while I am away."

The steamship *City of Paris*, bound for Liverpool, had scarcely pulled out from the pier before he began to feel sorry for himself. He went to his cabin to compose another letter to the only people in whom he constantly confided, his faithful managers.

"The agony is over and my Dear Friends that came to see me off have just gone home; and we are left to the mercy of the elements. I must confess that when it came to the final farewell a frog came up in my throat and I could say nothing but I have been trying hard since to get it out; and it will be all right in the morning. Frog up in my throat again; so I shall stop writing and mail this and go to bed. Good bye."

They ran into heavy weather from the start. After seventy-two hours, the seas were still mountainous, bouncing the ship around like a twig in a millrace. Frank's calm faded faster than his appetite, which was a bitter discovery for a man who liked his plate piled high; in the year since his illness, he had gained fifty-three pounds.

First day out: "On deck part of the day but awful sick from morning till night. Did not eat anything at all. I don't see any pleasure in going to sea. I wish I was home. Why was I such a fool to leave home?" His shipmate was a seasoned traveler, but he had never experienced such a storm. "Last night everything movable in our cabin broke from their fastenings and in the morning we felt we had been pounded all over."

Third day: "Pulled on my waterproof ulster and managed to get up on deck. It was the grandest sight I ever saw. The waves were mountains high, fifty feet I should say by actual measurement. . . . I am getting very weak and unless I eat soon I shall starve to death."

Fourth day: "The sea is calmer but still I can't eat."

Fifth day: "A fine bright day and the sea is comparatively calm. I'm still starving."

Sixth and final day: "Everything is calm and my sickness is gone. Have forgotten how sick I was already."

His first dry-land calls were made in Stoke-on-Trent in the heart of England's potteries, where smoke-stained kilns rose like a futuristic forest against the sooty Staffordshire sky. The gourmand in Frank arose, too. "I can eat now and never was so hungry in my life. . . . I am getting to be quite an Englishman and can eat Gorgonzola cheese, Stilton cheese, marmalade, cauliflower, mutton, pot pie, plum pudding, and several other luxuries. Cheese I eat every meal, same as the rest do. It is brought in in about 50 pound pieces and everyone digs out what he likes of it and in that way it is always fresh."

He inspected any number of china works, but he took his time about placing orders; food came foremost in his thoughts. "We went today to a hotel and ate in what they call 'The Ordinary.' It cost us two (*shillings*) and three pence and is patronized mostly by commercial men or travelers." Seated with fifteen other men at a long wooden table, he was fascinated by the ritual for electing a "president" as chief carver of the twin roasts of beef and mutton wheeled in by the waiter: the honor went to the diner whose stay in the place exceeded every other guest's. "The roast beef was the finest I ever ate. After that course was over they served puddings in the same way and then cheese, as Englishmen nearly always finish up on cheese. After all are through the waiter comes around with a silver plate and collects the two shillings, three pence, commencing with the President, after which the President thanks us very kindly and all is over. It is a very nice custom and I wonder it has never been introduced in America."

London made Frank feel like a boob. He could not understand a word the people spoke half the time, and they had the same trouble with him. He resented shopkeepers who treated him like a fool by trying to palm off stuff that would cost him a fortune in customs dues if he took it home with him. And the shops themselves did not compare with "our fine stores."

The compensations provided by breakfast, luncheon and dinner were not entirely dependable—he had the uneasy feeling of being underdressed. "We dined in a fashionable restaurant on the Strand. A fine orchestra discoursed fine music while we ate. Dress suits for Gents and Ladies is the rule there, but of course we had none to wear." With Hunt coaching him in the etiquette of the city, he "took lunch in a restaurant in the Old Palace of Richard the Third in the Throne Room. The bill of fare was dated 1466 but the meats and vegetables are comparatively modern."

The seed of an idea planted itself, though its germination followed considerably later. "I think a good penny and six pence store run by a live Yankee would create a sensation here, but perhaps not." He was thrilled to enter Westminster Abbey, since the flare-up of trouble in Ireland, "the guard at the door would not let me pass until I opened up my Kodak and proved to him there was no dynamite in it." Once he was inside, the sound of the great organ stirred him to the depths of his unlettered soul.

One other aspect of English living won his attention—the

women. A woman with a pretty face and a well-formed figure like Mary Creighton always appealed to Frank, and he found some dazzlers on view in London. "The ladies wear very low neck dresses in all public places here in the evenings, and we soon got accustomed to them." On a lower level of the social scale, "Mr. Hunt took me into the Bar Room of the Grand Hotel, which was fitted up fine, and behind the bars, dealing out liquids of all kinds, were handsome Bar Maids dressed up in the height of Fashion, as this is the custom in all bar rooms in England, large or small, to have female bartenders."

The two travelers, one worldly wise, the other innocent, bought first-class tickets to board the overnight steamer that carried them across the North Sea. But "of all the rotten accommodations we have had on our trip," Frank rated their stateroom the worst, and the breakfast served before they disembarked at the Netherlands port of Flushing was "rotten," too. "I did not eat it. You all know my weakness for good victuals and can appreciate my situation. To add to the horrors everyone was talking Dutch and even Mr. Hunt could not understand it."

Frank bridled again when the train bearing them to Cologne ground to a halt for customs inspection at the German border. "They went through my trunk and found a celluloid case with brushes etc. that Miss Creighton gave me for Christmas that looked too new to them. . . . They made me pay the enormous duty of five pfennings or 1⅓ cents just to show their authority."

After a change of trains in Cologne, they rode along the banks of the Rhine to reach Frankfurt that night, finding a beautiful city, a comfortable hotel and "last but not least good square meals and fine bedrooms heated with steam." There was only one drawback: "We could not speak their language and were obliged to depend upon Mr. Hunt entirely, and hung to him like a child for fear of getting lost."

Their goal was Sonneberg, capital of the microcosmic universe of dolls, that lies buried in a narrow valley in the forest of Thuringia. Frank was greatly impressed by the welcome the crowd at the station accorded Hunt, a familiar source of income for the town. "After the handshaking, kissing etc. were all over, we took the bus to Krug's Hotel, where we shall stay several days." He had his first sight of pinchpenny cottage industry as the two of them walked the streets, peering through leaded windows at men drinking beer while women and children put together, painted and dressed the wax figurines that they would afterward tote to the warehouses for shipment overseas.

A rare sense of injustice bubbled up in Frank. "Some of the women in America think they have got hard work to do, but it is far different than the poor women here that work day and night on toys, strap them on their backs, and go 10 or 20 miles through the mud with 75 pounds on their backs, to sell them." A Sonneberg *hausfrau* received three cents for a doll that would cost his customers a dime. Since she had to buy all the materials, she cleared approximately one cent.

"We saw a poor little girl that could not have been over four years old with a basket strapped on her back larger than herself and Mr. Hunt asked her where she lived and she told us a place about five miles from here, and she came alone. We gave her some money and she looked at it as if she never saw any of it before."

He struggled to learn enough German to strike his own bargains and buy direct from the women workers, and he laughed at himself for his blunders. "I came very near being thrown out of a window in one sample room while I was trying to get off my Dutch, as I told the man he was no good without knowing the meaning. Since then I have been very careful. They all have great sport with me trying to learn, but I don't care, but keep at it every day."

The menu at Krug's, heavy on sausage and sauerkraut, did little to enthuse him. "I cannot say that I have had what I call a good square meal since we left the Savoy Hotel in London." Before he left Sonneberg, he had placed orders for some 220,000 Christmas tree ornaments and earned a reputation as a public benefactor.

Compassion surfaced again when he rode with Hunt in an aerial car up pine-covered mountains to the little town of Lanscha, shopping for marbles and more tree ornaments. The marbles that cost him forty-five cents a thousand in America were worth only three cents a thousand to the young German girls who painted them. As for the tree ornaments, "they are made by the very poorest class there is in Europe and we were obliged to go into their dirty hovels to see what we could use. One place we went into we found a man and a woman in one room with six small children, the youngest not over eight years old, and both man and woman hard at work. It was the dirtiest and worst smelling place I was ever in, but they seemed to be happy in their filth and dirt."

The plight of the children of Lanscha affected him most of all. "The streets are full of them and most of them barefooted and bareheaded and the snow not all off the ground yet." That evening, after an acceptable dinner had lightened his spirits, he ventured to dance for the first time in his life, inviting a succession of *Fräuleins* to join him to the beat of a hotel band. "I do think a livelier crowd never struck the town."

Four days later, he was in Gotha, the ancient Thuringian town overshadowed by the castle of Friedenstein, "treated in royal style" by a manufacturer of children's tea sets, with a carriage and coachman taking Frank anywhere he fancied. His report of that day hinted that he was either lonesome for Jennie or regretful that his evening of fun in Lanscha had ended too soon. "Don't think many newly married couples come to Germany to spend their honeymoons," he grumbled, "for there is not such a thing as a double bed in the whole country."

Nuremberg, Munich, and then on alone to spend Easter in "Vienna, beautiful, magnificent Vienna, words cannot express the beauties of this city." Some of his appetites were quickly satisfied. "I never saw such good coffee before. It comes with a rich thick foam on top which seems to be the secret of its flavor. And the beautiful rolls that Vienna boasts cannot be beat." Other pleasures tantalized him: "the handsomest girls of any city in the world. They are one of the sights of the city and one can scarcely see on the streets an ordinary looking girl and as for real homely girls they are impossible to find."

Work and play could be combined; window-shopping and girl-watching went well together. "The store windows make the finest display of any city I was ever in. Everything looks so new and odd, and very tempting. It is all I can do to keep my money in my pocket. . . . The proper time for ladies to go shopping is between 4 and 8 p.m., and that is the time to see the people."

He wandered along the boulevards of the old Inner City within the tree-lined Ringstrasse, buttoned up against the raw March weather, listening for the chimes of St. Stephen's Cathedral to signal an approaching mealtime, aiming his Kodak at courtyards and churches, embassies and palaces "that were simply grand and must have cost a mint of money." He found it incredible when he tried to strike up a conversation that only a handful of Viennese spoke a word of English, though they looked so very much like Americans.

He patrolled the parks, the Hofgarten and the Volksgarten flanking the complex of buildings that comprise the Hofburg. "Children were playing with their nurses and by the way you should see the bright and gaudy colors the nurses wear, with dresses only to their knees, with red stockings and low shoes on, and nearly all wear hoops or something to make their dresses stick out all around like a ballet girl." He was enchanted to discover that in the Imperial Opera House he could listen to music while he eyed the ladies in their décolleté gowns. On a single night, he sat through three performances.

A drive to the outskirts took him to Schönbrunn and stirred the childhood memory of the Bonapartes which from then on would be a recurrent fantasy. "In the Emperor's bedroom saw the original bed that Napoleon first slept in when he occupied the Palace after he had taken the city. Napoleon must have been a perfect terror to all of Europe in his time, as we see his works nearly every place we go."

The weekend was over, and he had arranged to rejoin Hunt to attend the Leipzig Fair. "Oh, if I could only stay here longer," Frank wrote in farewell to Vienna, "but no use, I must go tonight sure, but I am in hopes of coming back again."

The contrast between *gemütlich* Austria and the commercial carnival in Saxony soured him. "Get out of the way, hustle up, tumble up, confusion. That is Leipzig during the Fair. If any one likes hard work and lots of it, let them come here and look over samples all day, up and down stairs, jostled about in the crowded streets, halls and sample rooms." He was beginning to question the drudgery to which he had once dedicated himself.

Work was laid aside when he and Hunt caught the train for Berlin and checked into a room at the Grand Hotel de Rome. Frank picked up a girl and gave his colleagues back home an ingenuous account of it. "Today I wandered into a show of waxed figures and while looking at a tattooed girl heard her drop a few

words of English. She told me she was an American and had come
to London with Barnum's show and will show in the various cities
of Europe.''

He also brought the Woolworth team up to date on another of
his pastimes. "Have been away two months and have had no
strawberries, celery, oranges, no beans, buckwheat cakes, oysters,
but they have lots of dishes here we don't. I have a good appetite
and can eat most anything but draw the line at sausage and caviar. The latter is composed of fish eggs, raw, soaked in oil and
looks like black tea. . . . Tonight we go to see Verdi's new opera,
'Othello.' "

He had just passed his thirty-eighth birthday when he finally
parted from Hunt and set off for an April weekend in Paris, as eager as a young man courting a sweetheart. He was down to his last
two francs in ready cash as he entered the Grand Hotel de
l'Athenée, 3,000 miles away from Brooklyn, and he spoke only a
single word of the language, but *oui* was enough for his purposes.
"All this did not worry me in the least and I put on as much
cheek as I would have done with a thousand francs in my pocket.
The first hard work I did was to order a *Table d' hôte* dinner."

Even the weather was kind to him, he thought, because the
rain "allowed me to see how the Parisian women expose their small
feet and ankles. Indeed, they take delight in exposing more than
the ankles. Nearly every one of them when the streets are wet
carry their overskirts over their arms."

The subject of toil and his temporary retreat from it came to
mind only fitfully. "I don't know what the people do for a living,
it seems to be all pleasure and no work." And of a tour of the
Louvre: "Rubens must have been a hard worker for he seems to
have more paintings in Europe than any other painter."

He learned French at the same snail's creep that had marked
most of his progress in anything. "The cabs here are very cheap.
You can ride anywhere in the city from point to point for one and
a half francs (30 cents) but the driver will call out 'Poor Boy'
which in English means a fee." The week was nearly over, and his
vocabulary consisted of *oui, non, garçon* and *merci* when he sallied
out for his first solo meal away from the hotel dining room.

"Well I managed to get soup, roast beef and coffee all right
but I wanted dessert and decided to go it blind. I pointed out an

article marked a franc and a half and thought I could stand that
all right. The waiter brought me the finest strawberries I ever saw,
served with the stems on in very small jars, containing about 5
strawberries each, and four or five jars in a small box filled with
moss."

He spent one dutiful afternoon prowling through Bon Marché,
which the Widow Boucicaut and her staff had built into the
world's largest department store. The statistics staggered him.
"They employ 4,000 people regular and feed them all in the same
building. . . . On the busy days the sales would run up to 1,500,000
francs ($300,000)." He perceived one flaw in the organization that
would never apply to a Woolworth's. "They use no cash system
whatsoever but each customer must go to the desk and pay for
what they buy. They are not allowed to pay the clerks who wait
on them."

The more he saw of Paris, the more spectacular it appeared to
be in its infinite—the word he chose was "grandeur." He had sampled the elation of high living, and he would never lose his taste
for it. Carriages to ride in, splendid restaurants, vintage wines,
music, luscious ladies to ogle—the trip had been what he termed
"a real eye-opener." He had arrived feeling he was a rubberneck,
a fish out of water, but next time would be better. "Nearly all the
men wear silk hats and gloves. In the evening dress suits are the
rule. If I ever come to Europe again I shall not leave my silk hat
at home and will surely bring a dress suit."

Three months had passed when he boarded the *Etruria* in Liverpool. In his luggage there was a big doll for each of his daughters on which, he grumbled, he would have to pay duty of $2.10.
He made no mention of a gift for Jennie. For seventy-two hours,
the return voyage was as wretched as the outward bound crossing
had been.

"The waves began to roll and the 1,300 stomachs on our good
old ship and I bid goodbye to breakfast and lunch." . . . "Stormy.
Ate nothing. The day has been so long. Will it never come to an
end?" . . . "A terrible hurricane with the sea boiling and foaming
and big waves breaking over it. . . . This has been the longest and
most disagreeable day I ever put in."

The three months he spent there—shopping for Christmas tree
ornaments and gimcrack dolls, sampling English roast beef and

Viennese opera, reveling in the luxury of grand hotels and the seemingly endless parade of enticing women—stirred his imagination. Not with the speed of a match applied to dry kindling, because he had not been an imaginative man. But the spark was there, the fire was smoldering, and eventually there would be flames. He boarded the steamship *Etruria*, westward bound from Liverpool in May 1890, dreaming of a business, perhaps on an international scale, pulling in a million dollars a year, enabling him to live in a style that suddenly appealed to him—in grandeur.

The daydreams were disrupted when the ship docked in New York. One face was missing from the little, familiar crowd that gathered to greet him as he ambled, heavy footed, down the gangway. "Such hugging and kissing I never got before," he exclaimed, but where was Sum? Fred Kirby, in from Wilkes-Barre, supplied the answer. Frank's brother "had been very busy in the past week and had succeeded in raising an eight-pound boy." So in his first-born child Sum had what Frank was short of—a son to follow him in the business. His comment was cool: "No doubt he feels very happy."

There was other news, but it was kept from him until he was home in Brooklyn and the remains of Sunday breakfast had been cleared from the table. The syndicate, he was told, had suffered its first fatal casualty. Hesslet, the prim little man with a goatee who had been partner-manager in Harrisburg, was dead, killed by a heart attack at the close of a working day.

"At first it seemed impossible that one of the best friends I ever had should pass away so quickly," Frank wrote that afternoon. Jennie would have to take the evening train to Lancaster with him, to make a joint appearance at tomorrow's funeral.

The loss of Hesslet was a double blow. Where could a replacement be found? Even more crucial, how was Frank to locate officers for the new outlets he intended either to initiate or acquire? There was too much catching up to do for him to take off on a fresh round of talent spotting, yet the only people to be entrusted with a manager's job were men like himself, his alter egos.

If Fred Kirby were available, he would make an ideal colleague. He had floundered for a while after the end of his partnership with Sum. Fred was downcast about his prospects the day he met a legless veteran of the war propelling himself along the sidewalk on a low platform fitted with rollerskate wheels.

"I got to comparing my condition with his," Fred liked to recall. "Right then and there, I decided to try harder. I had new strength, new determination, new confidence."

During the past two years, he had set up Kirby stores in other towns, and things were looking bright. It would be useless for Frank to ask him to drop everything and enlist as a lieutenant. There had to be a likelier solution to the problem of manpower.

Woolworth came up with the answer: the syndicate itself must raise the next generation of managers. Carson Peck, firm but friendly in relationships with everyone around him, was handed one more project. He was to supervise the training of young beginners whom Frank labeled "learners."

They were brought in raw and callow and put to work for minimal wages in stockrooms, tackling the same chores Carson and Frank had once been saddled with. In this way, the base of a pyramid of promotion was put together. When a manager was selected to run a new store, his assistant moved up into his place, and a new learner was picked to climb one step up behind him.

The structure was designed to have a boundless future. When the chain grew too big for supervision from New York, a senior manager was raised to the rank of area supervisor. When, in turn, their number became too unwieldy for centralized control, a district office was created, with a former supervisor put in as area manager. From the base up, another round of advancements got under way.

Profit sharing was the glue for holding the pieces together. A manager was treated more like a partner than an employee. Though he would fix wage scales for his staff and for the learners assigned to him, he would be paid no salary but commission calculated on the earnings of that link in the chain for which he bore responsibility.

On the face of it, the plan was foolproof. It took care of everything Frank was reaching out for: ability, loyalty rewarded in cold cash, a business made up of his own kind of man. *Man* was an operative word; no women were accepted as learners. The count of managers of their sex stood at two, Mary Creighton and Mrs. Coons, though it was women and only women who served behind the counters for $2 or a rare $3 a week. "We must have cheap help or we cannot sell cheap goods."

Peck's eagerness to help with the scheme came as instinctively to him as popping candy. Perched on top of the pyramid and holding title to most of it, Frank went on poring over census figures. "I am convinced," he announced, "that there are a hundred cities and towns where we can locate five-and-ten-cent stores." There lay the route to a million dollars a year.

Growth was essential in the country's creed for a businessman or the nation to achieve manifest destiny. Growth in industry and commerce would guarantee a better life for all and opportunity for a hard worker to get rich. Growth of population boosted America's power in world affairs. After the cruiser *Maine* settled on the bottom of Havana harbor, that particular growth brought a walkover victory over the Spaniards who ruled Cuba.

The census figures supported his conviction. The greatest mass movement of people across the face of the earth that had ever been known in an era of peace was under way. Up to 1846, immigrants to America numbered less than 1,600,000. Then the flood began, first with the Irish escaping famine at home, followed soon after by Germans in flight from political disorder. By the time Frank was plotting the currents on the charts hung on his office walls, the total of newcomers approached 16,000,000, more than fifty percent of them either British or German.

The charts and his breakdowns, city by city, of where the throngs were settling determined his strategy. Provided it was effectively located, a store's sales would probably grow at much the same speed as the town it was sited in. How rapidly he expanded his overall business was decided by the profits made by the Woolworth's already in existence, since capital must be self-generated, not borrowed from a greedy bank. Every new store was financed from the existing ones.

The advance into Massachusetts was staged on two fronts, Springfield and Worcester. Then came Virginia, first Richmond and three months later Norfolk. Blacks, in many cases poorer than the most poverty-stricken immigrants, flocked to the five-and-tens, but he found no place for them behind his counters.

In business terms, every Woolworth's was a profit center. As Frank dictated the rules, "Each store must be successful in itself. The separate stores are like a lot of barrels making up a raft—each barrel must hold itself up to a fairly high level."

Staying afloat was the individual manager's duty. He had authority to stock whatever items sold best, and showed the biggest return on investment. Standing instructions from headquarters compelled a manager to try out goods when New York shipped them to him, but he had leeway in reordering any experimental line unless it had proved itself with his particular customers.

Sheet music was an example. Frank, the frustrated piano player, added it to the general inventory in hope of its becoming a solid moneymaker. His managers convinced him that, instead, it was a "sticker," and he agreed they should order no more. (Eighteen years went by, Franz Lehar wrote "The Merry Widow Waltz," customers clamored for copies, and Frank had the pleasure of seeing sheet music restored as a best-seller. In one twelve-month period, the chain sold 20,000,000 sheets of music as well as 5,000,000 phonograph records.)

Turnover among his managers was low, and he credited his own astuteness for that. "I could always size up a man at a glance. And no one I ever fired ever made good anywhere else, so far as I know."

He bombarded them with directives. "You don't have to bark for customers. Draw them in with attractive window displays. Remember our advertisements are in our show windows and on our counters." He wanted the bait behind the polished plate glass rearranged twice a week. And then there was the matter of politeness to patrons. A telegram went out to every store: GOOD MORNING. DID YOU SAY GOOD MORNING TO EACH CUSTOMER THIS MORNING? F. W. WOOLWORTH.

Carson Peck, accepting that communication was a two-way street, urged the field staff to talk back. "Kick on every occasion that warrants it," he advised. "Kick intelligently so that your kick touches the right spot. If you don't like the goods we buy for you, kick. . . . We may kick back, but you're used to that."

One old-timer of the team who enjoyed freedom of action was Mrs. Coons, known in the New York office as "the Lady of Syracuse," where her hold over her girls was tight. A sales day she organized there drew a restless crowd before the doors were unlocked. "I sent for a policeman," she reported joyfully. "No sooner did he gaze upon these beautiful things than he was overcome and joined the mob. So this grayhaired lady formed herself into a police force and tried to keep the crowd from killing the clerks and smashing plate glass."

She was one of the troops pulled in by Frank to stake out

Rochester, New York. Carson Peck traveled up from his home in Brooklyn, and William Moore down from Watertown on the same mission. When Frank had originally seen the city, the $700-a-year rent for the location he wanted had scared him away. Now he was willing to pay $4,500 a year on a forty-four-month lease on East Main Street.

It was a commitment that alarmed his lieutenants. Perhaps he was gambling with trouble by overextending his resources. But he had listened too long in the past to ill-informed opinions, and he dispensed with any board of directors: they invariably complicated his affairs, he argued, and killed more good deals than they ever clinched.

"We have the biggest store in the biggest city in the Syndicate," he assured the skeptics. "Our location is prime. The store is large enough and the city big enough (138,000) to beat all records. We shall try to open three weeks from Saturday, August 22."

The days of cutting corners and running on a shoestring were over. The Rochester counters were craftsmen's handiwork, not packing cases covered with cotton cloth; the signs hung above them were not hand-lettered cardboard but stylish glass. Neither gas jets nor kerosene lamps but Mr. Edison's electricity lit the place. Merchandise was displayed in hardwood boxes instead of tin bread pans. With its sixteen stations and screwtop cylinders whizzing to and fro on overhead tracks, the change-making equipment was as fancy as a department store's.

Frank extracted Clinton Case from Allentown to take command, and Clinton felt safe in breaking the rule that only learners could find footing on the promotion ladder. The man he hired to help with the unpacking was no eager stripling but a former citizen of Watertown only three years younger than himself, Harry Moody.

Frank's nighttime comrade in Bushnell's cellar had gotten nowhere so far in his efforts to advance himself. He had long since quit Bushnell's and moved to Rochester, aiming to get out of dry goods by taking a course in stenography. But his studying had to be given up when his funds ran out. He took to the road as a traveling salesman and flunked again.

He was left with only one recourse—to go back behind the counter, this time as a clerk at Sibley, Lindsay & Kerr's, dry-goods merchants of Rochester. He jumped at the chance to work for Frank, no matter how far apart they were in income and status; somehow his old friend would open doors for him. Harry Moody was right in his forecasting: he would eventually be worth $3,000,000.

While his deputies drilled the newly hired clerks—five dozen of them in all—for impending duty, Frank proposed a raffle, everyone in the management group to hazard a written guess at the first day's sales and seal it in an envelope, prize for the most accurate estimation to be a ten-dollar bill—five girls' wages for a week.

Nobody hit the bull's-eye; nobody had imagined a five-and-ten bringing in $1,119.22 in twelve hours of trading. Frank spread the news: "We are the talk of the town. All wonder how we can pay such rent and sell goods so cheap. . . . We had customers from the moment we opened until we closed." But he was getting persnickety about close personal contact with the sources of his income. "In the evening there must have been over 500 people in the store at once and the heat and smell was awful."

In the spring of 1892, he engaged as a learner a Canadian teenager who, in the absence of a natural heir, was ultimately to head up the Woolworth empire. Hubert Templeton Parson, nineteen last September, had come down from Toronto to Manhattan in search of a bookkeeper's job. After Frank spotted the classified advertisement Hubert placed in the *World*, he summoned him to his office. Alvin could use some help, but Frank would do the choosing. As the interview was reported, he lived up to his claim to be a shrewd judge of men.

"What can you do for me?" he asked.

"Anything you've got for me to do."

"All right. I'll try you. The pay will be eight dollars a week."

Parson asked for twenty-four hours to think the offer over; he had another interview lined up. Frank consented to wait. Seldom headstrong himself, he appreciated a measure of caution in a young man. The next day, Parson persuaded Frank that he had rejected a better proposition because he wanted to dedicate himself to Woolworth's. The first career man in its financial history was engaged on the spot.

Friends or relatives filled most job openings at headquarters, and office romance blossomed. One more of Jennie's sisters, Henrietta Creighton, joined the stenographers' pool; Alvin Ivie, currently the manager in Albany, knew what his next ambition would be as soon as he met her on a scheduled trip to New York. Frank reported the consequences:

"At 4 p.m. today at 209 Jefferson Avenue all that remains of Alvin E. Ivie and Miss Et Creighton will be united in the Bans of Matrimony and will start immediately on their wedding trip. I understand that there have been several bushels of rice ordered and there have been several men employed for a week collecting old shoes. There has been talk of an invisible wire stretched across the door of the room where they are to be married. A balky horse has been engaged to take them to the station. A card has been labeled 'Bride and Groom' to hang on the rear of the carriage."

He could be much less jovial. Within a few months, Parson showed his aptitude for analyzing records, and perhaps he prompted Frank to circulate an end-of-the-year warning throughout the chain. "We pay out more than one third of our annual expenses for salaries. . . . When a clerk gets so good she can get better wages elsewhere, let her go—for it does not require skilled and experienced salesladies to sell our goods. You can get good honest girls at from $2 to $3 a week and I would not give $3.50 for any saleslady except in special cases. It may look hard to some of you to pay such small wages but there are lots of girls that live at home that are too proud to work in a factory or do housework. They are glad of a chance to get in a store for experience if nothing more and when they get experience they are capable of going to a store which can afford to pay good wages. But one thing is certain: we cannot afford to pay good wages and sell goods as we do now, and our clerks ought to know it."

The conversion of the United States from a land of farms and homesteads into a nation of cities and industry was progressing at a gallop, though neither Republican nor Democratic party recognized the stresses that were developing under pressure of relentless change. America's health and wealth were dependent now on big business, from the supply of raw materials right on down the line to the distribution of finished products. Farmers, impoverished by years of deflated prices for their crops, fought to hold onto a vanishing mode of life. The railroads had opened up the way for homesteaders to till the soil from Connecticut to California when the war ended. But now, as one farm journal declared, there was "a screw loose" in the economy. "The railroads have never been so prosperous . . . and yet agriculture languishes. . . . Towns and cities flourish and 'boom' . . . and yet agriculture languishes. Salaries and fees were never so temptingly high and desirable, and yet agriculture languishes." The Woolworth team could congratulate each other on having fled farming while the fleeing was good.

Discontent mushroomed in the factories, where pay stayed low and fear of competition from cut-throat immigrant labor increased. The Knights of Labor had discarded the mask of secrecy and emerged into the open as a union of all workers, skilled and unskilled, manual, clerical and professional, with nearly a million members and influence in excess of its size. Since 1886, the Knights had faced rivalry from the new American Federation of Labor, which looked to organize workingmen craft by craft as a prelude to confronting the bosses.

Of the nation's 60,000,000 and more people, many did not care which party was in power, and cynics offered their votes for sale, cheap. That made it easy for the Republicans to get their candidate, Benjamin Harrison, through the Electoral College to oust Grover Cleveland from the White House, though Cleveland ran ahead by almost 100,000 popular votes.

Frank took a certain professional pride in the victory. It was largely the work of a man who, like himself, had started as a storekeeper's clerk—John Wanamaker of Philadelphia, former president of the Young Men's Christian Association, now merchant prince, kingmaker and pride of the dry goods trade. The bulk of the party's war chest had been collected through his efforts, and his appointment as postmaster general was his reward. "Only the interest of the public service should suggest removals from office," said Harrison, but Honest John was a champion of the spoils system: every Democrat in his department was dismissed, 30,000 of them in the first year. The road to the presidency had entangled the party in such a thicket of political obligations that there was no other way out of it.

Another product of Honest John's energies aroused Frank's admiration. The Wanamaker store in Philadelphia, with its fountains, marble statuary and seating for 10,000 hungry shoppers in its Crystal Room, was the grandest showcase he knew of, apart from Bon Marché. Some day, Woolworth thought, he would like to see his name on a building like that.

By 1892, after four years of Harrison, the United States Treasury had been looted, gold reserves had fallen below the danger point, and the "Billion-Dollar Congress" had set a peacetime record by spending more than that sum in a single session. Spurred on by labor groups traveling out from the cities, the farmers were in revolt, hammering together a political platform that demanded free coinage of silver, a graduated income tax, curbs on immigration, an eight-hour day for factory workers, direct election of senators, nationalization of telegraphs, telephones and railroads. In November, Cleveland routed Harrison by a plurality of 400,000 popular votes, 277 to 145 in the Electoral College.

In December, before Cleveland returned to Washington, Frank ran into his first strike. Endemic unrest in the land caught up with him at last. Men like Carson Peck, seeing the dangers as well as the benefits of the changes that swept the country, could have been surprised only that it had taken so long when Woolworth considered salesgirls as disposable as wrapping paper.

The strikers were out for better pay, nothing more. They walked out spontaneously, self-organized, incited by resentment of long hours and skimpy wages. Their timing, however, was astute. Christmas shoppers made December the peak profit month for every Woolworth store.

Frank's response was cagey. Instead of firing the rebels on the spot, locking them out or hiring scabs as most employers would have done, he recommended jollying them along into believing they had a chance of winning. On the thirteenth of the month, he told his managers, "No doubt they will take advantage now while we are so busy, and think we will pay the advance. All such girls you should remember when the dull season comes and give them the 'bounce.' "

But skinflint methods could not endure forever. Beneath the glitter of Edison electricity, the new skyscrapers, the washing machines, bicycles and horseless carriages that were being hurried onto the market, a class war was in the making. Ten days before Cleveland took office again, the Philadelphia and Reading Railroad went bankrupt, with debts of $125,000,000. Immediately after his inauguration, panic struck Wall Street. Five hundred banks failed, and unemployment rose toward the 3,000,000 mark.

The country itself was on the brink of financial collapse, with insufficient gold in government vaults to redeem the currency notes in circulation. Only a handful of businesses escaped the effects of the slump; one of them was Woolworth's, rich in cash and free of debt. As factories faltered and wholesale prices sagged, Frank found more and more items dropping within his range. "We got another foothold," he reported happily, "and were able to secure large and fine goods to sell at our prices."

At Carson Peck's urging, the syndicate began to improve conditions for its girls. Managers eager to maximize profits were no longer free to cut clerks' pay. New minimum wage scales allowed nothing for overtime but left the top limits wide open. Vacations with pay—one week for everyone employed six months or more—were introduced by the middle of the decade, to be followed by Christmas bonuses: $5 for every year served up to a total of five.

These moves were made despite a sudden deterioration in the general business climate that threatened the very existence of the five-and-tens. The sheaves of documents delivered to Frank's desk every day showed a dramatic reversal of the downward trend in costs that, over the past two decades, had encouraged him to broaden the range and increase the quality of his stock. The charts he kept indicated a precipitous rise. Since his selling price was held at a dime, the margin of profit was shaved slimmer and slimmer.

But he had the weapon of buying power. Sales passed the $1,000,000-a-year milestone in 1895, and the figure was more than quadrupled four years later. The syndicate would absorb a factory's entire output under the terms of year-long contracts. Frank dictated the terms to those manufacturers; the price of their security was subservience.

His competitors fought back as best they could. If a rival five-and-ten lowered its prices, Frank declared war, commanding the local manager to undercut his opponent and go on undercutting, selling at a loss until a truce could be arranged. If an antagonist could be driven to the wall, a temporary dip in profits was insignificant.

The opposition tried another tactic. The rumor spread through the trade that Frank, a Yankee born and bred, was in fact a Negro. He laughed at the absurdity of it. Slurs like this were nothing compared with the threats against his life that compelled old John Wanamaker to engage an armed bodyguard.

Woolworth liked to rile people, competitors, manufacturers or his own staff alike—anybody but his customers, who must always be respected. He encouraged his underlings to confide suggestions and complaints directly to him. If one man leveled an accusation against another, he called them both in, happy to see them harangue each other. "Now I've got you," he would say. "You're losing your tempers and maybe we'll get to the bottom of this business."

Sometimes he took a different tack and stayed out of the way to check on how his team would manage without him. For once, he had Jennie and their daughters with him when he sailed on one of his annual missions to Europe in May 1895, leaving the August opening of the chain's twenty-ninth store—in Washington, D.C.—in the hands of his lieutenants.

The new manager there, originally commissioned as a learner, sensed the boss' hankering for glory. His cablegram to Frank proclaimed: ONCE AGAIN THE BANNER OF WOOLWORTH ENTERPRISE HAS BEEN PROUDLY UNFURLED TO THE WINDS OF TRADE—THOU TOO SAIL ON, O EMBLEM GREAT, WAVE ON AND KEEP THY PLACE OF STATE AT THE HEAD OF THE SYNDICATE.

Clinton Case's report came closer to matching Frank's homespun prose. "When I raised the sheet of paper covering the door my heart almost went out to the very end of my big toe. Great guns, what a mob! Women, darkies, police, enough to take the whole building and dump it into the Potomac River but we had to let them in. And they came like an Iowa cyclone and in less time than I can write the store was packed and we had to call on the police for help. All day a sweltering, perspiring crowd fought for bargains. The crush was so great that our glass side lights on both sides of the entrance were smashed. We took in $1,954.08, a new record."

Frank, back in harness, set about correcting a curious omission in the roster of his enterprises. Though he had become the grandee of the five-and-tens, there had been no store of his close enough for Jennie, a homebody, to shop in personally from the time the family left Lancaster. He nosed around the streets of Brooklyn, smelling out the territory. The Washington experience proved that money lavished on fitting out a store earned quick dividends. The merchant princes had learned this long ago. Now Frank put the principle to work in his own bailiwick.

Brooklyn, growing at the rate of twenty-five thousand more people every year, was the fourth largest city in America and fourth, too, in the value of its factory products. There was talk of its being merged with New York very soon, and more discussion of the need to build a second bridge across the East River. He found what he was after at 532 Fulton Street, a new, steam-heated building, three floors plus basement, located in a row of department stores.

Preparations began as soon as the lease was signed. Mirrors paneled the rear and side walls behind the display windows. Woodwork was painted and glazed in a semblance of mahogany. Counters were cut from cherrywood. Showcases for jewelry and candy shone bright with incandescent light. One hundred and sixty girls, chosen for their looks, were rushed through a training course.

The newspapers covered the opening as though it were produced by Gilbert and Sullivan. "The visitors," said one account, "were agreeably surprised when they found the big store stocked from floor to ceiling with useful and ornamental articles of almost every conceivable kind." Income on the first day broke another record: $3,139.41.

One more giant step forward had been taken. The Woolworth formula succeeded not only in farm and factory towns but in the heart of a metropolis, too. The manager he selected for Brooklyn stood higher than ever in his regard—Mary Creighton.

But the city was not grand enough for his personal tastes. Jennie's fading health was his excuse for moving his family into a furnished brownstone on Manhattan's lower Fifth Avenue, where the neighbors were men of stature and substance. Her doctor had recommended their leaving, Frank explained, because Mrs. Woolworth "has had trouble with her throat."

The home on Jefferson Avenue, complete with every piece of furniture, was a gift to Mary. It would be a convenient place to visit when he came over in his new carriage to keep an eye on the store and maintain his friendship with his admirable sister-in-law.

10

The Sidewalks
of New York

Wedding bells and nepotism strengthened the clan spirit among the management. After Henrietta Creighton became Mrs. Alvin Ivie, Hubert Parson, whose manner was as stiff as his collar and shirt cuffs were starchy, began courting Maysie Gasque, sister of one of the typists at headquarters, at the same time that Fred Woolworth, Frank's young cousin from Jefferson County, was taken on as Ivie's new assistant. Fred's credentials could not be questioned: he had worked first for Bushnell's in Watertown and then for Sum in Scranton.

The clan gathered for a day by the sea every summer, first at a cottage rented by Frank in Asbury Park, New Jersey, and afterward at resort hotels along the same shoreline. The carriage and pair he had bought were always on hand as evidence that he had joined the ranks of what he referred to as "the upper crust."

His ambition was to attract more people of that same class into shopping at Woolworth's. He delivered a brief lecture on the subject to his managers, whom he sometimes addressed nowadays as "my generals." "Be especially attentive," he said, "to customers who come to your store in carriages. This class of people likes to be petted and waited upon. Managers should never smoke or wear their hats. Sales ladies should be neat and clean and dressed in black."

All expenses were paid for at a seaside frolic. He would lower his increasing bulk into a beach chair or a rocker on the piazza to watch the ladies scurry into bathing machines and emerge, shrieking for joy, in serge suits and sun bonnets for a splash in the water, with a round of ice cream cones awaiting them as a reward for valor. For the men, straw hats were *de rigueur.* Kodaks clicked. Cigar smoke drifted on the breeze, along with choruses from such solid song hits as "Daisy Bell," "Sidewalks of New York," and "Hot Time in the Old Town Tonight."

He took his followers aboard a hired coach-and-four for drives along the sands, with one uniformed Negro at the reins and another tooting a hunting horn.

The souvenir snapshots had much in common: Frank sprawled grinning in the front row, flanked by Mary Creighton and Mrs. Coons; the tilt of the straw hats; the interlocked arms; the ogling of Mary. On these outings the dry goods business enjoyed something more exhilarating than branch water. Jennie was never to be seen.

On Sunday mornings, Frank conducted his guests to church as a man of his station should, yet there was a suspicion among some of them that they were out of place in exalted society. Alvin Ivie remembered, "We were still pretty much looked down on. When upper-crusters who knew each other would meet, each would pretend to the other that it was her first visit to the store—even though I'd seen both at our counters repeatedly."

William Moore hinted at a similar feeling when after one so-called "convention" he wrote: "The first day the Ocean looked like any Ocean and the thousands of nice-looking people did not look any better than our party and surely did not have any more fun."

When Clinton Case asked for an assistant to share the burden of European buying trips on which he substituted for Frank, the boss brought down from Rochester that companion of his youth, Harry Moody; after his stint at ripping open packing cases, he had been put in charge of the Rochester outlet.

Then Frank reckoned he, too, could use some help on the tours of inspection he made to ensure that every operation was conducted by the rule book. He turned to yet another ex-farm boy from New York State, Charles Griswold, who had left his imprint as "general" in Norfolk, Virginia. He would spend most of his time traveling the circuit and winning the nickname "Old Eagle Eye."

A letter to Frank was all that was necessary to give Clarion Bartlett Winslow a foot on the beanstalk that led into the land of giants. Winslow's qualifications were uncannily akin to Frank's. He was a farmer's son from Depauville, Jefferson County, a descendant of Edward Winslow, who had crossed from England aboard the *Mayflower* and served as the first governor of Plymouth colony. Clarion stuck to farming until he was nineteen, when he started in at the general store in the village: three A.M. to ten P.M. six days a week for $10 a month in wages. He had a notion that he had risen as high as he could three years later when he was up to $20 a month, with free meals thrown in.

The classes he signed up for at a Utica business college brought him the diploma that he imagined to be his key to the future. Instead, he was reduced to hanging wallpaper for a living before a summer job in Thousand Islands Park earned him a dollar a day. He tested his luck in Watertown next, and there it improved. When Clinton Case quit Campbell & Moulton's to join forces with Frank, Winslow was hired to replace him.

Parallels with Frank's beginnings extended beyond that. Winslow, another respectable Methodist, was a boarder in a Watertown lodging house. One icy Christmas night, he played Santa Claus at the Sunday school party. The buffalo coat was heavy, the white whiskers thick, the church overheated, and the sweat ran fast. Since his landlady owned no bathtub, he took a shower at the YMCA, then headed through the snow for Campbell & Moulton's to wrap himself in a blanket by a register that delivered warmth from the furnace in the cellar.

The thought of Frank's prosperity drove him, during the night, to write to New York, asking for an interview. The two-cent stamp won him the managership of the Holyoke, Massachusetts, store. The beanstalk kept on growing. A buyer's job was earmarked for him at headquarters, giving him an automatic share in profits. When he died one year short of his eightieth birthday, he left an estate of $3,000,000.

When outlays for merchandise, clerks' wages and profit sharing by the executives rose in unison, it was impossible to judge who was the sterner assessor of a manager's performance, Frank or Charles Griswold, although Frank stipulated, "We can't have all don'ts; we must have a few strong do's."

The pair of them made their separate calls like admirals on fleet inspection running white-gloved hands under galley sinks. Griswold issued reprimands about defective electrical wiring or snow left unshoveled on the sidewalk. He checked the level of water in the fire buckets and examined lamp shades for traces of dust. Was the jewelry free of tarnish? Were counter displays in apple-pie order? Wasn't that sign hanging lopsidedly?

Correspondence filed anywhere except in an office safe; rates omitted from freight bills; a yard measure 39½ inches long instead of 36—the list of offenses seemed endless. And perhaps the most heinous crime of all: "The candy girl wore one of the dirtiest aprons I've seen for some time, and her hair looked like 'sloppy weather.'"

That complaint in a Griswold report provoked Frank to add a few words of his own. "Glad the inspector called the manager's attention to the untidy appearance of the candy girl." He constantly suspected his competitors of prying into his affairs to tap his knowledge of how to get things done. "Why does the manager allow the general letter books to remain where persons that ought not can see them? These books and all private matters should be kept under lock and key. We hear too much about the secrets of our business leaking out."

As for the culprit guilty of using an overly generous yardstick, he deserved a flaying. "I didn't suppose there was a single manager in our Syndicate who is ignorant of how many inches it takes to make a yard, yet this manager has been giving 39½ inches of goods for the price of 36. Now I want every manager at once to see that he has absolutely correct measurements marked off on the back of the counter. For if you have been giving short measure you are liable to be jacked up by the sealer of weights and measures; and if you have been giving too much you have taken all the profits away from the goods."

The ingrained watchwords of childhood were never to be forgotten: *waste not, want not; look before you leap; too many cooks spoil the broth.* "If I had been willing to borrow," he reminisced, "the business would have branched out much more rapidly. But I stuck to my policy of paying cash and have never regretted it."

Only four new stores were set up in 1896, but he was delighted with the one in Boston. The carriage trade could not help but notice it when it was abutted on one side by R. H. White's venerable department store, founded the year after Frank's birth, and on the other by the premises of Jordan Marsh, started even earlier by a ribbon clerk from Maine. In Frank's opinion, it was the grandest location in the city, but for all that this manager was admonished like the rest of them to obey regulations: never neglect to weigh a letter prior to mailing; conserve your string and brown paper; make sure every light is out before you lock up for the night.

And next came New York City. Frank thought the two stories at 259 Sixth Avenue, near the corner of 17th Street, were worth every penny of the $20,000-a-year rent. Threading its way down the center of town, with horsecars, cable cars and an occasional automobile plying its length, while the elevated railroad rattled overhead, Sixth was a magnet for shoppers. Here, he was in the realm of those merchant princes whose splendor was already procreating legends.

Three blocks down from No. 256 stood "The Store of the Red Star," R. H. Macy and Company, with its indoor track on which enthusiasts were urged to try out a new bicycle unless professional peddlers happened to be staging an exhibition there.

B. Altman and Company, advertised as "The Palace of the Trade," reared its tan-colored facade a block to the north. Trim-bearded Bernard Altman himself, a lonely old bachelor, patrolled its four floors, constantly circling back to the third, which held his personally chosen displays of rare china, marble clocks, cloisonné enamels, fine French furniture and *objets d'art*. His private collections, given to the Metropolitan Museum before he died, were reputedly valued at $15,000,000. In 1896, he had just begun the secretive buying of parcels of real estate, one by one, as ground for a new store that would rise on East 34th Street, safe from the descending cinders of the El's coal-burning locomotives.

The signs at No. 289 spelled out the name of Bonwit & Company, a specialty shop for women. Competing with Altman's was uphill work. As Frank compared the number of Paul Bonwit's customers with the count of *haute monde* ladies stepping down from the landaus, broughams and victorias that deposited them at Altman's main entrance, he could foresee only disaster for the challenger.

Woolworth did not pretend that his spanking new premises were in the same league as "The Big Store—a City in Itself," whose six tower-topped stories filled the whole block between 18th and 19th Streets and reached half-way back to Fifth Avenue. Capitalized at $1,000,000, that fabulous figure that was always calculated to cause eyes to pop, it had been opened with a flourish of publicity one month ago by the patriarchal Henry Siegel and his partner, Frank Cooper, invaders from Chicago.

Each of its three entrance arches soared two stories high. Patrons on the 19th Street side passed under the central landing of the main staircase, whose marble steps and carved mahogany balustrade curved all the way to the top floor. At the heart of the main floor there was a terrace of white marble where the multiple jets of an ornamental fountain sent cascades of rainbow-lit water splashing into a seventy-foot basin around the base of a brass-and-marble Amazon known as the "Goddess of Light." "Meet Me at the Fountain" was one slogan of the advertising with which Siegel-Cooper deluged the city; "Everything Under the Sun" was another. The ice-cream sodas served at the little tables on the terrace, acknowledged to be the best available anywhere, were a favorite of weary shoppers, thirsty businessmen and young New Yorkers out a-courting.

Siegel-Cooper inspired Frank with a number of ideas for future application. "Everything Under the Sun," for instance, included the first lines of groceries to be sold in a department store: sugar-cured ham at forty-four cents a pound; Smyrna figs at $1.15 for a ten-pound box; and from the nearby liquor counters hundred-proof rye at $2 a gallon. Aisle demonstrations of kitchen products in use, with free snacks and tidbits handed out to draw an audience, were another Big Store innovation.

Frank had also heard the tale about John W. Gates, tycoon of the barbed-wire industry and compulsive gambling man universally known as "Bet a Million." He wagered with J. P. Morgan, the banker, that "Everything Under the Sun" could not possibly be true, then tried to prove his point by walking into Siegel-Cooper to ask a floorwalker for directions to the elephant department.

The stunned supervisor sent for the manager. "What color

were you interested in?" the manager asked Gates.

"White."

"We'll obtain one for you and let you know when it's in stock."

The bet with Morgan was all but forgotten when Bet a Million received the store's telegram: STEAMSHIP VAN DAM ARRIVING FROM CEYLON TOMORROW WITH WHITE ELEPHANT. WHAT ARE YOUR INSTRUCTIONS?

He made an appointment to go with the manager to the pier where the ship was to be unloaded. He waited long enough to see the elephant hoisted from the hold in a cargo sling and winched down onto dry land. He paid for the beast by check and turned away, but the manager had a final question for him: where was his purchase to be delivered?

"Give it to the Central Park Zoo."

Had he known it, Gates could have won in the first place by asking for a celluloid collar. Siegel-Cooper regarded them as a fire hazard for smokers, who sometimes set whiskers and collars on fire simultaneously.

A man shopping for a celluloid neckpiece could find one at Woolworth's.

*   *   *

Big as the business as a whole had grown, Frank's nervousness about his rivals in the trade drove him to go on aggrandizing it. There was room in most towns for only one dime store to prosper. It was essential to get in first to fend off the competition. The present program of opening them up one at a time left too many opportunities for the enemy to steal a march on him. The solution was to look around for a string of shops already in operation and buy them to add to his own. The closer he got to establishing a monopoly, the more secure Woolworth's would be from its adversaries, men like John G. McCrory, who had broken ground in Scottsdale, Pennsylvania, while Frank was still struggling to make a living in Lancaster, men like Sebastian Kresge, who had picked up some of Frank's secrets as a traveling salesman calling on Woolworth stores.

Even the attempt to create a monopoly was a crime subject to heavy penalties under the Sherman Antitrust Act, a curiosity of Benjamin Harrison's otherwise business-oriented administration, passed by an almost unanimous Congress in 1890. But the act was being employed principally against the labor unions, and Frank felt safe in ignoring it.

In 1898, the year of the trifling war that shattered the last remnants of Spain's colonial empire in Cuba, he struck a deal with Earle Perry Charlton to acquire nine of Charlton's retail outlets.

Charlton, a former drummer like Kresge on the five-and-ten circuit, was an oddment among the men who entered Frank's circle. He was born not in Jefferson County but in Chester, Connecticut. He made his start not on Public Square in Watertown but in a Boston dime store. The girl he married, Ida May Stein, was a Jewess, when Jews were outcasts in the retail end of dry goods. Ida shared her husband's hopes of putting down roots somewhere some day and owning his own show.

On a selling trip to Buffalo, he dropped in on Seymour Knox. Had he thought, Charlton asked, about expanding into Massachusetts, where the surface was scarcely scratched and there was the promise of easy money to be made? Seymour, as keen as Frank to boost his profits, invited Charlton to join him a double-barreled shot, Knox & Charlton, at Fall River, with a population of 100,000 and a labor force heavily engaged in spinning cotton.

The two of them scored a bull's-eye. On the proceeds, they took aim at Lowell, which boasted of having the biggest cotton mill in America. They hit their target again there and thrust southward into Connecticut.

After five palmy years, Seymour's history of entering into and walking out of partnerships repeated itself. When he and Charlton broke up, Knox held onto Lowell and Charlton took over everything else they had owned. Then Frank showed up, cash in hand, and Charlton was content to sell him stores in nine New England cities. The sudden surplus of ready capital stirred the wanderlust in him, and Charlton took to the road again, heading for the Rocky Mountains to sniff out opportunity there.

Woolworth's year-end report in 1899 exuded pride in the past, confidence in the future. "How little did I realize twenty-one years ago when I had that little tumbledown store in Lancaster and paid $30 a month rent with a capital of less than $400 that this business would ever grow to such stupendous proportions. And the end has yet to come."

"Our capital," he reminded his generals, "is $875,000 in stock and fixtures. You are the guardians of this enormous amount of money. I have faith in you and congratulate myself upon having secured such good and capable managers to conduct my business." The chain at present had fifty-five links; he wanted many more. "We are limited only in our physical ability to open all these new ventures without getting our fingers burned."

The memory of the singeing he suffered in those Lancaster days when he stuck a hand in the Wall Street boiler still rankled. A clause in the standard employment contract every manager signed stated: "I agree not to speculate in stocks, grains or securities or enter into any game of chance." Frank also had some specific advice to pass along: if any of them had money to spare, "put it into bonds or mortgages or something that does not fluctuate very much."

The "enormous amount of money" he boasted of was chicken feed to the hawks and vultures in the forests of finance, but he began to spread some of it around for the sake of gaining attention. On the eve of a store's launching, a kind of housewarming party was held with an orchestra on hand to play the new "Woolworth March." He went one better in the matter of music when a second link in New York City was added to the chain. An organ was a permanent installation there, piping out selections from Frank's favorites, classical or sentimental, to entertain his patrons. It was, according to the ballyhoo, "the largest ten-cent store in the world."

It was also rented space, like the rest of his fiefdom. Every store was being redecorated in a new shade of red to standardize the appearance and underline the fact that all of them were Frank's achievement. But since he owned none of the property, any store could be forced out by its landlord when the lease ran out. It was a situation that had to be remedied. He wanted his name attached to something more enduring, a building that was *his.*

Once again, he was copying the merchant princes who had felt the same urge before him. The greatest of them in his estimation were John Wanamaker and Marshall Field, whom he rated "the most successful merchants in the United States." Honest John had bought the Pennsylvania Railroad's gargantuan freight depot at 13th and Market in Philadelphia, to convert an area of almost three acres into what he advertised as "the largest space in the world devoted to retail selling on a single floor." Now he had taken over the ersatz marble palace of the late Alexander Stewart in New York City, less spacious but paying off just as handsomely.

Marshall Field, a melancholy man of simple tastes and sledge-hammer drive, had outdistanced Wanamaker in the storekeeping hurdles. Field, who left the family farm to earn $4 a week as a counter clerk in Pittsfield, Massachusetts, was the Croesus of the trade, with an estate of $120,000,000 at his disposal. The first monumental building that housed his operations in Chicago was a $50,000-a-year rental, with a booming retail and wholesale business. When fire ravaged the city in 1871, he assembled a platoon of volunteers to drape water-soaked blankets across his windows, but by morning the place was a smoldering ruin.

Within forty-eight hours, he rented a horse barn from the City Railway Company, and he was back to selling in less than two weeks. Six years later, a second landmark store, an Italianate pile on State Street, went up in smoke, too. "The destruction of St. Peter's at Rome," said the *Tribune*, "could hardly have aroused an apparently deeper interest than the destruction of this palatial dry-goods establishment."

The landlords, the Singer Sewing Machine Company, demolished what remained and replaced it with another mammoth structure. After Field rejected an invitation to sign a new lease—which his competitors at Carson, Pirie and Company hastened to do—he suffered a change of heart. It cost him $700,000 to buy the building outright, $100,000 more to oust Carson, Pirie.

Frank was aware of some of the legends concerning Field. The Chicago merchant found a sales clerk arguing one day with a disgruntled customer; Field's reprimand became the store's slogan: "Give the lady what she wants." His carriage brought him most of the way to work from his mansion on Prairie Avenue every weekday, but he always walked the final block or two to keep tabs on the shopping crowds. When a wheeled cart that two stockroom boys were playing with came hurtling forward to lay him flat in an aisle, his response was a mild, "Boys, don't forget to be gentlemen."

Style was increasingly important to Frank, though his approach was more forthright. "I don't want to find any girls under fifteen, especially those in short dresses, working in our stores," declared one admonition; the sight of girls' legs was unsettling to a Yankee conscience.

Most of his patrons might be farm workers, factory hands and immigrants, but they must always be considered *right*, exactly as if they were breathing in the scented air of Wanamaker's or Field's. Frank was emphatic about the cash benefits implicit in that policy. "We have found on investigation that the average customer prefers the small 6 inch nickel shears to the larger ones. Yet inspection shows that only two or three out of thirty or forty stores keep in stock the smaller shears, which give us much greater profits than the larger ones. This is only one item in our multitudinous line of goods, yet it shows you have been buying things the customer does not want."

The princes wooed their clientele with commissionaires to open the entrance doors and assistants to sweep the sidewalk clean of dust or snow. The princes provided carpeting on the floor, lounges and restaurants, free delivery. (When Field's stable of horses was infected with distemper, he had his wagons drawn by oxen.) At Woolworth prices, Frank could not match these embellishments, but he was game to try.

"Make your customers feel at home. Have waiting rooms and rest rooms. Encourage people to meet their friends in your store. Give them something free. I was in a store the other day where they furnished free ice water and made a hit. The same store set up a pair of Fairbanks scales with a sign: 'See how much you weigh? Free.' Both are good ideas for us."

Although the princes and Frank were united in holding down the wages they paid, there was a certain prestige involved in working behind a counter in a dry-goods palace that was altogether lacking in a five-and-ten. Pondering the disadvantage, Frank reached a startling conclusion. "We must pay enough to keep the department stores from taking away our best sales ladies. I would like to increase salaries but at present don't want to put down an ironclad rule other than the $3 a week minimum."

It was to Lancaster, scene of his first solid accomplishment twenty-one years previously, that he turned when he decided to erect a building and collect rents instead of paying them. Since his name would be on it, the structure had to be a *corker*, with a dime

store occupying the ground floor, four more stories of leasable office space on top of that, and a roof garden where light refreshments could be bought. It would not qualify him for membership
in the same architectural league as Field or Wanamaker, but for a
cash outlay of $300,000 it was a promising start.

His New York staff, caught up in the excitement, reacted like
proud fathers playing with a child's train set. When construction
began, everybody made a trip out to Lancaster. The store's windows, as always, were regarded as the magnet that would attract
the trade: show what's for sale, and people feel the urge to buy.
Frank hammered away at the point.

"You can pull customers into your stores and they won't know
it. Draw them in with attractive window displays and when you
get them in have a plentiful showing of the window goods on the
counters. . . . Let them look around to their heart's content. Don't
try and press goods on them. . . . Special sales are fine if the bargains are real. Be sure your ten cent specials cannot be bought
elsewhere for less than 20 or 25 cents. Remember our advertisements are in our show windows and on our counters."

The counters in Lancaster weren't real mahogany like the
princes', but they appeared to be. Once the cast-iron columns had
been raised to make the store a single unit of open space, Frank
hired a crew of Italians to hide the metal under the same mock
marble that had disguised the exterior walls at A. T. Stewart's. A
pair of hand-wrought bronze lions marked the entrance to the new
office provided for his convenience whenever he journeyed down
from New York. With its gold-leafed wall panels adorned with an
emblematic "W," it looked almost as grand as the suite he currently dwelt in at the Hotel Savoy. Those panels listed every link
in the chain, along with such braggadocio as "The Woolworth
stores require and employ five thousand people to sell one hundred million articles annually" and "Large purchases for cash direct from manufacturers explain the high values we offer."

He bent the rules and let nostalgia influence his choice of
manager. The original Lancaster premises had been on the route
of Harry Albright, mailman. Frank had kept in touch with him
over the years and eventually brought him into the syndicate as a
trainee. Harry was put in charge of the new store. The day was to
come when he was making $50,000 a year as a buyer in New York

and Frank would nudge him: "Did you ever stop to think that if it hadn't been for me you would still be delivering mail in Lancaster?"

Harry knew how to be grateful. "Not a day goes by, Mr. Woolworth, that Mrs. Albright and I do not remember the opportunity you gave us."

It fell to him to engage the musicians for the gala opening and lend the conductor the arrangements of "The Woolworth March." The scent of out-of-season roses, carnations and chrysanthemums set in ten-cent vases spread through the store. There were enough potted palms and ferns to fill a ducal greenhouse. Engraved invitations went out to the worthies of the city in what was known as "The Garden Spot of America." Frank's pet name for his latest creation tapped a similar vein: "The Gem of the Syndicate." The cigars he passed out had to be good—tobacco was a major crop in these parts. And only prime cuts of steak must be served when the time came to feed the guests, since here were the biggest stockyards east of Chicago.

In a cutaway coat and pin-striped trousers with a knife-edge press, he was the epitome of genial affluence as the orchestra played his anthem and he shook hands on the receiving line. Jennie, beside him, looked more nervous and withdrawn than in the days when she was a working housewife.

A turnout of the press included a representative of the respected *Intelligencer-Journal*, whose discarded issues he had once used as wrapping paper. He had a word or two for the reporters today. "We've got some of the best people in town here," he beamed. "Don't it do your heart good?"

The following spring, he moved out of the Savoy into his new mansion on Millionaires' Row as a neighbor of the very best people in New York City. But his arrival received little attention from them. He still had a long way to go before he was taken seriously as a newcomer among Manhattan's nouveau riche.

The way toward that goal, he thought, was to build an empire so big it could not possibly be overlooked. Up to now, he had been firm in his opinion that he must "fill up the East"—his words—before expanding further afield. He changed his mind when he learned how well Earle Charlton was faring as a pioneer.

Charlton, habitual flower stuck in his lapel, had struck it rich with the stores he introduced into virgin territory west of the Rockies and then in Canada, although it had been a risky undertaking when delivery charges over the distances involved put a squeeze on profits.

Frank concluded it was time to follow in Charlton's footsteps, but first he would settle the freight-rate problem. He laid down his terms to his suppliers: he would step up the size of his orders—on condition that they absorbed the extra costs of shipping merchandise across the continent. With that accomplished, he slipped off to Grand Central Station to catch a Friday morning train for Chicago along with his chief inspector, Charles Griswold.

Two weeks later, they had established a western chain of twenty-one more Woolworth's by buying them, ready made, from their various owners: two in Colorado, four in Illinois, two in Indiana, six in Iowa, two in Minnesota, two in Missouri, one apiece in Nebraska, North Dakota and Wisconsin.

With no feasible way of supervising them from New York City, Frank opened an office in Chicago's Railway Exchange Building, leaving Griswold there to oversee a staff made up largely of former employees of the businesses Frank had just acquired.

Besides tying them down with contracts, he cut them in on all Woolworth profits. Why? "I want my executives interested in every store we own. The prosperity of one is the prosperity of all." In an age of heartless laissez-faire, when survival of the fittest was the rule proprietors imposed on most managerial teams, it was a progressive philosophy, although "progressive" was a word repellent to a hide-bound Republican.

Only radicals were happy to call themselves Progressives, but their fervor set alarm bells ringing all over the country. Adherents of the Populist Party, which had polled more than a million votes in 1892, enlisted in the cause. So did the labor unions, farmers, Eugene Debs's Socialists and spokesmen like muckraking Lincoln Steffens, Upton Sinclair and Frank Norris. The Progressives clamored for a better deal for factory workers. They demanded that an end be made to bullying by management and to the pendulum swing of boom then bust that dizzied the economy. They aimed to break up the trusts in order to put a stop to control of the nation by big business.

Huge monopolies set their own prices and stifled competition from individually owned businesses. One gigantic trust, the $1,400,000,000 United States Steel Corporation assembled by J. P. Morgan, governed that entire industry. The meat packers regulated their markets by secret agreement. The exchanges of Wall Street were dominated by a few giants of finance enjoying an extended Roman holiday at the expense of gullible investors. The great insurance groups of New York consistently raised a fever of speculation in dubious stocks.

Frank's opinion of the Republican currently in the White House went unrecorded, but Theodore Roosevelt seemed as alert as the Progressives were to abuses that threatened to stir revolt against the very structure of America. Hedging his attacks on the "criminal rich" by vowing that his purpose was to save capitalism itself from the Socialists, he asserted that "of all forms of tyranny, the least attractive and the most vulgar is the tyranny of mere wealth, the tyranny of plutocracy." He swung a punch in passing at John Wanamaker, whom he charged with "slanderous falsehoods . . . sly intolerance, cruelty, and meanness that would be shocking to a barbarian."

But Frank found nothing amiss in his desire to be a plutocrat. There were too many dime stores blossoming over the land for one man to corner the market, but nobody owned as many as he did, not even Cousin Seymour, who in this February of 1904 concluded a merger that expanded his chain by twenty-two more links.

Not to be outdone, Frank went shopping again in Pennsylvania and Massachusetts, then added two units in the West and five in the East for a total of forty-four newly painted, bright red Woolworth's procured in a single year, his biggest splurge to date.

The count now tallied one hundred and twenty. He would have to do better than that.

FRANK WINFIELD WOOLWORTH: "Hunger for profits, pleasure and respect"

ON MILLIONAIRES' ROW: "The stairway was piped for music"

**FANNY AND
JOHN WOOLWORTH:**
"Hard living in a harsh climate"

FRANK AND SUM IN 1866

EDNA, HELENA, JESSIE: "Mother sewed the dresses"

UNG FRANK: "Authority in a new mustache"   JENNIE: "Out of touch with grandeur"

Elizabeth Woolworth   Jasper Woolworth

FRANK'S GRANDPARENTS

Kezia McBrier   Henry McBrier

BACKYARD REUNION: Brooklyn, 1889; Frank sits, hands on knees, next to Cousin Seymour

FIRST CONVENTION, 1894: Frank lolls down front between spritely Mary Creighton and matronly Mrs. Coons

ARCHITECT GILBERT:
"Patience was essential"

THE MONUMENT:
"The cash was waiting
when the bills arrived"

WINFIELD HALL: "Jennie was seldom in view"

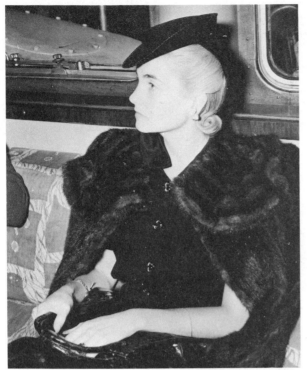

BARBARA:
"Rich little poor girl"

**FRANKLYN HUTTON,
BARBARA, REVENTLOW:**
At Lance's London christening

CARY GRANT AND BARBARA: "The wedding was discreet for once"

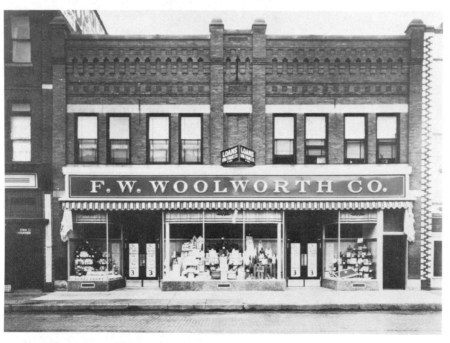

**VANISHED SPECIES: One of the last dime stores;
Oelwein, Iowa (population, 7,740)**

11

⚙] The Yankee Invader [⚛

It was the hardest lesson to learn in his life, but he was prepared now to accept the fact that the goad he applied to himself was threatening to kill him. After twenty-six years of trying, he was close to making his name a household word among the rank-and-file Americans. It had been done fairly and squarely, as he saw it, but on the cheap—by cutting corners, paring expenses, and carrying most of the burdens alone. The cost in human terms had been high. He had sacrificed virtually all normal family living, which had imposed a different kind of burden on Jennie. His pleasures were limited to his concerts on the magical organ, mountainous piles of food, and the fleeting company of agreeable women.

He was fifty-two years old, and depressed about the physical shape he was in, which was no better than might be expected in a man of his weight whose principal exercise was chomping on cigars. He fell ill again, and an old fear haunted him—"of the terrible responsibility resting on my shoulders and of so many people depending on my health."

He forced himself to a mournful conclusion. "Time is flying fast away, and I cannot expect always to be in control of this vast property." The syndicate in its present form was as overextended as he was. Some of his power must be shared with others, but in arranging the transfer, there would be the satisfaction of letting the nabobs of the city see for the first time what he was worth in hard cash.

His last letter written as sole proprietor arrived on the desk of every manager. "Hereafter I will write to you as a representative of a corporation. I am sorrowful, but modern methods must be pursued." On February 16, 1905, F. W. Woolworth & Company was incorporated, with principal offices in Mineola, New York, and executive quarters at 280 Broadway, where freshly decorated and furnished rooms provided privacy for every senior executive, which was a decided novelty.

"The corporation," Frank told his team, "is more expensive than the old way of doing business, but that is the penalty for security." Capital was set at $10,000,000, half of it common stock in which control was vested, half in seven percent preferred. "We could have capitalized for much more and sold stock to the public, but we're not going to do that." The public had the right to be customers, not part owners of his realm.

Except for Hubert Parson, appointed secretary-treasurer, every seat on the board was filled by an old hand from Watertown: Frank, president; Carson Peck, vice-president and general manager; Clinton Case, another vice-president; Harry Moody, a director. Their contracts bound them to Woolworth's for a further five years.

The newborn company proved more robust than the man who had founded it. In its first full year of life, sales edged up close to $15,000,000 and the number of stores increased to 160. Then, generated by the reaction of big business to Rooseveltian reform, panic struck Wall Street again. Starting with an abortive attempt to set up yet another trust, it brought about the collapse of the Knickerbocker Trust Company. Banking services had not been so completely disrupted since the Civil War. But Woolworth's business, unscathed, climbed past $20,000,000.

Out of the churning stock market came a candidate for the hand of his second daughter, Edna. Franklyn Laws Hutton was a broker's man, like his elder brother Edward. Both had arrived in the city as schoolboys in a family from Cincinnati. The Huttons' finances permitted only one son to go through Yale. The choice fell on Franklyn, while Ed was enrolled in commercial courses.

Woolworth's thought that living at the Savoy might draw Jennie out of her shell had not worked at all, but it was there that Franklyn met Edna, the most fragile of the three girls, who had her father's passion for music plus the talent for singing and playing it. Since she was as self-effacing as her mother, she declined to be coaxed into a concert career, though she may have been attracted by Franklyn's exuberant performances along vaguely similar lines: he liked to cheer up dejected colleagues by dancing a *pas seul* around the floor of the Stock Exchange.

The end of the financial crisis waited on the intervention of J. P. Morgan, whose associates in the steel trust simultaneously took over their last major rival, the Tennessee Iron and Coal Company, but Franklyn went ahead and resolved his personal shortage of cash by marrying Edna in Fifth Avenue's Church of the Heavenly Rest and moving with her into the new, fully furnished, five-story house at 2 East 80th Street that was a gift from her father, who lived around the corner. The city's newspapers again judged a Woolworth wedding unworthy of mention. Some time later, when Ed Hutton ran a brokerage house of his own, he followed his brother's example and courted an heiress of a fortune made from breakfast cereal, Marjorie Merriwether Post.

While money was sprayed out at one end of the pipeline, it was siphoned up drop by drop at the other. President Frank was delighted to hear about the extra $1,000 a week saved by the introduction of baling machines to compress packing paper and discarded straw into bundles of waste that fetched as much as thirty cents each, a vast improvement over having to pay garbagemen to cart the stuff away.

F. W. Woolworth & Company failed from the start to lift the work load off Frank's back. He was no more capable of giving up responsibility than of sticking to a slim-down diet. As soon as he felt well enough to leave the house, he was back at his desk, haranguing his troops.

"Some envelopes were furnished you to sell at two packages for three cents. At this rate they showed a good big profit. But there is so little difference between the two for five and the five-cent envelopes that many managers were tempted to put the two for fives on the five-cent counter. Now what sort of way is that to do business when you can go into any drug store or stationery store and get good envelopes at five cents a package? The same criticism goes for those of you who are trying to sell ten-cent goods that should be sold at five."

He lectured them about turnover, the number of times their stock was sold and replenished within a given period. They must try to maintain it at an annual figure of eight, since it "is our greatest means of giving the public economy."

Profits? Perfection lay somewhere between forty and forty-five percent. A manager who deviated on either the plus or minus side landed himself in trouble with the boss. If he toed the line, the man on the receiving end of the president's instructions would take home as much as twenty-five cents of every dollar netted during the year by the store in his charge.

Carson Peck, counselor of the trainees, rattled Frank with a report that some of them, wages controlled by the manager they were assigned to, were grossly underpaid. He cited the case of a learner who was started at $6 a week and then held down to that sum for eight months. "I would like to ask you what kind of enthusiasm that man can be expected to put into his work. How can you expect him to come one half-an-hour earlier in the morning and stay until ten or eleven o'clock at night?"

Frank laid down a new law. The pay of a learner must be raised by increments of a dollar a month until he was making a weekly $10. After that, the manager on the spot could decide how much more the recruit was worth. But reports on his progress must be filed with headquarters, and every youngster had the right to communicate directly with the president.

As he saw it, there was nothing in the world that could not be improved upon by trying, and this included the light show with pictures he could conjure up from the keyboard of his organ. What he yearned for was some Wagnerian *Sturm und Drang* to match the tumult of his moods. More wiring, more electric motors and some extra plumbing were installed in the drawing room. Now, at the touch of a button, he could startle his guests with flashes of lightning, rumbling of thunder, the hiss of falling rain. With music holding an equal place with gastronomy in his affections, he also had the main staircase, his clothes closets and the supports of the canopy over his bed equipped to supply harmony on tap.

In 1909 ambition spurred him into daring that dumbfounded his associates. In his fifty-eighth year, the chain stretched into nearly two hundred American communities, divided into regional administrations, each with its own head office in New York City, Boston, Albany, Philadelphia, Chicago or Omaha. His aim, he said calmly, was "to open a store in every civilized town throughout the world."

For a start on the advance overseas, he began collecting maps and vital statistics of England, analyzing them in the same way he had sited outlets in the United States. "A live Yankee," he had once noted, "would create a sensation here. . . ." When he broached the subject with his colleagues, they reminded him of the rest of that quotation: ". . . but perhaps not."

He brushed aside objections, and a call went out for volunteers to accompany him across the Atlantic on May 19. To a man, the senior staff declined. Profit sharing made them leery of embarking on a project more than likely to cost the company and themselves income.

Then Cousin Fred stepped forward, a young man who had added some weight to his bones and a mustache to his lip since he enlisted with Woolworth's. From assisting Alvin Ivie, he had been handed a manager's job, first in Maine and lately in the Sixth Avenue store. He was willing to join in testing British reaction to a live Yankee business.

Next to fall into line was Byron Miller, once an errand boy, then a learner, and currently superintendent of the Boston district. One last man was needed to go musketeering. Frank beckoned the manager of his 14th Street store, Samuel Balfour, originally hired in—where else but Watertown?

The four of them made London their base, rented a car and driver, rode the railroads constantly to take them out through the provinces as far as Southampton to the south and in the north to Manchester. "Trains and service are better than ours," Frank wrote, assessing everything he saw. "Trains go 70 or 75 miles an hour and are seldom a minute late."

He was less impressed by the sight of Harrod's, the upper-class emporium catering to the carriage trade on London's Piccadilly, which he inspected one day with one of his three-man team. He began by methodically pacing the sidewalk in front of and alongside the store to ascertain its measurements and jot down the figures in the notebook he habitually carried in a coat pocket.

"Three hundred feet of frontage, one hundred and fifty feet in depth. I always pictured it being bigger."

He peered into every window. "Not a price tag on anything. We don't have much to write home about this place."

He bustled through the main entrance, which a doorman sprang forward to open for the pair of them. Frank, resplendent in morning coat and striped trousers, was rapidly confronted by a floorwalker attired in equal splendor, lacking only a top hat. "Good morning, sir. May I assist you?"

"Quite unnecessary."

"Ah, a gentleman from America. Perhaps you will allow me to escort you to a particular department. You may have seen something of interest in one of our windows."

"No. We just came in to look around."

The floorwalker's manner turned icy. "Very well, sir. In that case you may prefer to be left to your own devices." He stalked away.

Frank was miffed. "The moment you go in," he grumbled to his companion, "you're expected to buy. Did you notice how he stared at us, as if we were a couple of muleskinners? He wouldn't last a week on my payroll."

"He was pretty sharp on the uptake, Mr. Woolworth."

"And snooty into the bargain. I bet he adds more to the overheads than he does to the sales. But Britishers are always slow to catch on to things like that."

The only department store bearing any resemblance to the home product was the palatial mishmash of architecture that had just been completed on Oxford Street, close by Marble Arch. Harry Gordon Selfridge's building, Frank recorded, "is five stories high with a fine roof tea garden."

Selfridge, nicknamed "Mile-a-Minute Harry," had until this time been the only American to make a success of the British drygoods trade. Impulsive and inventive, he was poles apart from Frank, who accepted at face value, as most people did, Selfridge's claim to have been a partner in Marshall Field's; he had actually begun there as an office boy, then wound up managing the store.

From his imagination sprang the idea of making Field's show windows so spectacular that merchants everywhere, east and west, felt compelled to imitate them. He dazzled his patrons with concentrations of electrical wattage focused on the aisle displays; he tripled the number of public telephones available to Field's shoppers; he dismantled counters so that goods could be piled high on tables for bargain-hunters to rummage through.

He argued his employer into multiplying the budget for newspaper advertising—Sundays excluded, because of Marshall Field's religious principles—and personally wrote much of the text. He also came up with the notion of a "budget floor," stocking the basement with cut-price merchandise—"less expensive but reliable," as the announcements said.

Mile a Minute was the originator of Field's third-floor tearoom, where within a year of its installation in 1890, 1,500 customers were served every day. When the World's Fair opened in Chicago three years later, Selfridge enticed the Infanta Eulalia of Spain into the store to make her contribution to its luster.

He had tried his hand as an independent storekeeper in Chicago for four years before he was ready for London. There, he had drummed up enough capital to erect his Oxford Street palace. Frank was dubious about Mile a Minute's long-term future. "He has been trying to float some stock in his corporation but without much success. Most Englishmen think he will fail. There seems to be a prejudice against him, in fact against all foreigners invading this territory. Americans in many lines of business have given up, especially manufacturers who have been trying to open a market here for American goods."

He was right in his forecasts about Selfridge, who made one fortune, which he lost, and then another, which disappeared down the same drain for the same reason: outgo surpassed income. He died in 1947, leaving an estate of only $6,000.

One lesson was already plain to the Woolworth quartet: the British preferred to buy British. The stores Frank planned here would be stocked from local factories; the goods, in any event, were cheaper and better made than American imports. He would form a subsidiary corporation, F. W. Woolworth & Company, Limited, with the usual distinction between common, voting stock sold at one share for a shilling, and preferred, nonvoting stock, going at ten pounds sterling a share. He would cope with anti-American hostility by adding an Englishman to the team. William Stephenson, buyer for an export house, came in to understudy Cousin Fred as managing director.

"British businessmen," Frank finally conceded, "are as bright, alert and smart as the average American. Some of their ideas we would do well to copy." That was a second lesson he had learned on the trip. "My opinion of the average Englishman being rather slow was an error." When it came to striking a deal, they were shrewd operators. "We may get done in yet."

He had thought at first that this would be only an exploratory expedition, but he could not resist taking the plunge in Liverpool, Lancashire's slum-girt seaport where, it was said, "trade is enthroned with cotton as prime minister." Its imports and exports exchanged with the United States were an important factor in his decision.

"At times," he wrote, "the difficulties we have encountered have seemed insurmountable. However, pluck and perseverance have overcome all obstacles so far. The buying power of the New York office is a great help now in securing low prices for goods we need."

He had survived similar challenges a hundred times before, so forecasts of imminent disaster could be disregarded now. "They remind me so much of what I used to be told so often in America." The lease on the premises that would house a "threepenny and sixpenny store" was dated Friday, July 13, "but we are not superstitious. I predict a moderate success here at first and eventually a big, assured success."

The timetable allotted four months for preparations, commissioning the counters and fixtures, installing lighting that was to be spectacular by native standards, and applying the coats of brilliant red paint. He could not possibly wait around for all this to be accomplished. With Jennie and their youngest daughter, Jessie, he took off for Lucerne, on the lake and in the Swiss canton of the same name, to unwind. He kept a Panhard car on tap for his European jaunts, together with two Renaults garaged in Manhattan. His chauffeur traveled with him, to serve on both sides of the ocean. Jules Billard, master mechanic and once a racing driver, had been hired in Paris, where Frank bought his first automobile, a Renault, to be shipped over to New York. Jules, with a keen eye for a handsome woman, was not treated as a servant but as a confidant, accomplice and friend.

Lucerne, a medieval town of winding streets and picture-book

houses, attracted all kinds of people, including a floating population of fortune hunters on the lookout for a girl like happy-go-
lucky Jessie, still single at twenty-three and blessed with a rich
father. Frank was not taken in by the attention that was lavished
on her. "These cheap titled people are after the American girl and
her money," he decided. "You must respect their judgment in
hoping to get both money and a fine-looking wife. But the poor
American father and mother over here have their troubles if they
are not sympathetic with this sort of courtship."

He plucked Jessie out of the circle of sycophants that was gathering around her and, with her mother, took her back to England.
The granddaughter who became the same sort of target was to be
born three years from now. When one of "these cheap titled
people," Alexis Mdivani, set his sights on her, Grandpa
Woolworth was no longer alive to fend him off.

Frank detected the odor of fortune hunting again when, extending the vacation, he drove out to inspect Blenheim Palace,
seat of the Marlborough dukedom at Woodstock in Oxfordshire.
The ninth and current duke, Charles, nicknamed "Sunny," had
won the hand of Willie and Alva Vanderbilt's only daughter,
Consuelo, along with a $2,000,000 dowry and a guaranteed
$100,000 a year from her railroad-rich spendthrift father. The
mournful marriage had collapsed, and Consuelo had fled to London.

"The Castle," Frank observed acidly, "is the home of the Duke
of Marlborough and *was* the home of the Duchess, Consuela [*sic*]
Vanderbilt, who now refuses to live with him. This famous estate
of 70,000 acres is sadly run down because the Duke is no longer in
receipt of enormous sums from his American father-in-law, W. K.
Vanderbilt. The Duke spends all he can get hold of in fast living
in Paris, London, Monte Carlo, etc. He has not the power to sell
his land or great works of art, sculpture or furniture."

Woolworth, despising "dudes," felt sure he knew what was
wrong with Marlborough. "How much better it would have been
for him if he had been obliged to learn the five and ten cent business at $6 a week and become a commercial man instead of as we
see him now—no use to anyone and no satisfaction to himself." On
that note, he and his wife and daughter sailed for home.

There was nothing that Lancashire people enjoyed more for

entertainment than a big brass band, so a big brass band played for the Liverpool premiere on November 5. The British link in the chain developed exactly as he had foreseen: off to a slow start, then gathering momentum week by week. He had to get back to the scene of action. He made one more Atlantic crossing to plan the spread of threepenny-and-sixpennies across the British Isles— and caught influenza.

Disdain for work-shy aristocrats was something he had in common with most British voters, especially in working-class areas like Liverpool. "Peers against people" was the complaint raised continually on public platforms by Winston Churchill, a temporary convert from Toryism, Lloyd George and their fellow Liberals. The party's leadership in the House of Commons had made moves not unlike some of Theodore Roosevelt's to fend off socialism: The Workmen's Compensation Act to help victims of industrial accidents; the Trade Disputes Act to arbitrate unrest in the factories; the Eight Hours Act to shorten the working day.

The country was in turmoil as a result of the House of Lords' counterattack, mounted to protect patrician society. Britain's unwritten constitution entitled them to reject outright any finance bill voted by the lower House. The Liberals' latest budget called for real-estate taxes which the Lords construed as a warranty of blood-red revolution. The action they proposed had never been dared in the past: they would simply throw out the entire budget to pull down the government and precipitate a general election. "The order of battle," as a noble backwoodsman declared, "was now fairly set for a campaign of class warfare."

Frank was still suffering the aftereffects of the flu when new outlets began to appear on an average of one a month. Preston and Manchester, both cities of Lancashire; another in Liverpool; in Leeds and Hull, two cities of Yorkshire—all were in communities where the laboring poor outnumbered the middle class and well-to-do. The American experience was about to be repeated, but the appeal of Woolworth's proved itself quicker here, where a threepenny-and-sixpenny store reflected the spirit of insurgent democracy.

That spirit was all too obvious on opening day of the second Liverpool store. A mob of barefooted women, with their usual knitted shawls about their shoulders, shoved counters around the floor; salesgirls swooned; and customers helped themselves without going through the formality of paying for anything they walked out with.

Frank believed, nevertheless, that some British institutions merited respect. Cousin Fred and Byron Miller had been clean shaven when they stepped off the boat. He commanded them to cultivate mustaches like his to endow them with the same look of hirsute authority as their British underlings. The new hair came off as soon as the boss finally sailed for home, but whenever word came of another impending visitation, the whiskers were grown again.

Three years after the first sortie, the British business had twenty-eight units in flourishing condition, all but two managed by Englishmen. Instead of borrowing money, it was being pumped into New York at a better rate of return than the American links of the chain could earn.

Though his colors had been successfully raised in Britain, his recovery from influenza was slow. He suspected that his rivals on the home front were taking advantage of his ill health to steal trade from him. Attack was the best defense. He declared war by slashing prices and sent out his battle orders.

"When your competitor puts a line of goods in his window, pick out the best selling items in these goods and put them in your window at just half his price; and keep them there just as long as he keeps similar goods in his window."

And: "Don't be afraid to lose a little money. First, it prevents your competitor from making money; second, it advertises our stores more than anything else could do and will make people talk about us for years to come. We have had fights like this before and have always come out on top."

When two of America's largest manufacturers of sewing thread raised their wholesale price to six cents a spool, he regarded it as "the opportunity of a lifetime." A directive went out immediately to his troops. "Keep very quiet about it but buy all the spool cotton you can from jobbers or retailers, even if you have to pay 75 cents a dozen; and sell it for five cents."

Managers must shop around for items retailing for as much as a quarter, then send samples to head office so his team of buyers might flex their muscles to persuade other manufacturers to reproduce the goods for sale at Woolworth prices. Reports of encounters with the enemy flowed in from the front lines. In Pittsburgh, Kresge's was taken on after nightfall one Saturday. Harry Albright, former mailman in Watertown, led the reconnaissance aboard a streetcar traveling a route past Kresge's.

"I noticed the lights were all out, everything dark, but saw persons moving about in one of the windows. We jumped off the car and peeked." The enemy was arranging a display of chinaware, "larger and just as fine as ours." Harry beat a path back on foot to change every ticket in Woolworth's window from a dime to a nickel, then doused the lights and, in the darkened doorway, waited to observe what came next.

Two Kresge infantrymen strolled by on their way home. The sight in the window sent them scurrying back to base, to cut the announced prices there to the same five-cent figure. Harry, guessing correctly what they were up to, altered his signs again: any *two* items for a nickel.

It was close to two A.M. when the Kresge patrol returned, only to retreat again to adjust their tickets to match Woolworth's bargains. Harry got off a final shot: any *four* articles for five cents now. "While it cost money we feel we won out. . . . We watched and waited half an hour or so. But they made no further move, so we went home."

Once in a while, the commander mustered his strength to arrive in person on the battlefield. The Lancaster store had been closed for enlargement and remodeling. Among its new enticements there was a refreshment room with walls, counters and tabletops of real marble and seating for 120, attended by twenty-eight waitresses. On the eve of its reopening, Frank took a walk to a local hardware store and cleaned out its stock of kerosene lanterns. He ordered them placed in the center of the five-and-ten's main window to intimidate his enemies in a war of nerves.

"Ten Cents While They Last!" the sign announced. "One To a Customer." Each lantern had cost him half a dollar.

12

❧ A Queen for a King ☙

Time is flying fast away. That thought had given him the energy
he needed to overcome the obstacles that cluttered the path in his
younger days. To an aging man whose ego expanded as his
strength faltered, the same thought was a torment. Nothing he
had accomplished so far was enough, he felt, to stand as a memorial to Frank Woolworth. Two ideas entered his mind. The first
was to assemble the giant corporation bearing his name in the
$65,000,000 merger with Sum, Knox, Kirby, Charlton and Moore.
The second was to erect a building as his monument.

His original fancy was to make it a structure of perhaps a
dozen stories in downtown Manhattan, where he had pounded the
sidewalks on the slow road to a fortune. Toward that end, he
bought a plot of land on the west side of City Hall. Then, as he
stared down at the lot from his office windows at 280 Broadway, *la
manie de bâtir* seized hold. He pictured a fortress-cathedral so tall it
would reach the clouds. "I want," he told a colleague, "to build
something bigger than any other merchant has ever done."

It would throw him into competition with everything along
similar lines attempted to date by Macy, Field, Wanamaker, Siegel-Cooper or Alexander Stewart. If he gave free wing to his imagination in hope of outdoing everybody, merchant or not, the task
would be overwhelming. The Metropolitan Life Insurance Company's tower at One Madison Avenue held the current altitude

record, topping the second-place Singer Building by some eighty feet.

The mania to build lay covered by the veneer of a businessman. His opening move showed caution. Woolworth's principal bank was the Irving National Exchange, later to become the Irving Trust Company; his account there was impressive enough to have won him a seat on the board. Although the Metropolitan Club, J. P. Morgan's offspring, was beyond Frank's social reach, he was a member in good standing of the Hardware Club. It was there that he escorted Lewis Pierson, a senior officer at Irving, to pose a question during the steady serving of courses.

"Assuming there might be a Woolworth Building, would your bank rent space in it?" Pierson replied that this was a distinct possibility. Back at his desk, Frank set the wheels turning to buy and demolish more property abutting his present parcel until it extended the full distance between Park Place and Barclay Street, land once farmed by Dutch colonists before it accommodated the house of Philip Hone, merchant mayor of New York and diarist of the early 1800s.

By the spring of 1910, Frank was ready to commission somebody to give professional form to his Gothic fancies. For the past several years, he had admired the creativity of Cass Gilbert as demonstrated in an edifice of pointed arches, ribbed vaulting and flying buttresses that had arisen at 90 West Street. Through the services of that building's owner, General Howard Carroll, Frank found the architect he needed, a man with whom appearance outweighed mundane practicality.

Gilbert's own appearance—noble brow, pince-nez spectacles, drooping mustache—was, according to his biographer, "purposely impressive" and "rather pompous." Fellow members of that association of writers and artists, the Century Club, their eminence in the arts attained by longevity as much as by talent, asserted that "he could give the most convincing exposition of the obvious that had ever been heard there."

Yet it was clear to him that, if his patience outlasted his new client's vacillations, they might together awe the nation with the breadth of their vision. He could not guess how severely his forebearance was to be tested.

In the first place, Frank could not decide how big a building he had in mind, though he knew it must bear the same overall look as the Victoria Tower of London's House of Parliament, a photograph of which he produced for Gilbert's inspection at their initial encounter. (The architect had to identify it for him.) Frank's thought was that something of perhaps forty stories would do the trick. Gilbert pointed out that two more would add enough height to overtop the Singer Building. Since Frank liked that idea, Gilbert promptly prepared for future exigencies by having precise measurements made of the Metropolitan Life's tower—seven hundred feet plus two inches from sidewalk to summit.

The two men agreed they should go to London for a close-hand peek at the source of inspiration for the proposed masterpiece. Seeing what had been achieved in the Victoria Tower without going anywhere as high as forty-two stories, the dime-store dynast declared, "Twenty-five are about as many as I can afford at present, though I want provision made for a possible tower, to go up later." Gilbert's designers and draftsmen—Tom Johnson, George Wells, John Rockart and Gilbert Junior—went to work on the necessary thousands of perspective drawings, detail sketches and blueprints.

As the weeks slipped by, the opus grew in Frank's fevered imagination. By November, so many floors had been penciled in, erased, then penciled in again that his paper palace surpassed the Singer Building by a matter of eight feet. Constantly demanding more speed at the drawing boards, he seemed satisfied with that, and Gilbert's crew began the slide-rule computations for designing the steel framework.

Frank took on the task of shopping for structural steel at bargain prices. "I calculate that the United States Steel Corporation might offer a discount for the sake of publicity." A letter was sent to Judge Gary, board chairman and near neighbor on Fifth Avenue, who promised that the corporation's bid would be tendered on that basis.

Mulling over the dimensions of the Metropolitan Life edifice that Gilbert had now thoughtfully supplied, Frank reconsidered. "Is a 620-footer actually enough when, with another ninety feet or so, I could have a record-breaker?" The architect, with his fee agreed at five percent of all costs, congratulated Woolworth on his perspicacity. Had he possessed greater patience together with sta-

tistics concerning the Eiffel Tower, it is conceivable that the
Woolworth Building on completion would have scraped clouds a
thousand feet up.

As it was, he felt compelled to advise Frank that further pro-
crastination would be prohibitively expensive. The site had long
since been cleared, and concrete was already being poured. If it
was to be a 700-footer, this was the time to say so, for the foundations would need strengthening to carry the extra weight.

Frank shillyshallied for a further month, "trying," as one report put it, "to get people to work for him for nothing or for a
fraction of what they were usually paid." What his heart desired
was not only the world's loftiest skyscraper but also the cheapest
giant of a building ever to be erected in New York City, since he
intended to pay for it like everything else—in cash.

In January 1911, while he was warming up to prepare for the
$65,000,000 merger, he finally gave what he said was approval of
sketches calling for a minimum of 750 feet. If Gilbert imagined
the worst was over, he was grievously mistaken.

Ignorance of the nuts and bolts of architecture did not deter
Frank from demanding that his building be not only magnificent
but a sure-fire moneymaker, which meant ensuring it contained
the maximum acreage of rentable floor space. This, in turn, made
it necessary to compromise with medieval Gothic standards and
place uninterrupted bands of windows around the structure so
that, no matter how each upper floor was subdivided, every office
would enjoy daylight and a view of downtown Manhattan.

Once again, the crew in Gilbert's office tossed out a set of
drawings and started over. Two weeks later, they were at a standstill, "sucking their thumbs, marking time," as their employer
noted in an acid memorandum to Frank, who was wondering
whether he had come to the right decision.

It was impossible to keep him out of Gilbert's hair. Frank insisted on having a hand in the choice of everything from elevator
call buttons to the style of the lobby directories, from the ornamentation over doorways to the width of the corridors—he wanted
to trim them by two inches to provide extra footage on tenants'
leases.

The selection of a contractor taxed him to the limit. After
months of irresolution, he concluded that the Thompson-Starrett

Company's bid should be accepted, but not at the stipulated fee of $300,000. He let Louis Horowitz, the firm's president, know that a competitor of his was "ready to do the job for nothing—for the sake of prestige."

Horowitz would not dicker. "I had the feeling," he reminisced, "that Mr. Woolworth was turning on me, as if it were a fire hose, his customary way of buying goods for his five-and-ten-cent stores." Frank backed off, and the first cut-price steel was hoisted into place.

"Pay as you go" was one rule applied, "a penny saved is a penny earned" another. Frank spent half his days poring over accounts from subcontractors, while the other half went to completing the union of dime-store chains. In September, when the founders were holding their last meeting as independent operators, he grumbled to Gilbert about the needless expense of paying a boy $2.50 a day to answer the telephone installed at the building site. The architect, patience worn thin, relayed the complaint to Thompson-Starrett:

"It would appear that this is a large price to pay for such services, and I would ask your explanation thereof and in doing so have no doubt that you can place before Mr. Woolworth information that will satisfy him or if some error has been made . . . that you will make correction accordingly."

Gilbert was due to have his own arm twisted. "There are plenty of other architects," Frank told him, "who would have been flattered to work for a fee of far less than five percent; perhaps it ought to be renegotiated."

"That," Gilbert replied icily, "is neither here nor there." He would never have taken on the assignment had he anticipated this happening.

In just ninety days, he reminded Frank, Gilbert's staff had "entirely reorganized the plans of your building"—an unprecedented task performed "to save you heavy interest charges on the investment." His draftsmen had labored around the clock, "and I have paid for the expensive overtime myself."

On November 15, thirteen days after Frank's announcement of the new corporation, the steel skeleton loomed into view at 233 Broadway. He dropped in on the Sanitas Manufacturing Company to examine its range of toilets and garner an opinion on whether liquid soap dispensers deserved a place in his washrooms. Three more months elapsed before he chose the handles that would flush the urinals.

"The greatest difficulty we had," Louis Horowitz recalled, "was to prevent Mr. Woolworth making decisions that only specialists were fitted to make. I grew very fond of him, though. Often he took me to his Fifth Avenue home and played his electrical reproducing pipe organ, the ducts of which were cunningly placed throughout the palace-like interior. Sometimes he would play for hours, not stopping until he was relaxed and easy in his mind."

The master of the household was uneasy in his mind when he gave Jessie in marriage on February 1. Before the ring was on her finger, he had opposed her engagement to James Paul Donahue. For one thing, the young Irish dandy came from what was now a decreasingly desirable section of Manhattan, the west side instead of the east. For another, his father ran a family business in the noisome trade of rendering animal hides and fats. ("Well, *somebody* has to do that," Jessie taunted him.) And for a third, the bridegroom showed a taste for extravagance beyond his capacity to foot the bills. Jessie's gifts to him outnumbered his to her.

The prospect of losing her to a potential wastrel aggravated the tension in him. He cracked under the strain. On the morning of the wedding, he stretched out on his office couch, weeping.

When the ceremony began at four o'clock, he had composed himself. He seemed calm as he escorted her into the drawing room, as resplendent in his morning coat as the bride in her white satin dress trimmed with *point de Venise* lace and veil caught up in a chaplet of orange blossom. It was a small gathering, made up only of family and friends. Her mother's absence was not unexpected.

All went off smoothly. Jessie was attended by her two sisters Lena and Edna, in matching outfits of white and purple floral chiffon. Lena's daughter, seven-year-old Constance McCann, served as flower girl in a long white gown, her five-year-old brother Frazier Winfield in a dazzling white suit as page. The bridegroom appeared little the worse for a late-night bachelor party at Delmonico's. The best man, his brother Frank Donahue, bore up well, too, though one of the ushers could have looked happier. The bride wore only one piece of jewelry from the collection she was amassing—Donahue's present to her, a diamond and sapphire brooch.

Jessie was kissed, the organ played, the wedding breakfast served, and Mr. and Mrs. Donahue left for a two-month honeymoon, anticipating life under Frank's wing in Manhattan. The newspapers covered the affair with a few paragraphs, but a dry-goods monarch who refused to buy advertising space was not about to receive free publicity for his line of business. "Mr. Woolworth," said the *New York Times,* "is the owner of the Woolworth Building, to be the tallest in the world, now arising at Park Place and Broadway."

The statistics of the construction could have daunted a man of much greater composure: 17,000,000 bricks; 24,000 tons of steel; 26½ tons of bronze and iron hardware; 7,500 tons of terra-cotta; eighty-seven miles of electrical wiring; twelve miles of marble wainscoting. Marble? "Couldn't we sheet every exterior wall with it?" Gilbert vetoed the notion: the foundations would crumble under such a mighty increase in tonnage.

The human aspects of the enterprise were no less intimidating. Recruitment started early to train a force of three hundred to service the building—security guards, cleaners, firemen, electricians, plumbers, carpenters, painters, elevator operators. There would be enough tenants to populate half of Watertown, needing rapid transit between floors whose number at this point remained something of a mystery. Another kind of record had to be established to cope with the impending situation: installation of thirty of the world's speediest elevators, the first ever to be monitored by signal lights blinking on panels in the lobby, the first to be controlled by a dispatcher talking by phone to the uniformed pilots should an emergency arise.

Vertical transportation had been commonplace in New York City since 1889, when Otis Brothers and Company produced a successful electric elevator. On crowded streets where land values were inflated, landlords jumped at the chance to reap bigger returns from real estate by building toward the clouds. But this form of architectural progress, like many other changes of this era, instilled justifiable fear in timid hearts. Elevators, in the popular view, were a risky means of travel.

The deaths of passengers trapped in plummeting cages were a steady, foot-of-the-page news item. In the past three years, 2,671 Americans had been killed or hurt in this manner. Since the engineers' specifications for Frank's express elevators called for them to zip between basement and top floor in approximately sixty seconds, prospective tenants had to be assured that their safety came first in his thinking.

The shafts were the secret, designed like cylinders in which the cars sped up and down like pistons in an engine. If cables snapped, governors on motors failed and automatic brakes malfunctioned in a compounded moment of disaster, then the car would behave like a compressor, creating its own cushion of air on which to make a gentle landing. The inventor himself, F. T. Ellithorpe, was brought in to conduct a demonstration.

He explained to assembled reporters that his practice for testing purposes was to replace the usual wire hawser with a rope before he entered the car at an upper floor, armed with a species of scythe. "I poke this pole through the top of the cage and saw away at the hempen cable. Strand by strand, it parts faster than I can describe it, and then, with a sound like a muffled pistol-shot, the last fibers yield under the tugging load of the car, and down the shaft the elevator goes whizzing."

On this occasion, however, Ellithorpe deemed it more prudent to make a further replacement—a glass of water and seven thousand pounds of ballast substituted for himself. The rope was sliced, and the car arrived at the base of the shaft with not a drop of water spilled.

Frank had lost contact with money in the everyday sense. He went around for days with his pockets stuffed with $212,000 of undeposited checks. His male secretary, relating the incident, reported having said, "Mr. Woolworth, would you walk to the window every morning and toss twelve dollars and fifty cents into the street?"

"Of course not, young man."

"Well, that's the amount you're losing in interest every day by failing to deposit those checks."

Frank appeared never to have considered the point. He rummaged through his jacket, saying nothing, and handed over the crumpled accumulation of income he had overlooked.

The first of his self-contrived memorials, the new corporation, was complete, but the skyscraper was only a shell, when the doctors calculated just how fast the time was flying by: only two more years left unless he changed his routines. He could afford anything in the world except an early death. He saw he had no choice but go to Carlsbad, as the doctors urged him to, with Edna and her husband to keep him company.

When she panicked at the thought of her baby being born in a foreign land and they left Frank alone there, he turned to Jennie for help. She must join him immediately, said his cablegram. Within forty-eight hours she was on her way, crossing the sea with Alvin Ivie to escort her.

Frank grew more peevish with every day he passed in bed, his legs supported by pillows to relieve the pain in his knees. Carlsbad in the summer days of 1912 was awash with visitors in chiffon gowns, white flannel suits and gaudy uniforms, most of them hoping that spa water contained the elixir of life. But he was not allowed to stroll through the streets or the terraced gardens. What pleasure he had came from hearing, filtering in through an open window, the music of concerts played on the lawns by orchestras competing one with the other in the magnificence of their uniforms and the glissando of their violins.

He was certain the cure was doing him no good. He yearned for a square meal, and he resented being deprived of authority over his surroundings. The only outlet for his malicious humor lay in pitting one nurse against the other until they reached the point of refusing to exchange a word between themselves.

Then, after Jennie arrived with Alvin, the most important subject to be discussed was a progress report on the Woolworth Building. Everything was right on schedule, Alvin assured him. On the first of July, the Stars and Stripes had been raised on top of the tower as a signal to New Yorkers that the steel was all in place. A brochure elaborating on the attractions of the finished product was ready to be mailed to prospective tenants. Frank argued that this should have been done already; he would be happy to see some leases signed.

Compared with the elegance of most of the women who flocked to Carlsbad in the summer season, Jennie looked dowdy. She had no desire to ride through the streets in a carriage like the rest of them, with their parasols and their pearls. In her speech, clothes and manner, her origins were obvious. She was beginning to lose track of what was happening around her. Would Edna's baby be the third or fourth grandchild? Fourth, said Frank; Lena had borne three.

In the shell of his skyscraper's vast lobby, stonemasons were uncrating golden-veined marble quarried on the Isle of Skyros in the Aegean Sea. On scaffolding forty feet overhead, other craftsmen were fashioning a vaulted ceiling of exotic flowers and forest creatures in Persian mosaics of blue and gold and green.

The entire twenty-fourth floor was reserved for company executives, but details of what was to be done with a thirty-foot-square room on the southeast corner were altogether lacking. This was to be Frank's domain, which he wanted to be "the handsomest office in the country and possibly the world," as he said. He had no idea how his goal was to be achieved. Neither was there any assurance as yet that he would survive the ten more months needed to complete his building.

He summoned his chauffeur to take him away from Carlsbad. Jennie and Nurse Salter, the more tolerable of his two nurses, traveled with him in the car.

The mineral springs of Marienbad on the outskirts of the Císařský Les were reputedly even more potent than Carlsbad's in tackling gout, diabetes, obesity and liver troubles. He could also experiment with the peat baths, rich in iron, that were another highly touted feature of the medical regimen of the Bohemian watering place. He ordered Jules to head south through the mountains to Marienbad.

In New York, his office colleagues stuck to the rule against sending him personal letters because they depressed him, but he insisted on progress reports on his unfinished skyscraper—they were better for his health, he vowed, than any amount of medication.

Woolworth's publicity department went on pumping out press releases glorifying the uncompleted building and the man who was paying for it—it was Frank's theory that the ballyhoo would somehow tempt millions of new customers through the doors of the chain. He was as far off beam in his assessment of his clientele as in his attention to checks. The five-and-tens, he declared, "are more generally patronized by the wealthy classes than by the poorer." But the data reeled off by his public relations chief, Hugh McAtamney, were impressive by anybody's standards.

The skyline queen had her own power plant roaring in the subbasement, with capacity to serve a city of fifty thousand people. Her roofs were sheathed in copper linked to grounded cables to protect her from the severest lightning. She weighed in at 223,000 tons, she had the strength to withstand hurricanes blowing at two hundred miles an hour. Most astonishing of all, not a single life had been lost in her construction.

Marienbad's most celebrated resident physician was old Dr. Gott, whom the late King Edward VII had consulted at least once every year. Frank, whose choice of hotel, the Weimar, was the same as the British monarch's, felt impelled to call in the same medical man. His prognosis was encouraging. Frank, he said, could perhaps be restored to health within eighteen months under proper care.

"But you won't recover unless you obey orders. Don't be like King Edward. He insisted on riding in open carriages and contracted pneumonia." That, said Dr. Gott, had been the cause of his death in 1910—a curious conclusion when British physicians, administering morphine to ease his pain, ascribed his end to a heart attack brought on by a lifetime of gluttony.

Frank, however, cheered up by this forecast, left Marienbad with Jennie and the nurse on an automobile tour of Switzerland and France, and promptly resumed his uncontrollable eating habits. In September, Mr. and Mrs. Woolworth sailed for home, with Jules and the nurse attending them. By October, whatever benefit Frank had gained from the doctor's attention was lost; he returned to Europe, without Jennie, to spend the winter in Pau, the French health resort in the Basses-Pyrénées.

He was there on November 14 when his granddaughter Barbara was born to Edna Hutton in New York City. Her zodiacal sign was Scorpio, which implied, as an astrologer told her later, that she must control her own destiny. In the year of her birth, Grandfather's company sold $60,000,000 worth of merchandise at a profit of $5,414,798.

In the early spring, Frank came home, no more obedient to medical orders than to any other kind of direction. One of his first desires was to inspect his skyscraper and determine exactly how big she had grown. An elevator carried him up to the tower. Then, fighting for breath, he walked down every flight of stairs to the subbasement. "Hereafter," he gasped, "this will be known as a sixty-story building."

He took another ride in the direction of heaven with a fellow enthusiast of the pipe organ who, on the top landing, noticed a ladder propped against an open trapdoor. He began to climb it, and Woolworth dragged himself up after him. Hunched in crawl space under the tower's pointed crown, he suggested they should inscribe their names on the rafters. "Frank Winfield Woolworth," he wrote in his curlicued Spencerian script, to which his companion added, "Frank Taft."

Stage-managed by McAtamney, Woolworth's night of triumph arrived on April 24, when at seven-thirty Woodrow Wilson pressed a button in the White House to light up the building's 89,000 bulbs. In an improvised banquet hall on the twenty-seventh floor, the orchestra struck up "The Star-Spangled Banner," and nine hundred guests rose from their chairs to drink a toast to their beaming host. In the city and its suburbs, said one exultant account, waiting thousands saw "flashing out in outlines of fire, the greatest mountain of steel and stone ever erected by man."

The dinner was professedly held to honor Cass Gilbert. Once calm had been restored and napkins reapplied to laps and under chins, the diners began plowing through caviar, green turtle soup, guinea hen, terrapin and squab, washed down by amontillado, chablis and port. Everyone wore a four-leaf clover, presented as a memento of the celebration. It was not, strictly speaking, the proudest occasion of Frank's life; nothing remotely like it had happened to him before.

McAtamney had culled the audience from the arts and sciences, politics and industry, letters and the law. Judge Gary was there, and so was another man in the same business, Charlie Schwab. Financier Otto Kahn was present; J. P. Morgan was not. Governor Eugene Foss of Massachusetts was absent, but his lieutenant governor was pinch-hitting for him. The nation's capital supplied three senators and seventy-eight congressmen. A poet arrived, Edwin Markham, who had once composed some verse the host was not likely to be familiar with:

> Why build these cities glorious
> If man unbuilded goes?

In vain we build the world, unless
The builder also grows.

Richard Harding Davies, reporter of past wars with one more awaiting him, sat at a table with Charles Dana Gibson, his fame earned by drawing idealized society girls. Banking was represented by Lewis Pierson—a noble marble stairway led up from the lobby to the opulent quarters leased by Irving National Bank.

On a preview tour through the lobby, the guests' attention had been directed to the gargoyles, carved in stone, that seemingly supported the crossbeams. One was a caricature of Frank counting his nickels and dimes, a second of Pierson fingering stock ticker tape, a third of Gilbert contemplating a model of the edifice as gravely as Aristotle studying a bust of Homer in a Rembrandt painting. If, as someone suggested later, the sculptor was "teasing mammon," Frank did not interpret it that way. On first sight of the effigies, he laughed himself into tears and commanded that they never be removed.

The first of the speakers introduced by the toastmaster was "a new man . . . an all-round American . . . born on a farm up in our State . . . a plain farmer boy who has kept ahead of the procession."

Sentiment prevailed. Frank quickly asked William Moore to present himself for applause, followed by Perry Smith, Moore's partner of long ago. Sum Woolworth—"I believe they call him my brother," Frank joked—was asked to stand, succeeded one by one by the rest of the founding fathers. "I do not wish to be egotistical," said the host, "but if I have had any ability, it has been in the selection of good generals of the little business I started."

Gilbert, when his turn came, found no reason for similar modesty, since the latest product of his talents had already been favorably compared with the Colossus of Rhodes and hailed as the "crowning glory of the builder's art." The same booster spirit inspired another admirer to remark that western civilization as a whole would now have no alternative to admitting that "for ingenuity, daring and effectiveness the American architects and engineers are far ahead of the master builders of this or any other age."

From Frank he received a silver loving cup of a size to slake the thirst of an elephant. William Winter, retired drama critic and elegist of the *Tribune*, recited a poem he had written in honor of Gilbert, who in Winter's view had been destined from birth "To hail the future and ordain/Triumphant Beauty's perfect reign."

It was unquestionably a building that stirred the imagination. One writer fancied it "conveyed the uplifting thought that business enterprise in America was more than just a sordid struggle for material gain." An earlier reporter came up with the following dialogue, allegedly exchanged between two awestruck cleaning women as they stood on the sidewalk and looked up at the queen standing tall against the midnight sky:

"How is it any man can build a buildin' like that?"

" 'Tis easy explained: your ten cents and my ten cents."

Frank was so delighted with what was alternately dubbed "the Cathedral of Commerce" and "the Eighth Wonder of the World" that he ordered tinted photographs of it run off in the hundreds of thousands for distribution throughout his empire.

The question of how his office was to be decorated remained unanswered when his doctors demanded that, unless he was looking forward to an early grave, he must take another course of treatment an ocean away from the scene where his addiction to work and eating made him impossible to deal with. This time, he was admitted to a nursing home on the shore of Lake Geneva for three weeks in bed and a further two weeks of submission to the fleeting benefits of spa water.

Jennie and a married sister of hers went over toward the end of July to join him on what had become a ritualistic convalescence, touring Europe in the Panhard. During his latest spell of seclusion, he had brooded over the tales he had listened to in childhood about the attainments of the Bonapartes, memories sparked by a fellow member of the Hardware Club who had taken to addressing him as "the Napoleon of commerce." When the Panhard delivered Frank to the summer resort of Compiègne, where a bridge dating back to the reign of Louis Quatorze crossed the River Oise, he headed straight for the palace built there for the same monarch and then glorified by Napoleon, emperor of France.

As Woolworth ambled through its Empire Room, the pieces suddenly fell into place in his fancy. This was the way his office must look, a setting he deserved. He ordered his chauffeur to drive him to Paris so that a start could be made on combing antique shops for the furnishings. What couldn't be found there, Frank would pick up from New York dealers in relics and *objets d'art*.

Within six months, the dream had become megalomaniac reality. Polished Vert Campan marble covered the office walls under a gold-embossed ceiling. The bronze panels on each door framed golden figurines—lions, lyres, laurel wreaths. Napoleon in his coronation robes (a copy of a portrait of Versailles) stared down from the west wall at a century-old mantel clock he had allegedly received from Tsar Alexander, a life-sized bust of the Corsican posing as Julius Caesar (imported from Paris) and two tapestried armchairs, reproductions of the throne chair in the Palace of Fontainebleau. Astride a horse, he was represented in the bronze inkwell that stood on a bronze-mounted Empire desk of 4,050 square inches. An antique paperweight was also adorned with his profile.

Every item in the room was listed in the blissful letter from the Napoleon of commerce to each of his stores. "There is also a beautiful fireplace capable of burning real wood or real coal as the President of the Company sees fit. . . . Off the Empire Room is a nice little office for the secretary to the President, decorated very simply in cream and gold with a handsome rug and Empire furniture."

How much time his health would let him sit at his desk basking in splendor was problematic. That summer he was back for another spell of bed rest and baths at Evian-les-Bains on the French side of Lake Geneva, with Jennie playing her role as nurse.

When the pistol shots fired in Sarajevo set the guns of August thundering across Europe, the two of them took refuge in neutral Switzerland; they were stranded there until the last week of September. The company had no stores in Germany—1927 was the natal year there—but Woolworth buying offices and warehouses were forced to close as employees answered the call to Kaiser Wilhelm's colors. Frank and Jennie managed to make reservations aboard *La France* and reach Le Havre in time for the sailing.

One surviving document indicates no concern about his health, the war or its effects on his business. Instead, he was preoccupied with finding the right class of tenant for 233 Broadway and mixing with such distinguished fellow passengers as Anne Morgan, daughter of the unapproachable J. P.

"Miss Morgan has a charming personality and devotes much

of her time taking care of young shop girls. She appears very en-
thusiastic about her work and wants me to give her some room in
the Woolworth Building." What a coup that would be when her
father had never entertained the idea! Philanthropy blossomed for
a moment. "Of course I had to consent to it."

The fighting in Europe posed two serious problems for Carson
Peck and the others who ran the company. The British navy's Atlantic blockade effectively halted the inflow of goods already
bought and paid for. Inflated prices in the United States threatened to crack the ten-cent ceiling that was an article of faith for
Frank.

The first of those challenges was met by sending an emissary to
persuade the British to give clear passage to cargoes bound for
Woolworth's. Then, drawing on everything that company buyers
overseas had learned of manufacturing processes, Peck set up a
program to teach American businesses how to turn out Christmas tree ornaments and celluloid dolls to retail for no more than
the mandatory dime. "Woolco" made its first appearance on
spools of crochet cotton spun in United States mills instead of
being imported.

While war wracked Europe, the chain's expansion did not falter; neither did payment of its dividends every January, April,
July and October. The Woolworth Building brought Frank all he
had hoped for in personal publicity. Suddenly, he was a national
figure, the subject of countless articles in newspapers and magazines: *King of the Ten-Cent Bazaar . . . Man Who Saw Millions in a
Nickel . . . Big Dreams That Came True.*

He was portrayed as a twentieth-century folk hero in *Current
Opinion, World's Work, Hearst's, Everybody's, McBride's, Literary Digest*
and a host of similar publications. Editors fed readers' hunger for
personal prosperity with stories of go-getters with the will to suc-
ceed, like Frank. (His fame outlasted that of some equally celebrated confrères; among them was William B. Walker, former
cowhand, who trapped Wyoming prairie dogs to peddle as pets to
greenhorn tourists, then shipped carloads of buffalo skeletons, collected alongside the railroad tracks, to New Jersey glue factories
before he settled down to make his real money from patented
Thermos flasks, an idea he picked up from Rheinhold Burger, a
German glass manufacturer.)

Frank's credo found its way into print: "Of course you will be discouraged, but keep on. . . . If you believe in an idea, give it a chance. . . . Supervise details, but don't let them absorb you." A biographer tackled, but did not complete, the writing of Woolworth's life story.

Since his customary vacation lands were sealed off by war, he bought a retreat at Glen Cove on Long Island's north shore, re-naming the white stucco house with its eighteen acres "Winfield Hall" and equipping it with another roll-playing organ. The urge to build overtook him again. He bought four older houses that stood in a row next to Franklyn and Edna Hutton's on East 80th Street, dwellings rendered out of date by the tide of change. He had them razed and replaced with a pair of handsome new man-sions, one apiece for Lena and Jessie and their families, at a cost of $750,000. The Woolworth compound now occupied twenty-six feet of Fifth Avenue and spread for a further two-hundred and fifty feet around the corner.

Beyond a shadow of doubt, Frank had made his presence felt in America. With equal certainty Jennie, after forty-six years of marriage, was losing her mind.

13

◁] In Memoriam [▷

Her faded blue eyes, someone said, were "as vacant as an abandoned house." She would sit in a tapestried chair, hands idle in her lap, staring for hours at the elaborate wallpaper of a house that had never appealed to her as her own. If Frank strolled in for a minute to have a word with her, she would look up sometimes and ask, "Who is it?" Their daughters met with the same response, but they had more patience with her than he did.

At the age of sixty, she looked thirty years older, a senile woman incapable of walking anywhere without help from a nurse, unable to dress or attend to herself in any way. Her memory of the past, the years of seemingly endless struggle and then of empty triumphs, was erased, along with her ability to remember events of a few moments ago.

The luxury surrounding her meant nothing; she had never demanded material possessions. She had served her husband with unquestioning devotion, and she had been repaid in what to her was worthless currency. She had been made a kind of sacrifice to his success. Her love for him had long outlasted his for her, but now it did not matter; her heart was as drained of emotion as her mind was bereft of thought. In personal property, she was worth $5,000, though title to the old house in Brooklyn in which Frank had installed her sister Mary remained in Jennie's name.

The most likely diagnosis of her condition reached by a later generation of doctors would be early senile dementia or possibly atherosclerosis, the thickening of arteries that gradually lessens the flow of blood, in this case to her atrophying brain, in much the same way that hard water furs the inside of copper tubing. They would have checked her medical history, seeking evidence of high blood pressure or heart attacks, and studied the possibility that accumulated mental stress was a factor in the onset of a disease as baffling today as it was then.

Analyzing the symptoms listed by her physicians, specialists now find some justification for extending a further theory: she may have been suffering from a venereal disease. Neurosyphilis can destroy the substance of the brain while syphilitic endarteritis, destroying the blood vessels by infection, can cause the same blocking of cerebral arteries that afflicted Jennie, producing identical reactions in a patient. In younger people, "apoplexy" was almost invariably traceable to syphilitic endarteritis or to embolism, the obstruction of an artery.

If Jennie had in fact been infected in her younger years, the only likely source would be her husband. Extramarital sex was a concept totally alien to a woman of her docile, unassuming nature. In Frank's case, however, there are grounds for speculation. "Nobody ever got on," he had said once, "who was in bondage to the body. You can't build a business on thoughts of having a good time." But the statement was made after the business had been built, when he showed no restraint in his appetite for food, luxury, power and perhaps sexual adventure.

Hotels and the women who frequented them had fascinated him ever since his nights in the St. Nicholas, long since demolished. On his excursions to Europe, his companion was Jules Billard, whose role was enigmatic. He had been an ace driver on the Renault racing team before Frank hired him away. The new job must have held some special attractions for him to have given up the excitement and prestige of the old one. In the guarded words of the only "official" biography of Frank, "A fancy lured Billard into becoming the millionaire's chauffeur, and he remained with Woolworth for many years. They became cronies. A bit of a D'Artagnan, Jules was daring, efficient and hardboiled. Woolworth never questioned his decisions in the 'motor department.' "

Did his services in the "motor department" cover the procurement of women? Another quotation from the same source only obscures the answer: "Another man whom Woolworth, strange to say, never sought to roil was his swashbuckling Franco-Swiss chauffeur, Jules Billard. Jules was now wed to Mlle. Ducharme, a member of the Metropolitan Opera cast." The likelihood of her marrying a run-of-the-mill chauffeur would seem questionable. But Billard was responsible for organizing Frank's enjoyment. Every spring, he crossed the Atlantic ahead of his boss to "map out the summer's touring schedule."

According to one internist's theory, the slow spread of venereal disease could account for Frank's behavior and state of health in old age—irrational, forgetful, deluded, self-indulgent. No autopsy was conducted either on him or on Jennie, so the truth remains hypothetical.

As things stood in 1915, Lena and Jessie played for time, putting off the day when their mother's condition must be confronted. Edna was of limited help in the situation; she had problems of her own to contend with.

Franklyn Hutton was rapidly establishing himself in the brokerage business and simultaneously developing a taste for hard liquor and the soft embraces of other women. Love had disappeared from the household in which three-year-old Barbara was growing up, "glutted with privilege," as she remembered, "softened by luxury, weakened by indulgent nannies, and made to feel special by all my governesses and chauffeurs and personal maids."

The policeman who patrolled the stretch of Millionaires' Row in the Eighties saluted the chubby child with big blue eyes and thick black brows when a nursemaid took her out walking with one of her trunkful of dolls. One of her few affectionate memories of her father concerned the white ermine coat and matching hat he bought her when he took a turn at giving her an airing. Otherwise, she sensed she was a pawn in an incomprehensible game played between her parents.

In her fourth year of life, her mother moved with her out of the house Frank had given the Huttons on East 80th Street; from now on, they would stay in a suite at the Plaza. Her grandparents were distant, almost unknown people to Barbara. Jennie had difficulty recognizing anybody. Frank was preoccupied with his health and the pursuit of glory.

Death among his comrades pulled him back to earth. The disease that afflicted Carson Peck, detected earlier, had been ascribed to the gross amount of candy he had sampled; candy was now earning the empire $3,347,000 a year. The onset of diabetes was a secret he kept from his colleagues. No effective treatment existed until insulin's role was proven six years afterward.

On January 4, the twenty-fifth anniversary of his arrival at headquarters, a luncheon was held for him. Then gangrene developed in a scratched finger, demanding its immediate amputation. His right arm was still in a sling bandage when he appeared at a mid-April directors' meeting. A day or so later, he collapsed and sank into a coma that preceded his end. He was fifty-seven years old.

His wife Clara and their two children, Fremont and young Clara, saw him buried in Brookside Cemetery, Watertown, before they built and endowed in his memory a $4,500,000 hospital in Brooklyn, his adopted home. Frank ordered every store and office of the chain closed for the hour of the funeral, then resumed nominal command of the company.

After an interval of two weeks there was a similar shutdown for the burial of Seymour Knox. With the merger accomplished, he had retired, in failing health, looking forward to enjoying the results of his labors in dry goods, along with dividends from his holdings in banking, railroads and lumber companies. He had lived as if he had been born to wealth, breeding racehorses at a stud farm in East Aurora named for his first stallion, "Prince Ideal," where he built a dirt and a cinder track with stabling for thirty thoroughbreds and pastures for his brood mares. Every Fourth of July was race day at Ideal Stock Farm, where Seymour mowed hay behind a team of horses—he never learned to drive the automobiles he owned.

He died at his home on Delaware Avenue, Buffalo, aged fifty-four, leaving his money to be shared between his widow, Grace, and their three children, Dorothy, Seymour Junior and Marjorie. The village of Russell, where he was born, had already received a new town hall from him, together with a high school, to which his name was given.

Frank acknowledged the loss of "two wonderful businessmen" with a few added words of reassurance to the staff. "But there are about ninety heads of different departments in the corporation, and our business will go on. This is not a one-man business any more than is the Standard Oil Company."

The reshuffling of executives was accomplished without the introduction of any outsider. Hubert Parson climbed one more rung to become treasurer as well as secretary. Charlie Griswold took over as general manager and straightaway began peppering his men in the field with terse bulletins. "Warning. A manager accused a lady of stealing in Dayton, Ohio, store. She sued the firm for $25,000. We defended the suit and won, but the total charges we had to pay were $555.41. Wise man that bridles his tongue under provocation."

The deaths of two intimates younger than himself turned Frank's thoughts deeper inward. It was time to demonstrate that, like them, he had a charitable heart. After a rare visit to the farm once owned by his father, in his grave for nine years now, he decided to donate a chapel in memory of both his parents.

A private palace car of the New York Central carried him and his party up to Great Bend for the organ recital, banquet and oratory attendant upon the September dedication of the Woolworth Memorial Methodist Episcopal Church. His own speech—"You may ask the reason why I gave the money for the construction"—from its beginning to its close showed an odd absorption with the theme of finanace. His intention, he made clear, was to contribute only a share of the overheads.

"For the maintenance of the property I am not going to provide entirely. I know that you want to bear some of the expense, so I am now going to present to the secretary of the trustees an endowment of $20,000 in five percent bonds for the maintenance of the church so that it will not become a burden on the congregation and the trustees. I hope that in time it may become too small for the congregation." The interest would amount to a less than overwhelming $1,000 a year.

His success had exemplified what his generation accepted as an immutable law of economics: the survival of the fittest. The expansion of his empire was irresistible when frailer merchants in the dime-store trade could not withstand the force of the competition he brought to bear on them. Now he was confronted with another law that said, rich or poor, all men were mortal. Those who enrolled in Frank's service had the opportunity to make a fortune, but it entailed the risk of working themselves to the cemetery.

Charlie Griswold was next. He had been Woolworth's general manager for only eight months when he died of a heart attack. Hubert Parson's ascent continued with his election as vice-president and Griswold's successor. That year, when the Franco-British and German armies were mired in the mud of the Somme, the number of Woolworth stores in North America fell eighty short of a thousand, registering sales of $87,189,270.

"Overhead in most retail stores is too high," Frank pontificated to Parson. "In factories, they do things much better. When motions are found to be repetitive, they are handed over to a machine designed to go through those motions." While automated selling might be the ideal, turnover, "our greatest means of giving the public economy," must be set at eight times a year, a goal attainable by working the counter hands to the limit of their ability.

Frank fell ill again that spring, but no matter how listless he was feeling, he showed up at virtually every monthly meeting of the board. A round trip to the west coast, with Harry Albright, Mrs. Albright and a nurse taking care of him, was scheduled to return Frank to Watertown in time for the company's annual meeting on May 17.

His headaches and gastric troubles were no better than on his departure from New York City when the train pulled into the Watertown depot. As he stepped down onto the platform, he thought he heard the bells of Trinity Church, where William Moore was senior warden. He looked around for the old man, but for the first time in years he was not there with his automobile, waiting to welcome him. A stroke had left him paralyzed.

Frank told the rest of the story in his suite at the Hotel Woodruff the following day. "When I arrived last night I heard he was better. Half an hour later I saw Louis [William's only son], and he said his father was much better. The next thing I heard he was dead."

Could the tolling of the bells have been a premonition? He didn't know about that, but he was sure his old mentor had not died of heart disease, as the doctors claimed. A dentist had just lately extracted most of Moore's teeth. It was dentistry, Frank insisted, that had killed his friend.

Woolworth, plagued by toothache, had always shied away from dentists. Now he felt justified in his evasions. As cavities increased and his gums grew pulpy, he turned to a diet of soft foods that became more and more restricted until he was subsisting largely on mashed bananas.

He paid a concluding tribute to the second dead founder of the empire. "I have never met a man so truly honest and upright as Mr. Moore. I owe my success to his influence, and had it not been for him, I would probably be working for ten dollars a week in Watertown."

Moore's will divided a $250,000 estate between his son and daughter Clara, Trinity Church, a local cemetery, and City Hospital. His summer place had been deeded in advance to the church men's club as a campground, complete with cottages, boathouses and clubhouse. The girls of Trinity had been given a two-story building he owned, the city's dental and tuberculosis clinics supplied with other property of his, as well as with gifts of equipment. In the old man's belief, it was more blessed to give than to receive.

Frank stayed on for the funeral, laying the groundwork for Moore's memorial: the ancient Corner Store must be demolished, and on the site there must rise another Woolworth building, six stories high.

A further building job, his last, was put in hand in November. "It's not the money," he said after a fire, started by a short circuit in the wiring, destroyed his Long Island sanctuary. "It's the fact that it's my home." The loss was estimated at $300,000. The new Winfield Hall, designed by long-suffering Cass Gilbert, would be valued at almost three times that figure, and Frank wanted it ready by the following summer at the latest.

Where the Woolworth skyscraper had been mock Gothic, Gilbert applied a fine Italianate hand to this new commission. The outcome, a flat-roofed, three-story pseudo-palace in Frank's preferred white marble, was artfully positioned for maximum effect at the end of a serpentine driveway in the midst of landscaped gardens, dense with yews and manicured flower beds, that harbored a summerhouse also of marble, two greenhouses, one fountain, a statue of Neptune, and an eighteen-car garage.

It was, in a sense, an anachronism, a throwback to the previous century when Vanderbilts and Astors vied with each other in exhibitions of architectural extravagance. The *Architectural Record*, after an inspection of the place, sniffed, "The country residence of the American millionaire will, we may confidently predict, again become a smaller and more informal and a less pretentious building."

With ten master bedrooms plus fifteen servants' rooms, the interior was a museum of decorating styles. Raised gold letters on the outer side of each door spelled out the particular period—Sheraton, Louis Quatorze, Louis Quinze, Marie Antoinette, and half a dozen more. "It was all very unusual," said the Fifth Avenue decorator charged with the task, "but Mr. Woolworth wanted it that way." The *Architectural Record* judged that "the design of some of the apartments is hurt rather than helped by the amount of ornamentation."

Frank's second-floor suite was, of course, Napoleonic, from the canopy over the bed (a similar one had hung over his hero's throne) to the marbled, gilded and mirrored bathroom, which was an enlarged copy of Bonaparte's own. Most of the house was wired for music and stormy sound effects supplied by the $100,000 organ that was the showpiece of the biggest and most elaborate chamber of all. The carved lacework grilles of this music room concealed an alcove from which a private detective spied on the guests. The Bohemian crystal of the Brobdingnagian chandelier was set tinkling whenever the master started a roll revolving at the touch of a console button.

He was so enamored of his palazzo that he conducted visitors on lecture tours, reeling off the credentials and provenance of pieces in every room. But the pillared porch with its ponderous wrought-iron lanterns and floor of Spanish tile was off limits when Jennie sat out there, staring at nothing in particular, rocking restlessly in a wicker chair.

One daughter did not live to see the house. Edna Hutton was alone in the drawing room of her suite in the Plaza on the afternoon of May 2, her husband away in their Long Island summer home, her four-year-old daughter in charge of a nursemaid. Edna left no note, or if she did it was destroyed, so what drove her to death had to be surmised. Her suspicions that Hutton was an adulterer were confirmed when she discovered a letter from him to his current mistress. Possibly she had come to feel, as her daughter did as an adult, that her life was as loveless now as it had always appeared to be, leaving her defenseless in adversity.

Three explanations were given for how she reached her end, clad in a white lace dress with a broken parasol at her side. The coroner's was the least convincing. Edna, he said, was found on a carpet by the window by a maid; Barbara used to assert, not always persuasively, that it was she who made the discovery. The cause of death? Mastoiditis, the coroner said, which "had caused contraction of the tongue muscles and consequent suffocation." As an adult, Barbara was certain her mother took her own life by poison. A third theory held that she had leaped from the window and then been spirited back into the room, dying or already dead. Barbara clung to the belief that, whatever had happened, her father was to blame. The greatest desire of her life, she once said, was to get even with him. "If I was incapable of love, it was because I saw no love around me."

Her childhood might have been happier if either of her aunts had taken over the care of her. Jessie had a second son, Jimmy, born in Greenwich, Connecticut, in June, 1915. Barbara could have played with him and his older brother, Woolworth, only seven months younger than she. Lena had a daughter, Helena, even closer to Barbara's age, as well as three other children. (The youngest, Gladys, died the following year.)

But Grandpa took his sad motherless granddaughter under his wing, to raise her in his eccentric, childless household. No nursery had been planned for her. Instead, she was provided with a room whose windows were of stained glass, curtained with Renaissance tapestries, while carved oak paneling covered the walls. When the thunder of the organ downstairs broke her sleep, she trembled with terror. She welcomed it, though, if she had been dreaming of her mother, running into the empty room that she knew only as a dream, calling to Edna, "Wake up; don't leave me!" The household rule was that her mother was not to be spoken of in front of the child. Otherwise, the pupils of her eyes would dilate with a look of madness.

She ate in vast dining halls where footsteps echoed from the vaulted ceilings and the long tables were set as if for a banquet with flowers, crystal and silver, while her grandparents sat apart, each with a nurse in attendance. "He was a little loony, but he was sweet to me," she recalled. "Grandma had lost her mind."

Even more marble had been added to the house on Fifth Avenue. She nestled in his lap there when he recited the story of each composer before Grandpa set the music rolling and the thunder roaring. "Barbara," he would tell her, "you're going to be able to buy the whole world."

It had been possible to hush up the circumstances of Edna's death, but in the following month Jennie's condition became public knowledge, though the headlines were more subdued than the banners of black type that dominated front-page dispatches from Château-Thierry: *Our Gallant Marines Drive on 2½ Miles, Capture 300 Prisoners.* Through his attorneys, Frank was petitioning the Supreme Court of New York on a crucial question of common law—dower, the life interest of a widow in a third part of her husband's property. He acted, his statement said, to his "very great regret and sadness," in the belief that, ill as she was, she could conceivably outlast him. To secure the disposition of his estate in his own hands, he was seeking the appointment of "a committee of her person and property" to sanction his lawful release from dower obligations.

Witnesses told of her existence under round-the-clock nursing care. Dr. George W. Jarman vowed to the court that she was not insane but suffering "what is popularly known as softening of the brain," an affliction caused by "lime salts in blood vessels."

"Her senility," he testified, "is similar to that of a person more than ninety years of age. She is cheerful but incapable of mental processes, cannot comprehend what is going on about her clearly, and is usually unable to recognize her husband and children distinctively. The condition is incurable."

The petition was granted, uncontested, and the dower abolished on payment of the $498,700 Frank deposited in her name to provide her with income for the rest of her life. Then he called for his attorney, William C. Breed, to prepare a new will to replace the sheet of paper Frank had written in 1889, bequeathing everything unconditionally to Jennie.

She was still treated handsomely in the new testament, but it took account of his astounding wealth by leaving millions to Lena and Jessie, setting up trust funds for each grandchild, donating lump sums to old friends and to charity. This masterful document was treated like the hoard of checks—tucked away, unsigned, into a pocket.

Company dividends hovered around six percent when the first Liberty Loans were issued by the United States Treasury at 3½, which was a distinct improvement over the three and even two recently paid on other government bonds. Frank, a good patriot, bought $600,000 worth of the new issues, enough to earn $21,194 in interest every year. He also offered to serve in an organization known as the Four-Minute Men whose speakers, in moviehouses, theaters and similar meeting places, stood up to deliver a few brisk words extolling the Liberty campaign. It was a useful contribution to the war effort when Wilson's aim was to raise only a third of the cost of fighting the Germans from taxes, the rest to come from loans.

Frank, lost to reality and dejected by family tragedy, summarized his thinking in two sentences: "I am a great believer in thrift. War is the great business of this country, and nothing else counts." He made a valuable recruit to Wilson's cause. Before Americans arrived on the battlefields of France, there were only 350,000 bond investors in the United States; the number had risen to 25,000,000 by the time the armistice was signed.

Victory over Germany gave him one reason to celebrate; another was the opening of his thousandth store. His fellow directors questioned whether the site, on Fifth Avenue opposite the Public Library, was a wise choice when the rent ran so high. He scoffed at their timidity. "I've been studying the location for five years. It is one of the cheapest sites I have ever attained. The business will be immense. Fifth Avenue is changing. It is going to be more and more a thoroughfare of business."

As a homeowner further up the avenue, the implications of change worried him. Was No. 990 secure against the northward advance of shopping crowds and commercial traffic? He was smitten with the idea, planted by his inventive decorator, Helwig Schier, of erecting a new marble palace to live in, a dwelling as big as a department store, covering a whole square block.

This attack of construction fever came too late to rouse him from his increasing lethargy, but Schier found ready customers among Frank's colleagues, who were eager to copy some of the style of the boss. Fred Kirby became one of Schier's clients, Sum Woolworth another, but Hubert Parson was the decorator's pride and joy.

First, he moved into a mansion close to Frank's on Millionaires' Row and commissioned Schier to make its every room more impressive than anything in sight at No. 990. Then he took over Shadow Lawn, Woodrow Wilson's former home on the New Jersey shore, and Frank, with very little to amuse him these days, laughed himself into tears.

Frank still nursed a thought that, provided he could apply it, would result in the biggest bargain ever offered in dime-store history. He had discussed it time and again with manufacturers in Switzerland and Germany. They invariably told him it was impossible, but he refused to believe them. "I'd be happy," he repeated, "if I could sell a watch for a dime, a watch that really worked and kept good time."

The watch remained a dream, and his own time was running out when he ordered a $100,000 granite tomb with doors of bronze to be erected with all possible speed in Woodlawn Cemetery, the Bronx. He was crankier than ever, and his mind wandered like a sluggish stream. His doctors had traced the trouble to rotted teeth that they said were poisoning his body, but he cut off the discussion. He had lost the one companion he relied on to cheer him up with her presence: Barbara had been taken off by her father to Altadena, California, and deposited there with an aunt, Grace Middleton. His granddaughter would see him only on his infrequent visits west or when she traveled east on the way to summers in Europe.

Her cousin Jimmy Donahue was undergoing an equally disturbing childhood. Jessie lavished gifts on everyone around her— her sons, herself and her husband. Jimmy was effectively sealed off from reality by the sheer pressure of her generosity, brought up to believe that work of any description was unnecessary to a fortune's heir.

His father's influence was more vicious. Jimmy Senior had emerged as a homosexual with no pretense about it. He preferred to flounce around night club dance floors rather than pretend to earn a living. He cruised the speakeasies of Manhattan and Palm Beach in search of fleeting affairs with chorus boys, sailors and any other young man whose favors he could buy with Jessie's money. His behavior was no secret to his sons. Young Jimmy was marked for life.

Frank spent his last day in his astonishing office on Wednesday, April 2, 1919. He might have heard from Parson the up-to-date story of what had been achieved. Sales exceeded $100,000,000. Almost all the 22,000,000 families that comprised the United States were Woolworth customers. In that year, 600,000 babies wore gold-filled rings bought for a dime. Profits were bulked out by selling 26,000 tons of candy, 100,000,000 postcards, 25,000,000 toys, 15,000,000 bars of soap and 10,000,000 packages of chewing gum, which was a wartime novelty.

But Frank swung aimlessly in his swivel chair, asked for a secretary to report to his house tomorrow to tackle unanswered correspondence, and called for his chauffeur to take him home.

The weather was cold for a weekend in the country, but on Friday he felt he must get out of the city and the mausoleum that was his home. Jennie would have to be left with her nurses. He was shivering and the pain in his throat made it impossible for him to swallow when he reached Winfield Hall. His fever mounted through the next day. When he lost consciousness on Sunday afternoon, Dr. Zabriskie, summoned from Glen Cove, diagnosed his patient's ailments as uremia and stones in the gall bladder. Frank responded briefly to medication, while Lena and Jessie made a hasty drive to Long Island. On Tuesday afternoon, they were there with the doctor when their father died.

The obituary was relegated to an inside page in Wednesday's newspapers, which had more momentous events to report. *Wilson Hopes by Plain Truth to End the Peace Crisis. Italians Still Hint at Withdrawal from Paris. Appeal for End of Delays. Reparations Almost Fixed. German Reds Wait Chance. Riots and Loot in Saxony. President's Ship Will Sail Friday.*

Dry-goods merchants advertised some bargains that morning. Franklin Simon and Company at 8 West 38th Street offered men's hand-tailored topcoats for $30. Gimbel Brothers at 32nd and 33rd Streets promoted carpet sweepers at $1.44, food choppers with four separate blades at $1.24, and "slightly marred" washtub covers ("also used as pastry and meat boards") at 85 cents.

The *Times* listed Frank's hard-won financial and social credentials in a single sentence. He was "one of the largest stockholders and a director of Irving National Bank and Irving Trust Company, a member of the Chamber of Commerce of New York, the Union League Club, the Lotos Club, the Hardware Club, and a director of the Pennsylvania Society."

Company headquarters stayed closed until the next Saturday. Activity in the Woolworth Building was halted for five minutes while the rites were said in the music room of the house on Fifth Avenue, where the organ pealed under the hands of his friend, Frank Taft. Woolworth's staff concluded afterward that "one of the great honors" came from Frank's direst rival, Sebastian Kresge. He, too, had the doors of his stores locked during the funeral service.

The order for the Woodlawn tomb had been placed too late. Until it was ready, the embalmed body was stored in a humbler rented vault. The new will had also been uncompleted. Without his signature, it was meaningless. The document filed with the probate court of Nassau County was the thirty-year-old hand-written page that made Jennie, senile and disoriented, the sole legatee.

14

❦] The Inheritors [❧

So much had been left unfinished by him that nobody could accurately foretell the consequences. To the end, he had held onto everything he owned, disregarding advice about how to minimize the inevitable tax bill. When the estate passed in its entirety to Jennie, first estimates were that federal and state inheritance taxes might amount to a round $1,000,000, a record for the day. Eventual payments were, in fact, an awesome $8,900,000.

He had shown limited patience with directors' meetings held in the ornate boardroom of his own design on the twenty-fourth floor of his skyscraper and had trained no one as his successor. So management had to be restructured, with Sum, respected for his integrity, coming in as the company's first chairman. Hubert Parson, making it up the final rung, was appointed president to serve under him, after Fred Kirby declined the job. Everything in the Empire Room was preserved intact except the painting of Napoleon, which was replaced by a portrait of Frank of similar dimensions.

Ownership of the building itself was in question. Frank's equity in it was assessed at $10,490,095, his holdings in the company at $13,181,172 in common stock, $2,201,100 in preferred. No one knew what should be mortgaged or sold to meet the demands of the tax collectors. The fate of Winfield Hall, valued at $852,666, and the $460,000 house on Fifth Avenue was equally uncertain.

The month after their father died, Lena and Jessie were afraid the problems would be compounded by the early death of their mother, a victim of influenza in the third successive wave of the disease that swept the world in a postwar pandemic, killing more than half a million Americans among a total toll of 20,000,000.

Lena and Jessie petitioned the courts as Frank had done, seeking to be named the "committee of her person." Their qualifications were spelled out by counsel. They were "upwards of thirty years of age, in perfect health, and have the love and affection for their mother which one would expect. They both have large and independent fortunes of their own in addition to what they will naturally receive upon the death of their mother. They inform me that it is their intention to have their mother live with each of them the alternate six months of each year." No more had to be said to persuade the judge to grant the petition that made Hubert Parson the third member of a benevolent triumvirate.

Jennie recovered and clung to life for five more years. Her end came in neither daughter's home but in Winfield Hall, with Lena and Jessie in the bedroom. She was buried next to Frank in Woodlawn Cemetery. The inheritance was diminished by another levy of taxes, but the committee of three had been prudent, raising the cash to settle the charges incurred on Frank's departure by disposing of real estate, not Woolworth stock. No. 990 Fifth Avenue had been sold to Jules Bache, a Wall Street broker. The Woolworth Building was mortgaged for $3,000,000 at six percent to the Prudential Life Insurance Company of Newark, which was busily investing its accumulations of capital in Manhattan hotels and office properties.

The era of peace and abounding prosperity coincident with Warren Harding's presidency was working wonders for the Woolworths. The wealth of the country had almost doubled in the past decade, and the population had long since soared beyond 100,000,000. The stock market was hyperactive, but sales continued to increase, making every day a blue ribbon one for the bulls, who relied more and more heavily on brokers' loans.

When Jennie's estate was tallied, it was appraised at $78,317,938. It slipped, unnoticed by her, through her hands to her eleven-year-old granddaughter Barbara, to Lena and to Jessie, split three ways between them, after a final obstacle had been removed by the courts. Jennie had written out her will on the same day in 1889 that Frank had executed his. She had bequeathed everything of hers to him just as he had done for her.

It was a tight knot that must be cut, and only a battery of lawyers could advise how the cutting should be done. Otherwise, the three apparent heirs would be caught up in endless litigation, with the Woolworth fortune captured between two pairs of lifeless hands. "It can be resolved simply by a finding of the court that the will is invalid," said counsel.

"How could that be," asked one of Jennie's daughters at the first of a series of conferences, "when Mother was no more than thirty-four at the time and perfectly normal, and Jessie was only three?"

"Reasonable grounds can be presented for invalidation," counsel answered. There was no alternative.

Justice Howell agreed when the case came up in the surrogate court. The few possessions Jennie had owned a generation ago bore no relationship to the present size of the estate. Therefore, she had no concept of the implications when she put her signature to the will. She had not recognized then what she was doing any more than when she married Frank or when she drifted into mindless death. Lena, Jessie and Franklyn Hutton could breathe more easily.

Barbara had not seen her grandmother since the day her father took her to Altadena. She knew nothing of the sequence of accidents that made her one of the wealthiest heiresses in America.

Her father would only hint at the scale of her fortune: "If you want anything, buy it and never mind the cost." The New York courts allowed her $12,000 a year and Hutton $35,000 for her support after he removed her from her aunt's care and put her, with a French governess, on an estate near San Francisco in the little town of Burlingame, to attend the first of a series of private schools for girls. There, at Miss Shinn's, Barbara, plump and plain, was badgered so relentlessly about her money that she begged her father to give it all away. His solution was to find a new school for her, in Santa Barbara.

Lena handled her inheritance with such style that it was hard to imagine her original circumstances. She was a soft-spoken, kindly woman like her mother. With her family, she lived, until she died in 1938, in the house Frank had bought her. Charles McCann, attorney, was drawn into Woolworth business as president of a corporation, the Broadway-Park Place Company, that for a while owned the Woolworth Building.

The Catholic McCanns bought a Long Island estate, Sunken Orchard, in Oyster Bay, where Lena grew prize-winning roses and held fund-raising parties for the charities on her list. The Metropolitan Opera and the New York Philharmonic stood high in her favor, as was becoming to a *grande dame* welcomed into the ranks of the Daughters of the American Revolution. She provided her own memorial to her father—an organ donated to Princeton University's chapel.

Only one of her three surviving children would gain attention from glossy society magazines and the daily newspapers; Helena, wife of Winston Guest, who was a dashing figure in the international polo set, with a fellow member, David, Britain's Prince of Wales.

Jessie, perennially blonde and bubbly, had the flamboyance that was missing in Lena. Of all the Woolworths, Jessie seemed to know best how to enjoy a fortune: spend it without worrying about it. She paid $50,000 for a railroad palace car to give her husband, James Paul Donahue, and she named it *Japauldon*. One million dollars went to buy Wooldon Manor, Southampton, Long Island; two million for the Palm Beach retreat she called Cielito Lindo, "a taste of heaven."

He repaid her by devoting himself to roulette, baccarat and constant flirtations with young men. She consoled herself for what was missing from the marriage by collecting Russian sables and jewelry, with a special passion for emeralds and pearls, one rope of which bore a $600,000 price tag. Jim Donahue was as profligate with her money as she was. "From now on, darling," she was reported to have said to him after he had gone through a prolonged losing streak at the tables, "you must not lose more than $25,000 a night."

She made conscientious efforts to stay in touch with Barbara, who in the years to come acquired Jessie's taste for collecting. "My jewels are a great comfort to me," Barbara would acknowledge when she kept to her bed for weeks at a time in some hotel suite, alone with the boxes full of treasures a maid had brought up from the safe. Like her aunt, she liked on occasion to wear trinkets picked up at a Woolworth's counter.

Both Jessie and Lena had seats on the company board, where Sum preached honesty as the essential creed for success and Parson thrust on with expansion overseas, helped by a new vice-president, Byron Miller, called back from England; he was replaced there as managing director by William Stephenson, a threepenny-and-sixpenny Croesus in his own right. A nephew of Jennie's, Roy Creighton, was assigned to start operations in Cuba. The first German store was opened in Bremen.

With an iron jaw jutting over his stiffly-starched collar, President Parson was never reluctant to see his name in print. "Frank W. Woolworth," he said in the course of one extended interview, "was exceedingly human, although he was not very capable as a salesman."

He was asked whether Frank's sacred barrier, one slim dime, might be abandoned now that Coolidge was in the White House and prosperity was fueling inflation. "We are more fixed than ever," Parson intoned, "in our determination to stick to the price class we selected." That "we" was accepted without question by the interviewer. "Fifty or a hundred years from now, so far as I can see," Parson added, "our top price in the eastern United States will still be ten cents."

There were rumors at one time of a rift between the management and the two Woolworth daughters, but he quickly denied them.

The third heiress, Barbara, was plucked out of boarding school in California and tucked away in similar Eastern establishments for young ladies, first at Miss Hewitt's in Manhattan and then Miss Porter's in Farmington, Connecticut. For some vacations her father took her home; for others he did not. Her Uncle Ed and Aunt Marjorie Hutton, inheritor of the Post cereal fortune, filled in a few of the gaps by inviting her to their Fifth Avenue triplex apartment, their summer place in the Adirondacks, or their gargantuan Palm Beach mansion, Mar-a-Lago. Aunt Lena and Aunt Jessie occasionally drove out to Connecticut to see her, but her schoolmates, raised to detect vulgarity in ostentatious displays of riches, sniggered at their Rolls-Royces, minks and diamonds.

Frank had left his building, the stores and the company itself as his memorials, but in another respect he had been deficient. Other merchant princes bequeathed hunks of their fortunes to worthy causes. The Metropolitan Museum had Altman's art collection. Field had set up a charitable foundation. John Wanamaker had poured out millions in philanthropy. But Frank had been generous only in spending on himself and his daughters, and in giving his intimates a like opportunity.

Though it remained in essence a family business, the process of fragmentation was picking up speed. Barbara was two months past her fourteenth birthday when Franklyn Hutton had Goldman, Sachs offer 50,000 shares of her Woolworth common stock on the market, by far the biggest single parcel put up for sale to date. Immediate demand kited the price to $200, which made her $10,000,000 better off by accountants' standards, before it fell to $160 some weeks later. In the boardroom on the twenty-fourth floor, Parson and his colleagues flinched as rumbles of discontent sounded on Wall Street.

Family stock continued to be sold, lot by lot, until eventually only Jessie, in old age, would cling onto a block described as "sizeable." Barbara's went early and fast. In March 1926, she acquired a stepmother, the former Irene Curley Bodde, a divorcée her father met in California. In his new marriage, he concluded that his daughter should have her own twenty-six room duplex in the 1020 Fifth Avenue cooperative owned by the Franklyn Huttons, and he asked the surrogate court to release $250,000 of her sequestered funds to pay for the remodeling.

"My daughter," said the petition, "for her own safety and welfare in later years, must be brought up surrounded by the luxury and comfort to which her income entitles her, so that upon attaining the age of twenty-one, at which time her fortune is to be turned over to her unrestricted control, she will have no desire or reason to embark upon a scale of expenditures in living to which she has not been accustomed during her formative years."

He also sought $60,000 for maintenance of his child in accordance with the style he set for her. Everything he asked was granted.

What had died together with Frank was the sense of destiny. Among his direct descendants, Woolworth had vanished as a family name, though it persisted as a given name of three of his grandchildren. There was no observable pride among them in his achievements. That was left to the men who ran the company, forever paying their respects to his memory and what one brochure called his regard for people. *"People,* as customers, dictated his every move; and *people,* as managers and friends, formed the nucleus around which his organization grew and prospered. *People* have remained equally important in Woolworth's operations ever since."

The inheritors of his millions behaved as though they preferred to forget how it had all been made in nickels and dimes, the same source as the dividends that flowed in every three months, as dependable as a tide table. The empire he had spent fifty years of his life assembling was important to these second and third generations because it spelled money.

Other men of wealth and power had more to show for their labors. In Dearborn, Michigan, Henry Ford, eleven years younger and considerably richer than Frank, followed the path of dynasty. His son Edsel was president of the family business, and *his* son, Henry II, was being raised toward the same end.

The DuPonts, after setting up a powder mill on the banks of the Brandywine in Delaware at the start of the nineteenth century, had handed down undiluted control of an armaments and chemicals kingdom from one generation to the next, disciplined against competing with each other so as not to fritter money away, and there was more of that in the family than Woolworth's might net in a lifetime.

Among the Rockefellers, old John D., born in 1839 and still the patriarch, was giving away millions of his accumulated $900,000,000, but the bulk of it was destined for his children and grandchildren in obedience to what his biographer, Allan Nevins, described as his "instinct for the future."

Frank's heirs faced and then skittered away from the fact that "Woolworth" stood for nothing as substantial as automobiles, armaments that had conquered the Germans, or a network of oil and banking interests. Woolworth's manufactured no products of its own, apart from a deserved reputation for selling candy and kitchenware, brushes and stationery at hard-to-beat prices.

Yet a tradition of a kind was taking root within the company. When Lena and Jessie stepped down from the board, sons of Frank's comrades and their sons in turn established a line of succession. Carson Peck's son, Fremont, followed him as a director, and a Carson Peck of the next generation became a vice-president. Allan Kirby, son of Fred, filled the place left open by his father's death, with Fred Kirby II coming along behind him. Cousin Seymour's heir, Seymour Junior, took over in the same manner, and Seymour Knox III, like Fred II, sits on the board today.

The 1920s had opened with a slump in trade darkening the profit picture generally, though not for Woolworth's. The Depression of the next decade engulfed the world, but not Barbara Hutton. In 1930, she rounded out her second year as a boarder at Miss Porter's. "I have finished school," a new petition to the courts stated, "and am now about to make my debut at a large dance which my father is giving for that purpose at the Ritz-Carlton."

She listed the Franklyn Hutton homes: Fifth Avenue; Palm Beach; Newport, Rhode Island; and a 5,500-acre plantation outside Charleston, North Carolina. In all of these places "my father will entertain extensively for me." It would entail a great deal of travel to and fro. Therefore, she said, she wanted her own private railroad car, like Aunt Lena and Aunt Jessie. It shouldn't cost more than $120,000 outright, plus $36,000 for expenses, and it "will give me, as well as other members of the family, so much pleasure that I do not consider it an extravagance for one of my position and means."

As an afterthought, she also requested $10,000, "to be given in our family's name," to help the jobless. "It is the duty of people situated as fortunately as I am, to aid in the relief of those less fortunately situated."

By official count, there would soon be twelve million of them, bereft of any sort of direct or indirect relief, since the dole was anathema to Herbert Hoover's belief that "the sole function of government is to bring about a condition of affairs favorable to the beneficial development of private enterprise." Nearly two million became hobos, roving the countryside hunting for work or if no work could be found, then handouts of food. Bankruptcies soared, factories were padlocked, farm-belt communities abandoned. Prospects for recovery appeared as black as night.

The bill for Barbara's railroad car had run up to $125,000 when it was completed, with bedroom suite, three baths, dining salon, galley and enclosed observation platform. Hutton borrowed his wife's maiden name and part of his own to christen it with the acronym *The Curleyhut*. It was, as Barbara had foreseen, one means of "giving employment to others instead of adding to my own fortune, which is already amply large."

During the week before Christmas, more work was provided for the needy when $60,000 was spent on her debut, $3,000 of that sum going for eucalyptus sprays shipped from California and mixed in with silver birches and pink and white roses to transform the cream-and-gold pillared ballroom of the Ritz-Carlton into "a costly bower of flowers and trees," as one reporter gasped. Prohibition as well as the Depression was ignored that night. A thousand guests sat down to a champagne supper at tables adorned with white lilac, gardenias and more roses, her stepmother's favorite flower. Then they listened or took a turn around the floor to the three orchestras and the tenor voice of a new wonder of the entertainment world, twenty-nine-year-old Rudy Vallee.

"The Man I Love" was the tune that lingered longest in the memory of the wide-eyed girl, whom the newspapers invariably referred to as the dollar princess, the Woolworth heiress. Another song hit of the day, "I Met a Million-Dollar Baby in a Five-and-Ten-Cent Store," was not performed on this occasion.

In the dank night outside, another crowd, just as big but less resplendent, waited behind police barriers on Madison Avenue for a glimpse of her. Its mood was as apathetic as the spirit of the country. There was no cheering but no hissing or catcalls either.

Inside, at eight in the morning, breakfast was served—caviar, scrambled eggs and more champagne. At nine, the fleet of limousines returned to collect the celebrants. The party, Barbara decided years later, "was a terrible slap in everybody's face." She realized it had "made me a sitting duck. . . . Very definitely my life began on the wrong foot." And for this she blamed her father, although he had acted in strict accordance with what Grandpa Woolworth came to believe: if you've got money, there's no point trying to hide it.

But in the aftermath of that night, millions of Americans began to change their opinions of what Woolworth's represented. Frank had always claimed, and they believed him, that he had assembled his empire as a kind of public service. Most of them regarded his wealth as a just reward for hard labor, which in no way applied to a spoiled child of eighteen who seemed hell bent on enjoying herself while the rest of the world struggled to survive.

In April, Uncle Jim Donahue took the path her mother had chosen. His final liaison, with a young seaman, had been broken off. Jilted at the age of forty-four, Donahue found his brand of happiness no longer worth pursuing. He offered his apologies for leaving the card game he was involved in at the 80th Street townhouse. In one of the bathrooms, he swallowed the contents of a vial of bichloride of mercury. When she went to look for him, the sight of him writhing on the tiled floor traumatized Jessie. They were carried off together to the same sanitarium. After four days of sedation to ease his suffering, he died, muttering that he could not explain what he had done.

As soon as she was discharged, Jessie closed the house and never returned to it. Her Manhattan address now was a place farther downtown, which her two sons shared with her.

To all appearances, she made a quick recovery, comforting herself with more jewels. With her sons, she roamed the fashionable, less hidebound international circuit—London, Paris, Monte Carlo, the Venetian Lido, Biarritz—as footloose as the wanderers who rode the rods, free of charge, under the freight trains that crisscrossed America. She was as bountiful toward her sons as she had been with her first and last husband. One of their aims was the same as his—"to avoid the nine-to-five syndrome."

The circle of gadabouts in which they traveled was chic but not exclusive. Admission to it was readily obtainable by laying out money in sufficiently impressive sums. Noble birth was not a requirement of membership, although a title, either honestly inherited or thoughtfully invented, helped to gain instant entry. A refugee king or an exiled queen was a focus of attention, especially for the camp followers who sold tidbits of gossip to the newspapers.

It also helped somewhat to be rated "bright," which meant being chatty and gregarious, not necessarily overburdened with native intelligence. Fellow travelers prided themselves on being worldly, sophisticated and up to date on the latest scandal concerning anyone within the circle. In their specialized vocabulary, "boring" was the ultimate condemnation of anything or anybody.

Most of them, with manservants and maids in attendance, crossed the seas aboard one of the fleet of liners—British, German, French, Italian and sometimes American—that competed with each other in providing ease and luxury for privileged passengers.

Greater prestige was incurred by sailing as owner or guest in a private yacht like *Sea Cloud*, the 350-foot, four-masted barque bought by Aunt Marjorie Hutton.

For land travel, a gadabout relied on chauffeured limousines, on sporty automobiles more suited for the race track, or on private railroad cars like *The Curleyhut* that supplied cushioned comfort on a par with that of the ocean liners.

Movement from city to shore and from continent to continent, as dictated by the social calendar, was one means of filling in idle time. So were appointments in beauty parlors, shopping expeditions, and hosting or attending parties, preferably in some specified period costume. They sunned themselves on Mediterranean beaches remote from the tourist trade. They exchanged wives, husbands and lovers with less care than they chose new clothes.

It was, by and large, a motley crowd. There were princes, dukes, counts, tycoons and ne'er-do-wells among them, White Russians, French, Greeks, Italians and citizens of nations drowned in the flood of the past war. There were cadet sons and daughters who lived on their wits and on remittances sent by British and European bluebloods in gratitude for their offspring's uninterrupted absence from home. There was a revolving contingent from the theater and what was then called "the silver screen"—Douglas Fairbanks and Mary Pickford, Adolph Menjou, Gloria Swanson, Pola Negri and many more. There were buccaneers of all four sexes, confidence tricksters, card sharps and an eternal representation of fortune hunters on the prowl for any prospective bride or groom eager to pay for a hoist up the social ladder. A tireless chronicler of all the goings-on was a large and forceful American, Miss Elsa Maxwell. The most sought-after guest at most gatherings was the man his intimates knew as "David"—His Royal Highness Prince Edward, the next king of England and its empire overseas.

One ambition of young Jimmy Donahue's was to see Cousin Barbara married to an English duke. Another was to become, as he said, "best friends with the Prince of Wales."

A tentative step was taken three weeks after his father's funeral when Barbara, chaperoned by her stepmother, sailed for England for presentation as a debutante, gowned in virgin white, to King George and Queen Mary at the Court of St. James's. She was eager for marriage not to an Englishman of any rank but to a rich

American of the globe-trotting set, Phil Plant, husband of Constance Bennett, who was a slinky motion-picture star. Though Barbara may have told Jimmy that Plant would be on board the same ship, it came as a surprise to her father.

Franklyn Hutton missed her London debut, but he arrived there in time for the announcement that his daughter and Plant were engaged, an arrangement he objected to so vigorously that Plant surrendered and fled for home.

The men who ran Woolworth's were tormented by the continual appearance of Barbara's name in headlines, tarnishing the image they strove to impress on the public—that theirs was a democratic institution devoted to delivering the best values obtainable to anyone with a little loose change to spend. For the present, however, a weightier question had to be tackled in the boardroom: how much longer could the ten-cent ceiling last?

They delegated one of Cousin Seymour's old hands, Charles W. Deyo, to study the market and prepare a report. The move was a challenge to the unqualified forecast of President Parson that "fifty or one hundred years from now" a dime would still be the limit.

Deyo, pince-nez spectacles sparkling, had made a late start as a twenty-one-year-old assistant stockman in the London, Ontario, store of Seymour Knox in 1902. After the merger, Deyo's career put on speed, taking him up through the ranks until he held the title of supervisor of buying and a directorship.

He felt that the price barrier had to be breached or else the company's growth must falter. Bigger variety, better values—the only way to ensure them was to raise the sights. Parson might disagree, but his reputation was past its peak, anyway.

The Napoleonic complex that unbalanced Frank had the same impact on his ex-bookkeeper. As the millions poured into Parson's bank account, he poured them out in a compulsive effort to live like a king among princes. He built a mansion in Paris, though he had neither son nor daughter to inherit it. When Shadow Lawn, his house on the Jersey shore, burned down, he cleared the site to erect a Parson's palace more magnificent than Frank's Winfield Hall.

It was finished, furnished and decorated just before the roar of the twenties dwindled to a whine and the market collapsed, with stock prices down by $14,000,000,000 and 16,000,000 shares landing in the hopper on a single October day. The bills for Parson's palace were not much less than the cost of the Woolworth Building. He was swamped by debt when Deyo came forward with his recommendation that Woolworth's, which had held out far longer than any rival chain, should make its top price twenty cents.

Parson was ousted, with the official explanation that his health was failing, although as a courtesy he was to retain his directorship. Byron Miller, once a learner in Frank's original Brooklyn store, moved up into the presidency under Chairman Sum in June 1932, and Deyo won a place on the executive committee. One more contest of wills was in the making, between Miller, a traditionalist who accepted twenty cents as an essential new creed, and Deyo, a pragmatist who pressed always for policy to be dictated by conditions on the marketplace. He established his track record when new items tagged at twenty cents added $1,000,000 a month to the company's cash accounts.

Every surge in unemployment, fresh bankruptcy or foreclosure of another farmer's mortgage intensified the company's problem with the public image of Barbara. Hoover had forecast an early end to poverty in America once he was elected. Instead, people waited in bread lines or sold trinkets on street corners and improvised means of staying alive. Tin Pan Alley, struggling to lighten the gloom, scored a hit with "On the Sunny Side of the Street," which sold for a nickel as sheet music across Woolworth's counters.

Other products of the times were not kept in stock: "Hoover blankets"—newspapers tucked inside clothing to conserve body heat—or "Hoover flags"—empty pockets turned inside out—or "Hoover hogs," which were jackrabbits served up as stew. The president was commemorated in another way; the shanties tacked together out of tar paper and packing crates by down-and-out Americans with nowhere else to live were "Hoovervilles." One of the biggest of them, built by army veterans, sprang up across the Anacostia River from Washington, D.C., while Woolworth's was raising its price ceiling. Troops under the leadership of General Douglas MacArthur burned it down, and the President thanked God for giving the country a government "that knows how to deal with a mob."

That same summer, Barbara gave her thanks to Elsa Maxwell for introducing her to an athletic Russian émigré whom she watched playing polo on the field at Biarritz. Alexis Mdivani owed his title of "prince" to his mother, Nina, who had whimsically registered herself with the Paris police as "princess" after the family fled the Bolsheviks. Two of his brothers had already entered the marriage market, Serge as the bridegroom of actress Pola Negri, David as the husband of another motion-picture star, Mae Murray.

Some of her friends detected in Barbara a thirst for publicity, to spite either her father or her grandfather's business or both. She slaked it by making sure that the reporters who stayed on her trail covered every step of her courtship by Mdivani, unimpeded by the fact that he had a wife in Louise, the former Miss Van Allen, whose mother had inherited Vanderbilt money.

The exploits of Barbara by contrast with the plight of the country she appeared to have deserted outraged a majority of Americans. They looked to one much younger girl to help them forget their troubles and flocked to watch Shirley Temple on the movie screens. They turned en masse against Barbara, whose antics were rated intolerable. On one side of the street there was little Miss Sunshine; on the other side of the ocean there was Jezebel, slated to become another "Princess" Mdivani.

The simplest solution in sight for company management was to get her disassociated from Woolworth's by encouraging her to sever all ties and unload the rest of her stock. Selling it meant giving up assured income and taking her chances on new investments when uncertainty was roiling Wall Street. The company's 1930 sales of $289,000,000 fell below the figure for a preceding year for the first time since 1883. The decline bottomed out at $250,000,000 in 1932, but throughout the dismal decade dividends held steady at $2.40, with a bonus thrown in when part of the British holdings were liquidated when the company there went public.

The pressure to close out Barbara's investments in the Woolworth corporation increased when Franklin D. Roosevelt's first hundred days as president saw passage of the National Industrial Relations Recovery Act. The new law set up the National Recovery Administration, charged with regulating competition within industry and guaranteeing labor's right to organize. Paying union wages would add $4,000,000 a year to Woolworth payrolls.

The sources of her income meant very little to her. It did not matter where the money came from so long as it was there to draw on. Her thoughts were concentrated on her forthcoming wedding. The first time Mdivani proposed to her, he still had a wife in Louise. After she ended that marriage with a Netherlands divorce, he showered Barbara with proposals and love letters. She fled back to New York, bidding for time to decide her future.

The hostility she met with there made her fearful of going out alone. Jimmy Donahue took on the role of protector and escort, but it did not save her from being trapped in her limousine after an evening at a theater on West 44th Street. One woman in the screaming crowd threatened to throw acid in her face. Poison pen letters were mixed in with the usual pleas for handouts that turned up in the morning mail.

This was the year, 1933, when she would be twenty-one and come into her inheritance, destined, in her cousin's words, to be "the greatest sucker in history." He was well rewarded for his devotion to her. She took him on shopping sprees at Cartier's, buying gifts for him and for the young men he consorted with, running up a bill of $98,000 one afternoon.

Mdivani followed her to New York. Reporters tracked him to the Hotel Savoy Plaza, and a group of onlookers had gathered outside, waiting for a glimpse of him, when Barbara and Donahue arrived. Once again, an angry throng closed in on her Rolls-Royce, beating on it until the chauffeur could edge it clear and take her home.

She felt she must leave the city and make for San Francisco, to set off from there on a cruise around the world. Mdivani's pursuit of her continued by plane. He caught up with her in Bangkok, Siam, and the chase was over, the prize his. He talked with her father by radio-telephone. Barbara, said Mdivani, was willing to have the United States consul marry them on the spot unless Franklyn Hutton agreed to announce to the press that he gave them his blessing.

Hutton accepted those terms, hoping that as soon as he had the pair of them back in New York, he could rout Mdivani as he had once routed Phil Plant. A petition to the courts from Barbara disclosed the outcome of the meeting between the two men. "I did not anticipate that I would marry before coming of age. I am, however, engaged to Prince Alexis Mdivani, who resides in Paris,

France, and our marriage will take place there on or about June 20, 1933. My marriage to Prince Mdivani, and the plans which have been made in connection with the intervening months before I come of age, will necessarily entail heavy additional expenditures, which were not anticipated by my father.

"I have discussed the amount of these necessary expenditures with my father, and both he and I estimate that they will amount to at least $100,000.

"Even with this additional allowance, I will still be spending, in the year preceding my majority, only a fraction of my income, and my fortune is so large that I see no necessity why, upon my marriage, I should not immediately enjoy the luxuries which a fortune such as mine will enable me to have when I enter into possession of it."

Father and daughter walked together over the brand-new red carpet, presented to the parish by Mdivani, that was laid over the sidewalk outside the steps of the Cathedral of St. Alexander Nevsky on the rue Daru. In her wake came her attendants, gathering up the eight-foot-long train of her cream satin gown, a creation of Jean Patou's. The two hundred grim-faced gendarmes were outnumbered twenty to one by the surging mob of Parisians. She also wore a diamond tiara, a diamond bracelet and a strand of pearls, valued at $1,000,000 by the newspapers, which estimated a price of $20,000 for her lace lingerie, the work of a dozen nuns.

The show of gifts in the permanent suite she had leased at the Hotel Ritz gave the rooms something of the look of a jewelry department as it might be pictured in the dreams of a reader of the *Arabian Nights.* Most of the silver was early Georgian, the toilet sets gold, the crystal Baccarat. David Mdivani sent a Cartier clock inlaid with jade and diamonds, Serge a ruby-studded vanity case, their mother Nina the heirloom dresses embroidered with pearls in what had once been the kingdom of Georgia, which was now a republic of the detested U.S.S.R. Had Frank Woolworth been alive, he might have noted that the diamond bracelets numbered "one ½ doz." The bridegroom contributed one jade necklace—bought for $40,000, the reporters ascertained—and her father another, along with an additional keepsake, a Chris-Craft speedboat. The Argentinian polo ponies purchased by the bride for her pseudo-prince were excluded from the display.

Lilies smothered the cathedral's altar. Bills from florists and for the hire of the White Russian choir amounted to 8,000 francs, but Mdivani neglected to pay for the day's rental of the church or to provide a *pourboire* for the six attending priests. Twenty newsreel cameramen covered the hour-long ceremony, recording bride and groom sipping consecrated wine, kissing icons, circling the mosaic floor, and then standing beneath golden crowns held by her cousins, the two Donahue boys, while Jessie stared quizzically at her niece.

According to one account, Jimmy at one point whispered, "Are you pregnant?" Barbara's reply was emphatic: "Certainly not."

A discreet crown and her new initials, "B.H.M." identified the thirteen pieces of luggage, each as new as the sidewalk carpet, with which she left the Ritz that evening on the way to a European honeymoon. A Woolworth-style inventory of her trousseau would have included: "Gowns, dresses, suits (Patou and Chanel), 40; hats, 2 doz.; wraps, ermine; beach robes; bathing suits; miscellaneous accessories (all marked with embossed or embroidered crowns)." Cousin Jimmy's offer to travel with the bridal couple was turned down, but he was invited to join them when they reached Venice.

Five months later, a different crowd clustered on the sidewalk in another city, but the faces of some of the corps of reporters and photographers were familiar to her. Her twenty-first birthday party brought guests by the dozen to her apartment at 1020 Fifth Avenue. Adolf Hitler had been Reichschancellor for almost a year; Germany had just quit the League of Nations and the World Disarmament Conference; the American president, scenting danger ahead, was about to accord diplomatic recognition to the Soviet Union. The champagne poured at the Mdivanis' was still constitutionally prohibited, but the Eighteenth Amendment was due for repeal three weeks later.

A final petition to the surrogate court, filed when she and her husband were halfway home across the Atlantic, declared that "as I have attained my majority I am entitled to the possession of all the property which my father and general guardian now holds for me." Eighteen months earlier, she stated, she had retained her own attorneys to investigate his handling of her finances. "They have reported to me that my father and his counsel had displayed conservatism and wisdom in the management of my property, and that I was very fortunate that it was then in this situation, notwithstanding the vicissitudes of the past few years.

"I have agreed with my father that his account as general guardian be settled out of court, and upon delivery to me of the principal and income belonging to me, which my father now holds in his hands, I am prepared to deliver to him . . . a general release releasing him, his heirs, executors, administrators and assigns from all liability and responsibility whatsoever."

Hutton deserved her praise. He had piloted her ship of fortune through the hurricane of Depression while other craft had foundered. The brightest of blue-chip stocks had been battered--American Telephone and Telegraph down 34 points in a day's trading; General Electric down 47½; Eastman Kodak 42; New York Central 23; Westinghouse 34½. Men who had once been rich stood on line for a bowl of charity's soup.

As a result of his efforts, her inheritance from Grandma Woolworth had been almost doubled in nine years. By playing the market with funds raised from the sale of Woolworth stock, Hutton had $40,000,000 ready for his daughter, and it was increasing at the rate of $2,000,000 a year.

Hutton received $5,000,000 from her for his services, along with rare words of thanks. Mdivani, on whom she settled $50,000 a year on the eve of their wedding, was paid the $2,000,000 agreed to in advance as his fee for making her his princess, if gossip was to be believed.

Asked to name the richest woman in America, most of the public would have answered "Barbara Hutton," but this was untrue. Since the rich are as reluctant as other taxpayers to unveil their assets for scrutiny, exactly who had legitimate claim to the title was a matter of doubt. It was probably held by Doris Duke, the tobacco heiress who had made her curtsy as a London debutante shortly before Barbara. Doris, though, shied away from publicity, so it was Barbara who was the primary target of speculation and those eager for handouts, including Serge and David Mdivani.

Her attitude to her acquired millions was ambivalent. She complained to Cousin Jimmy, "All I ever do is write out checks." On the other hand, she was squandering money so recklessly that wiser friends wondered whether it was done to show disdain for the man who had multiplied her legacy and for the legacy itself, which served to cut her off from most normal human contact, as she had discovered in her schooldays.

Jimmy Donahue envied her because his only income came from his mother, but he came closest to filling Barbara's dire need for a trustworthy companion. He alone in the circle that enclosed her could understand the trials imposed on a Woolworth heir. At eighteen, he was a dropout from Choate School in Wallingford, Connecticut, and much like his father in a variety of ways.

He had the same slim build, the same soft handsomeness, the same taste for liquor that hinted at future alcoholism. He haunted the same sleazy bars and dubious nightclubs for the same purpose that had driven Jimmy Senior—soliciting men who, when they discovered his identity, sometimes tried to blackmail him. If there was any focus to his life, it was his desire to work in the theater, starting—and maybe finishing—as a chorus boy, buying instead of selling homosexual favors.

There were people who pitied him and blamed his mother for his problems. They speculated that he patterned himself on his father in resentment of the manner in which she had raised her son. They also wondered how far Jimmy would go in following the elder Donahue: would he come to a similar end when middle age overtook him and life began to pall?

He was the spare man when Barbara and her husband, bored with each other after seven months of marriage, decided on a second honeymoon, beginning aboard *The Curleyhut* departing from Grand Central Station for San Francisco, where they would embark for Tokyo on the Japanese steamer *Tatsuta Maru*. At Mdivani's insistence, she had dieted down from 150 to less than 100 pounds. Any one trunk of the forty they took with them weighed more than that.

At their stop in Chicago, Jimmy, lanky in blue silk pajamas, appeared alone on the observation platform and stuck himself with the label by which he would be known in the press thereafter. "I am," he told a reporter, "the court clown." In Sacramento, California, he disclosed another facet of his career: he had spent ten days working as a Broadway chorus boy in a musical called *Hot and Bothered* before it folded. But his yearning to be in show business endured. He played a record on a portable phonograph and danced a few steps to support his point.

That was the day Barbara spoke for the first time in public about her inheritance. "It's like any other fortune. It can be put to good use. It can be a blessing or a curse. It can bring happiness and pleasure, or distress and unhappiness. I'm trying to do good with mine, for myself and others." Her anonymous donations to charity were an annual $50,000. That summer, she paid $86,000 for a centuries-old Venetian palazzo, the Abbazia San Gregorio, the deed to which Mdivani carefully registered in his own name.

Then, for a change, the Woolworth company shared headlines with Barbara. A parliamentary commission in Ottawa began probing into the workings of the chain in Canada. It was disclosed that while profits stood above twenty percent of sales, wages had been cut by twenty cents on the dollar north of the border and clear across the United States.

The blame fell on Barbara. The effort of disposing of her every share of stock in the company availed nothing. So far as most Americans were concerned, *she* was Woolworth's, flaunting her millions while its counter clerks wrestled with the problem of survival. Frank, dead now for fourteen years, was all but forgotten, and the good will he had generated for the business during his lifetime had turned into disdain. She was hissed and spat on when she showed herself in public; stones were flung at her cars. "I am not America's richest woman," she decided bitterly, "but America's most hated girl."

The simmering conflict over pricing heated up in company headquarters between Byron Miller and Charles Deyo. Since the twenty-cent policy had arrested the dip in sales figures in 1932, why not go the whole hog and abandon all arbitrary ceilings? This was the argument advanced by Deyo, complacently sure that the facts supported him. Miller, grey and grizzled at fifty-nine, took an opposite stance: fixed prices were a hallowed Woolworth tradition, dating back more than half a century.

Other members of the board found the compulsory retirement rule a convenient means of ending the friction. Sum Woolworth, eighty next birthday, chaired the meeting that resolved "the selling price limit of twenty cents on merchandise be discontinued." On reaching the age of sixty one month later, President Miller retired and surrendered all executive functions. Deyo, who succeeded him, moved up from the presidency into the chairmanship when Sum's health began to fade in 1944. Since the top man in any organization can usually win stockholders' approval for writing his own rules, Deyo put in half a dozen more years of service before he quit at the age of sixty-six, to continue as honorary chairman until he died in 1952.

In the new regime, the five-and-ten as Frank had propagated it slowly disappeared from view, though his name was still spread across the bright new stores and the updated older ones. Most goods sold for a dollar or less, some for considerably more, and there were perhaps 5,000 essentially different items in stock. Sheer weight of numbers had been paramount in his dream of doing business, as he said, "in every civilized town throughout the world." Deyo steered the company onto a different course.

Emphasis shifted from the number of outlets to stores of greater size, better equipped to handle expanded lines of merchandise and bigger products brought in with higher price tags. The little hole-in-the-corner shops that Frank had started with passed into history. The buildings the company sought for its operations looked as solid as any bank from the outside, and the air-conditioned interiors glittered with glass and chrome.

Financing the program demanded another break with Frank's principles of doing business by and with cash. An issue of $10,000,000 in Woolworth debentures went on the market in 1937, to be retired three years afterward with part of the proceeds of a second offering, $22,000,000 worth.

So what had once been a nickel-and-dime enterprise moved out to run in competition with department stores, and shudders shook the entire dry-goods industry. Other chains were fearful for their profits. Smaller retailers anticipated bankruptcy.

Frank's rivals had hit back at him in his early days by spreading the rumor that he was a black. Independent merchants responded to the current threat by raising a hue and cry in state legislatures for laws to penalize Woolworth's and other giants like the Great Atlantic & Pacific Tea Company and United Cigar Stores.

The favored weapon of the antichain movement was taxation, usually on a graduated scale, starting with, say $25 for the first store, then rising by geometric progression to as much as $1,000 for every store above a predetermined level. Missouri wanted to set the tax on each one beyond nine at $6,400. A second device was a levy on profits, one percent to be collected by the state, under the terms of one proposal.

Frank had never known this kind of attack. Five hundred anti-chain bills were introduced in state houses across the country between 1934 and 1941. Thirty-two of them were voted into law. Along with legislation already on the books, this made a total of twenty-eight states where Woolworth's and similar enterprises were under fire.

In more than four hundred cities and towns, organizations sprang to arms to battle "the chain-store menace." Over one hundred newspapers pitched in to help. Radio stations from coast to coast were glad to sell air time to the assailants after a Shreveport, Louisiana, grocer, W. K. Henderson, owner of his own station, KWKH, enrolled local storekeepers, on payment of $12, into "The Merchants' Minute Men." More ammunition was shot off in the form of broadsheets, pamphlets, advertisements, convention speeches, and mail campaigns.

"The chain stores," said one letter distributed in Indiana, "are undermining the foundation of our entire local happiness and prosperity. They have destroyed our home markets and merchants, paying a minimum to our local enterprises and charities, sapping the life-blood of prosperous communities and leaving about as much in return as a traveling band of gypsies."

Woolworth company commanders had known calmer days than those in the spring of 1935. One New York newspaper carried the headline HOUSE INQUIRY IS ORDERED ON RETAIL GROUP over a report that read: "Congressional investigation of the newly created American Retail Federation on charges that it represents a 'super-lobby' backed by chain store interests was ordered by the House of Representatives today through the adoption of a resolution presented by Representative John J. Cochran, Democrat, of Missouri." Woolworth's was a contributor to that "super-lobby."

The latest exploit of "the Woolworth heiress" made more titillating reading and was accorded bigger headlines. She had arrived in New York, hiding below deck in the crew's quarters of the German liner *Bremen*, while Donahue waylaid reporters in her suite of cabins. Then he had driven her from the Fifth Avenue duplex to the Newark, New Jersey, airport and flown with her to Reno, where she was waiting out the required six weeks before going to court.

Divorce was another thing alien to Grandpa Woolworth's experience.

15

❧ ...On With the New ₰

These cheap titled people who are after the American girl and her money— But for the fact that his title was spurious, Mdivani had proved himself an exemplary specimen of the fortune hunters Frank had encountered a generation earlier. With belated respect for her grandfather, Barbara sometimes toasted his memory in champagne.

She had come to realize, as she said, that to her husband she was "the golden goose." At his urging, she had written checks to bail out his brothers after David had bilked his wife, Mae Murray, of $3,000,000 in stocks and bonds, and Serge had swindled both the women he had married in turn, first Pola Negri and then Mary McCormick.

Alexis's prescription for keeping Barbara happy was to encourage her to go on spending, while he rarely paid for so much as a pack of cigarettes. The parties she held in Paris reminded some guests of similar entertainments in the "let them eat cake" days preceding the French revolution. As a hostess in New York, she enraged readers of the *News* and *Mirror*, which kept close watch on how she frittered her money away.

Her Aunt Marjorie, as her father pointed out, was far and away richer than Barbara, but she preserved herself from public attack by making herself a less obvious spendthrift. His daughter paid no more attention to him then than she had done before.

191

Disillusion with Mdivani did not set in until he began casting around to find other women to satisfy his rampant sexuality.

Elsa Maxwell scented an opportunity to provide a new husband for Barbara: an older, less flamboyant man. Her candidate was forty-year-old Count Kurt Haugwitz-Reventlow, proprietor of an estate in Denmark and holder of the Iron Cross for heroism in battle with the German Life Guards.

After Barbara's arrival in Reno, she performed an unintended service for the Woolworth company throughout the rest of the year. Headlines focused on her, not on disclosures of the company's role in the superlobby when hearings began in Washington. Representative Wright Patman of Texas replaced John Cochran as chairman of the Congressional subcommittee, apparently less concerned with seeing justice done than with proving that every chain store's goal was "to eliminate as many people as possible between producer and consumer"—an explosive claim when jobs everywhere were hard to find.

Newsmen were pleased to report that she walked into Reno's Woolworth's and left without spending a nickel. The insignificant anecdote served as a warmup for the main event, the dissolution of her marriage to Mdivani on May 13. "The money," she reflected, "did something to Alex, and he began to throw it around like confetti."

The divorce was only a few hours old when Reventlow showed up in Nevada according to plan. There had been no preliminary announcement of their being engaged, but on the morning after the divorce they were married in the house of her attorney's doctor under surveillance of photographers perched in the trees outside the backyard.

PRINCESS BABS BECOMES COUNTESS BABS, said one tabloid's headlines; WOOLWORTH HEIRESS TAKES ON NEW TITLE, said another's. The count, it was learned, received $1,500,000 from her, along with entitlement to the proceeds from a $500,000 trust fund. A fifteen-car motorcade took the honeymooners over the Sierra Nevada Mountains to San Francisco, to board *The Curleyhut* for the journey back to Manhattan. COUNT AND COUNTESS WILL LIVE IN EUROPE FROM FEAR OF GANGSTERS IN AMERICA. It was not gangsters but everyday Americans that Barbara was afraid of.

Mdivani made his final exit the following August. He was

driving by night from Spain across the French border toward Perpignan with the woman he was courting, the Baroness Maude von Thyssen, wife of a German armaments manufacturer. At eighty miles an hour, his Rolls-Royce slid off the road and hit a tree. Mdivani was decapitated, his companion maimed and blinded in one eye. When his will was filed for probate in New York, it was disclosed that the once poverty-stricken émigré had left an estate of $2,000,000. Black Gothic type pinpointed another story for devotees of the Woolworth serial.

Wright Patman's investigation reviewed a new five-reel motion picture whose purpose was to nail the chains with responsibility for the sorry state of the nation. Wherever it was shown, local storekeepers handed out free tickets to their customers. With the chairman's approval, a promotion piece for the production was read into the record:

"At last here is the dynamite that will blast the chain stores and mail-order houses from your community. Mr. Independent Merchant, here is your opportunity to recapture your birthright and regain your former prosperity. . . . If you want to know the truth about the Depression, see *Forward America*. If you want to know who is to blame, see *Forward America*. If you want to know how it was started and how it is being continued, see *Forward America.*"

One superlobbyist summoned to testify was Robert W. Lyons, an attorney who listed Woolworth's as a client, together with thirteen other retail chains. He acknowledged that one of his functions was to engage local counsel who knew their way around the state houses, paying them handsomely if they succeeded in blocking bills hostile to his clientele.

Patman pounced. Hadn't Lyons also written to those fellow lawyers, "If we cannot stop this bill, we will have it so amended so it will be unconstitutional?"

"I would not be at all surprised if I had," Lyons replied. "I advised them to do everything they legally and properly could."

"You felt that it was ethical?"

"Yes, sir."

The chairman turned to the matter of suppliers' discounts and allowances that were granted to the whales of the trade but withheld from the small fry. NRA codes had branded this practice unfair competition, though Frank had made discounts a cornerstone of his enterprise. Atlantic & Pacific admitted that it received $6,000,000 a year from its suppliers as an inducement to stock and advertise specific brands plus another $2,000,000 for "brokerage." Woolworth's also figured on the "preferred list" on file with the Patman committee of chains that manufacturers courted with price concessions.

It was exactly what the chairman was after. On the day after its filing, he appeared in triumph before the House Judiciary Committee to speed passage of what twelve months later became the Robinson-Patman Act, making it a crime for a manufacturer to discriminate against lesser customers by lowering his prices to big-volume buyers or awarding advertising allowances or paying "brokerage" fees.

In the fall of 1935, Barbara's doctors advised her she was pregnant. In the same year, when Lena and Jessie each owned nearly 800,000 shares of Woolworth stock, Lena divided $15,000,000 between her children and was charged an additional $3,000,000 in federal gift taxes. Jimmy Donahue was still dependent on his mother and on Barbara.

"Nothing infuriates me more," she once commented, "than rich people who keep saying they're unhappy because they have wealth. I always tell them they should go down on their knees and thank God they have money."

She resented every ounce of weight she was gaining in pregnancy. Reventlow persuaded her it would raise her spirits to get away from Paris for a vacation in Rome. Jimmy tagged along with them. From an upper floor of the Grand Hotel he briefly diverted attention away from her onto himself. In the street below, a battalion of Fascisti was shouting its support of Mussolini's invasion of Ethiopia, scheduled to begin within the next four days. In the royal suite, where the Reventlows were hosting a party, Jimmy fortified himself with brandy, then carried a siphon to the open window. "Long live Ethiopia!" he yelled as he doused the demonstrators with soda water. Two uniformed Blackshirts put him on a train back to Paris in the morning, under orders never again to set foot in Italy.

She wanted her baby to be born in England. Reventlow agreed, sharing an opinion widely held among British aristocrats

that one's position in society was all-important and that there was
no higher society than in the realm of the middle-aged bachelor
king, Edward VIII. She had a selection of houses in the western
world, but none here. Her son Lance was delivered by Caesarian
section on February 24, 1936, in a rented London townhouse in
Hyde Park Gardens. Jimmy Donahue improvised bulletins for the
newspapers.

Lance was less than two weeks old when a garbled letter was
delivered to her, warning that the baby would be kidnapped unless the anonymous writer was paid the equivalent of $1,000 in
British Treasury notes. It was a ludicrous sum to her, but she was
terrorized by the memory of what had happened to the Lindbergh
baby in 1932.

With Reventlow serving as stalking-horse, the police arrested
the amateur extortionist, but Barbara's fears could be allayed
only by building a retreat more secure than any rented place.
Fourteen private acres of Regent's Park promised to provide what
she was seeking. The century-old Regency mansion that stood
there was torn down, and Winfield House rose on its freshly laid
foundations, three floor levels underground. By this time, estimates of the final cost had reached $3,000,000.

She wavered just as her grandfather had done over any building project. The plans were revised and revised again exactly as
Cass Gilbert's had been. Fifteen rooms grew into fifty and then
sixty, each of them with its own telephone, while the number of
stories climbed from three to four. The completed nursery suite
was white and turquoise, and turquoise was the color of the immense swimming pool. There were music rooms, without a player-
organ, and more than enough marble to have satisfied Grandpa
Woolworth's whim. She shopped every day for treasures in furnishings, delighted on one expedition to find for the parquet-
floored drawing room an enormous carpet originally woven to the
order of Louis Quatorze. Reventlow grumbled that stepping on it
made him feel "as though I was walking on thousand-dollar bills."
The tennis courts were designed *in situ* by Baron Gottfried von
Cramm, a champion player in Hitler's Germany, who was another
of Barbara's husbands farther down the line.

While she had Frank's craze for building, his urge to get things
done and over with was altogether missing. Almost two years

passed before the house was finished in 1937. George VI was king now after the flight of his elder brother, dubbed the Duke of Windsor, to marry the former Mrs. Wallis Warfield Simpson of Baltimore, Maryland. Jimmy Donahue's desire to be his friend was inching along toward fulfilment.

For a while, the newspapers' stories of "the Woolworth heiress" took second place to coverage of the turmoil among employees of the company. Sitdown strikes had spread from France to America and into New York. Fifty clerks seized what Frank had once claimed to be "the largest ten-cent store in the world." The premises on West 14th Street were the site for a combined sit-in and hunger strike for a union shop and a rise in wages to $20 with the work week reduced to forty hours. A hundred more workers on the payroll paraded on the sidewalk outside on St. Patrick's Day. Placards held high above their heads asserted MISS HUTTON COUNTS MILLIONS WHILE FIVE-AND-TEN GIRLS COUNT TEN AND TWELVE DOLLAR SALARIES. The strike committee cabled Barbara, urging her to use influence she didn't possess to intervene with the management on the strikers' behalf. She sent no answer, but one more article in Frank's creed was about to be scrapped under pressure of protest—cheap labor.

One of his creations, the Empire Room, seemed isolated from the lashing storm of progress, like a ship model sealed in a glass bottle. Between the pilastered marble walls, everything but the portrait remained exactly as he had seen it on his last day at the desk that was now Charles Deyo's. A strict routine of cleaning and waxing kept "the handsomest office in the world" as pristine as when it had been assembled. There was a difference, however, in Deyo's increasing girth.

In these Napoleonic quarters, he was beset with as many problems as Bonaparte himself in his advances against the Russians at Poltusk and Eylau, but it was the Germans who daunted Deyo. Income from the eighty-two stores over there—nearly $2,000,000 in 1937—had to be excluded from company accounts because Hitler forbade the draining away of Reichsmarks.

Then Wright Patman introduced what was labeled "the death sentence bill." H.R. 9464, cosigned by more than seventy other congressmen, called for punitive taxes on all the chains. The formula was ingenious and lethal: $50 each on the tenth to fifteenth outlets, then progressive jumps in the levies until every outlet after the five-hundredth would pay an annual $1,000. Once a total had been computed on that basis, it was to be multiplied by the number of states into which the chain extended.

Woolworth accountants presented Deyo with their dismal calculations. In 1938, when the company had 1,864 stores in all forty-eight states and profits stood at $28,000,000, the tax would add up to *$81,000,000*. Only one other operation was threatened with a darker fate: with 12,000 groceries earning a little more than $9,000,000, the A. & P. would have to come up with $471,620,000.

A magazine of the trade, *Retailing,* concluded: "Chain stores are now confronted with the executioner's axe. If the bill just introduced by Representative Wright Patman is passed in anything like its present form, chain stores, as we know them, will pass out of the business picture within two years."

Recognizing that "a mighty effort is under way to smash the chains," *Business Week* summarized what was at stake. "Upon this effort the public must render judgment. It must make up its mind whether all the benefits of mass buying, mass distribution and mass retailing shall be destroyed in order to ensure that a multitude of small retailers, who are for the most part bad merchants, poorly financed, and ill equipped to give service, shall be subsidized at the expense of the ultimate consumer or whether the government shall permit some progress to be made in the direction of efficiency and cost reduction for the benefit of the people who go into stores every day and pay in pennies and nickels for the necessities of life."

For the present, H.R. 9464 stayed in the hopper. Deyo and his team kept the dividends flowing without interruption while they slowly realized that the bill offered the chains as a whole a rare opportunity to gain public support. Orchestrated propaganda over the radio, in the press and from the lecture platform spelled out the consequences of what Patman was attempting.

But Barbara was a constant hazard to every goodwill effort. When she appeared at the federal courthouse in Foley Square to declare herself a Dane, not an American, Woolworth workers in Brooklyn and Manhattan walked out on their jobs. BABS RENOUNCES AMERICAN CITIZENSHIP BUT NOT PROFITS, said the signs, and the strikers chanted, "While we're on strike for higher pay, Babs takes her millions and runs away."

If she hoped renunciation would preserve her marriage to Reventlow, it was a failure. The parting came after he threatened to shoot a Nazi admirer of hers, Prince Frederick of Prussia. She swore out a warrant for her husband's arrest on a charge of promising bodily harm to a British resident. Under the terms of separation, Lance would spend nine months of each year with her, three with his father, until a divorce emerged from the Danish courts.

Reventlow accepted the $500,000 she offered as the price of letting her take their son with her to safety after a call to Winfield House from Roosevelt's latest ambassador to Britain, Joseph Kennedy, warned her of imminent war with Germany. The rooms were stripped and the furniture carted off into storage. An armored car carried her jewelry to a vault in Coutts bank. She would donate the house and grounds for future use as the United States Embassy and never enter it again.

The fighting on land had come to a temporary standstill after Poland fell to the Nazi invaders, but U-boats prowled the Atlantic shipping lanes when the Italian liner *Conte de Savoia* brought Barbara and four-year-old Lance from Genoa to New York. Woolworth strikers closed in on the limousine that bore her from the pier to the Hotel Pierre on Fifth Avenue across from the Plaza, where she had lived at the age of four. In all her years she had never been exposed before to such venom—the screaming, the picket signs jabbed at her. BABS HUTTON FLEES EUROPE'S WAR, SEEKS PEACE. BUT HOW ABOUT PEACE WITH THE UNION? . . . BARBARA HUTTON! IS EIGHTEEN DOLLARS A WEEK TOO MUCH? . . . BABS! WOOLWORTH'S AGREED TO ARBITRATE YET REFUSED TO ABIDE BY THE AWARD WHEN IT LOST. IS THAT THE AMERICAN WAY?

"Do people realize," she snapped, "that I have no more to do with running the Woolworth stores than I have with the running of the British Empire?"

Aunt Jessie had her to dinner that night in the Donahue apartment at 834 Fifth Avenue, a duplex furnished gloriously but gloomily in the mode of Queen Anne, its walls hung with portraits of English nobility painted by eighteenth century masters. Jessie had two points to make. "I have found one husband to be all I wanted, and for you three is out of the question." She also recommended her niece try improving her reputation in America by hiring a specialist in that field. Steve Hannagan, public relations counselor, filled the prescription. Barbara paid him $60,000 a year for picturing her as a woman not entirely alien to the common run of humankind.

Jimmy Donahue was surprising those he termed "all the beautiful people" by taking flying lessons, training that would qualify him as a pilot in the Civil Air Patrol in the early days after Pearl Harbor. But the effort was not enough to save him from the draft. Jessie would provide the money to buy an airfield in Florida, seeking his deferment by claiming that his work in developing the facility constituted a "major war effort." His draft board disagreed; he was inducted into the Army as a PFC.

Hannagan did such a convincing job for Barbara that the Woolworth board might have been willing to vote him his fee. She took up knitting for French war relief and made an appearance with Lance at the New York World's Fair after it reopened in May 1940. She accepted Hannagan's advice to refrain from flaunting the biggest and best of her jewels in public, and she was suddenly more discreet about mentioning the parties she attended or gave. An item planted in a syndicated gossip column avowed that she had already donated $15,000,000 to worthwhile causes, which covered buying two dozen ambulances for the British and contributing to the American Red Cross. His influence led to her being listed among the world's best-dressed women, running ninth behind the winner, the Duchess of Windsor. Now and then, Barbara stumbled, as she did in the Hotel Mark Hopkins, San Francisco, when she presented a $10,000 bill to a bellboy.

More of the good work was undone on the death of her father. She was reluctant to fly down to Charlestown to see him on his shooting preserve outside the city, but she was talked into going. In reference to "my beloved daughter Barbara," his will declared, "any bequest of a monetary nature that I could make would be quite inconsequential. Therefore, I will to her a loving father's blessing for her future happiness." She proceeded to sue his estate for the return of an earlier loan she had made him. The court awarded her the $530,000 plus accrued interest at five percent.

Company rules were amended to retain Charles Deyo in office when he passed his sixtieth birthday in the same year that he celebrated victory in the struggle for survival under Wright Patman's challenge. The chains had obtained what they wanted—extensive public hearings—before his bill came to a vote. The sessions of a ways and means subcommittee lasted through most of the spring of 1940. The Department of Commerce spoke out against Patman, and its acting secretary, Edward Noble, explained why: "Failures due to unfair competition can find relief in laws already on the statute books prohibiting discriminatory selling practices, misleading advertising and other unethical methods of doing business."

On June 17, John W. McCormack, chairman of the subcommittee, pronounced a providential sentence of death on the "death sentence bill." The next ten years would be easier on Deyo than the past four had been, even when almost half the men who worked for Woolworth's went into uniform, four hundred women took on managers' jobs and dividends fell from an annual $2.40 to $1.60.

Of the six founders of the company, only Sum was left alive to see the New Year in. Fred Kirby, a widower, succumbed to pneumonia in October. His manner of living, calm and unpretentious, had been so unlike Frank's that they might have been born at opposite ends of the earth. The contrast showed up with equal clarity in the actions of their heirs.

Fred had given away more than $8,000,000, most of it for the advantage of his adopted hometown, Wilkes-Barre, which proclaimed a "Kirby Day" to honor him. Wilkes-Barre had a park and a $2,000,000 health center as a result of his charity. He conserved the startling flow of Woolworth cash by investing it in banks, railroads, lumber, telephone, gas and electric utilities—and poured it out into colleges, churches, hospitals.

His home, Thurlow House, was the pride of the local historical society. His most conspicuous extravagance was his yacht *Suzanne*, with a crew of fourteen. In the previous war, it had been refitted and handed over to the United States Navy. In the coming war with Japan and Germany, the Navy would see both his sons, his principal heirs, in uniform.

Sum Woolworth reminisced about a lost friend. "He walked to and from work every day, even in bitter winter weather such as we used to have in northern New York, through deep drifted snow. I often went home to spend the night in the Kirby's old fashioned, one-and-one-half story stone house. His mother was one of the nicest women I ever knew, a woman of fine character. I remember especially that each morning for breakfast we had toast, Fred's favorite dish, and nothing ever tasted so good."

Cast in a mold like Kirby's, Sum was signing away millions, too, for schooling, medical care and church groups in Scranton. He earmarked $100,000 for Syracuse University because it extended "splendid opportunities to the young people of my old home county of Jefferson."

Of Frank, Sum, Seymour, Earle Charlton, and Fred Kirby . . . Fred's grandson and namesake wrote in 1981: "In all previous, published accounts I have read, the importance of the contributions of the last four has been underplayed in dramatizing the remarkable talents and performance of the first one."

16

❦ Ends and Beginnings ❧

The signature of King Christian of Denmark on a sheaf of lawyers' paper put an end to Barbara's marriage to Reventlow on grounds of "incompatibility of temperament." It was a news item relegated to a paragraph or two. The Hannagan defense line protecting her from adverse publicity held firm.

Cracks in those defenses developed when she rented the house once owned by Buster Keaton on Benedict Canyon Road in Beverly Hills, California, and invited a few hundred people to the party she gave to celebrate the thirty-seventh birthday of a debonair, dimpled actor, the former Archibald Leach, known now as Cary Grant.

She had met him on a similar social evening in New York when the hostess was Dorothy di Frasso, who was as partial to matchmaking as the acknowledged champion at the game, Elsa Maxwell. Grant, in Cousin Jimmy's opinion, was the most charming fellow he had ever seen.

She was delighted to travel through Mexico with her new admirer, the only man in what became a string of seven husbands who could afford to support himself in Hutton style without being subsidized. Cuernavaca, an hour's drive from Mexico City, left such an impression on her that she decided to build a house there.

The tabloids tagged them "Cash and Cary" when they were pronounced man and wife in an unheralded six-minute ceremony

202

at Lake Arrowhead on July 8, 1942. The only available photographs were distributed by the motion-picture studio for which he was starring in a production entitled *Once Upon a Honeymoon.* Barbara, her son and the bridegroom settled down in another rented place, this one on Amalfi Drive in Beverly Hills, where Douglas Fairbanks Junior was their landlord.

Grant, who shied away from publicity, thought she was throwing money away on her public relations counselor, so Hannagan was promptly written out of the script.

She concluded later in life that Cary was the husband she had loved best. She wanted a child by him, but she declined a course of treatment her doctor urged on her. After three miscarriages, she gave up that ambition. She played at being a homebody, knitting socks for Cary while he spent the evening studying the script for his next day's work. Party-going did not appeal to him; at the few they went to together, she was bored by the endless shop talk about movies and the people who made or financed them. She missed the company of the idlers and intriguers who were her only friends, Elsa and Dorothy and the rest of them who lived as if the war against the Nazis and Japanese were being fought on a different planet.

Under all his professional charm, Cary, she decided, was a businessman. "All the men I know are businessmen," she complained, "or want to be businessmen. Once they marry a girl, they wrap themselves up in their business." She owed the material things she possessed to a man of business named Frank Woolworth, but she preferred to dismiss the thought over a martini or two before dinner.

The defense line developed by Hannagan was weakened again when Drew Pearson, a Washington columnist who specialized in unearthing scandal, disclosed that American intelligence agents had recorded the telephone calls she had been placing from Cuernavaca to a German baron whom he identified only as a Nazi. The point was clarified later: the baron was Gottfried von Cramm, just released from a year in prison following his arrest by the Gestapo on a charge of pederasty.

In a Los Angeles courtroom on August 30, 1945, her allegation of "mental cruelty" went uncontested by Grant. It took her ten minutes to obtain a decree of divorce from the only spouse who neither asked for nor received alimony of any kind. "I shall never remarry," she said. His hopes for her, expressed afterward, were appropriate. "I shall be so pleased," he said, "when I see her smiling and happy with someone she loves or even smiling without someone."

The service flag of Woolworth's was emblazoned by then with 5,848 stars, and sales that year touched $477,000,000. Charles Deyo's presidency was nearing its close. Hard-eyed Alfred Cornwell, who had been introduced to the business as a learner in the stockroom of the Worcester, Massachusetts, store back in 1905, would take Deyo's place.

Next spring Barbara, eager to be interviewed, was back with Jimmy Donahue in her familiar suite in the Hotel Ritz. "All my life," she said, "I've been bullied by men—first by my father, then by my husbands, because unfortunately I'm the sort of person who can't stand scenes. At least, that's how it was until a few weeks ago. I never expected to see Paris again, and here it is. . . . It's like a city in a dream."

She roamed the streets alone and unnoticed, clad in plebeian ankle socks, tennis shoes, shorts and sweatshirt. She strolled back one morning through the main entrance into the hotel lobby, where the visiting king of Cambodia was being welcomed with full protocol by morning-coated ministers of the French government. When a foreign ministry staff man tried to steer her away from the group, she stared him down. "Excuse me, I have the same rights as a king."

A former sovereign came into closer orbit in those days. The Duke of Windsor and his duchess made it a practice to spend winters in New York, summers in Europe, though never in England. Jimmy Donahue, on a similar timetable, gravitated toward them like a shooting star.

The strain of his finances was relieved when he inherited $15,000,000 at the age of thirty-five. Since he had always behaved as if he were already a multimillionaire, the windfall brought little change to his personal style, but he could play the host now more often than the guest. He dabbled as both producer and backer of shows on Broadway. Instead of giving shape to his own fantasies in marble and mortar, he bought a ready-made house from Alfred Gwynne Vanderbilt for $400,000, then spent as much again on refurnishing the twenty-nine rooms of Broad Hollow on the hundred-acre property near Cedar Swamp Road in Old Brookville, Long Island.

There was one clear distinction between the way he and Cousin Babs entertained. Jimmy was inclined to invite "all the beautiful people" in for the sake of a charity he supported—as an example, the Metropolitan Opera House at Lincoln Center, New York, for which he raised $100,000. He was also more willing than Barbara to scurry in and out of spotlights as a public benefactor. He made telethon appearances for the Cerebral Palsy Fund, drumming up pledges phoned in by the audience by promising to match them, dollar for dollar.

Jimmy, also linked in the public's mind with Woolworth's, gave the company board no cause for concern about invidious publicity. Marriage held no attraction for him, and his affection for men was a matter of gossip among the beautiful people, never referred to in headlines.

He served the Windsors much the same as he did Barbara, as the dependable, accommodating third member of the party. "Jimmy," in a columnist's arch comment, "escorts the D. and D. everywhere and stays up playing cards with the duchess even after his Royal Highness has retired."

In New York, the duchess and the Windsor's newfound friend dined together in such modish chophouses as Le Pavillon and the Colony, where one evening he brought in a musical trio to serenade them at their table. He took her dancing at El Morocco and Gogi's Larue. On a Christmas Eve, he led her and the duke, once the temporal head of the Church of England, into St. Patrick's Cathedral for a midnight mass in Donahue's own Catholic faith.

He was at their side all around the circuit, in Paris and San Sebastian, Spain. He infected Wallis with his enthusiasm for collecting eighteenth-century snuffboxes, which were a conversation piece in his Old Brookville house. One of them, purportedly used by an earlier king of England, George IV, and bought by Jessie, became one more gift of his for the duchess.

Jessie, delighted by her son's eminence in reflected glory, was alleged to have offered to pay for redecorating Wallis's bedroom in the old *moulin* that the Windsors took over and renovated at Marly-le-Roi, a few miles outside Paris. With her wad of

Woolworth stock, Jessie was better placed financially than the duke, whose private fortune was estimated at only $5,000,000, supplemented by untaxed income of roughly $250,000 a year.

The pumping out of company dividends, fifty cents a share every quarter, never skipped a beat as the 1940s gave way to the 1950s. The presidency passed from Cornwell to one more former bookkeeper, James Leftwich, and the rumblings of a revolution in retailing began to sound on every Main Street in America. The mass movement of population out of the cities into the suburbs was as significant for the future of Woolworth's as the inflow of immigrants had been to Frank.

Traffic downtown was getting so snarled that shoppers stayed clear whenever they could. Sprawling conglomerations of stores mushroomed in what had been cow pastures and orchards a decade earlier. Within a few years these malls, as they came to be called, would account for more than $50 billion in annual sales, twenty-five percent of American retailing.

The five-and-ten as Frank had envisioned it was crumbling like a sand castle caught by the tide. Inside any one of them, things seemed much the same. The air still smelled of cosmetics and candy and toast and coffee on the burners behind the luncheonette counters that stretched along the walls.

Everything for sale was arranged precisely—alignments of pots and pans, ranks of laces and ribbons, platoons of notebooks and Fifth Avenue Linen stationery, brigades of rainbow-colored plastic utensils for kitchen, bathroom and yard. No displays impeded progress through the aisles. There was a girl ready to wait on every customer—self-service was a concept whose time had yet to arrive.

It was no more than truth to state, as a latter-day brochure did, "What the bazaar was to the Middle East, Woolworth's was to America." But the variety store as a species was endangered.

The company was slow to assess the gravity of the challenge. Some analysts blamed that deficiency on a legacy of Frank's, the system of promotion. When only a learner could expect to occupy the president's chair, the result was bureaucracy, management made up of discreet, soft-spoken "Woolworth men" with a civil service mentality. They played it safe, sheltered from the outside world, stiff and closemouthed with shareholders and the press. Then, though Woolworth's had 2,850 stores and sales of

$700,000,000, the challenge of change could be ducked no longer if the company hoped to save itself.

Barbara also persisted in her established way of living. Now she owned a Moorish palace in the native quarter of Tangier, bought for $100,000, which was one of the few bargains ever to come her way.

She had gone through two more marriages, the first to Igor Troubetzkoy, whom Elsa assured her was a prince of royal Lithuanian blood; he had also once been the ace racing bicyclist of France before their wedding in St. Moritz, Switzerland, in February 1947. She arranged the usual celebratory party at her habitual lodging place in Paris, the Hotel Ritz, and ordered a repetition of the menu served at her twenty-second birthday gathering, now thirteen years past. This romance and her physical condition ebbed together. The three bouts of surgery she underwent left her sterile. Troubetzkoy was paid off with a $1,000-a-month trust fund.

She had been freed of him for a year when she went with Elsa to watch an afternoon of polo played on the field at Deauville. One of the riders was a Dominican friend of Troubetzkoy's, overbearing, overmuscled Porfirio Rubirosa, ex-husband of the French actress Danielle Darrieux and of Doris Duke. Elsa experienced a feeling of *déjà vu*: didn't Rubi remind Barbara of Alex Mdivani? A man like Rubi would do her more good than any doctor's prescription.

She wore Balenciaga black to the New York ceremony on December 30, 1953, and she broke an ankle that night in a bathroom of the Hotel Pierre. His attentions to her were diverted by his preoccupation with Zsa Zsa Gabor, a Hungarian by birth and an actress of sorts who vowed that Rubirosa loved her, not Barbara. Seventy-three days of it was enough. The parting payment of $2,000,000 he received from his dejected wife had been lost in gambling when—*déjà vu* again—he died behind the wheel of an automobile.

Aunt Jessie wrote her, "You absolutely cannot get married a sixth time," but when Gottfried von Cramm showed willing so did Barbara. He bore a strong resemblance to Reventlow except in the matter of sexual preference, and she felt it safer to relive the past than take chances on an uncertain future. Only her choice of site for the wedding was different: it took place in Versailles, close by the palace built by Louis XIV that Grandpa Woolworth's hero, Napoleon, allowed to fall into disrepair.

Her latest husband took her to meet his family in Germany. She tried to gain their affection with a gift of $1,000,000 for the restoration of bomb-damaged castles the von Cramms still owned, but to these defeated Germans an American heiress was less lovable than a mongrel dog. The settlement she made on him when they were divorced in 1961 was a standardized $2,000,000.

"We live Woolworth," said the new occupant of the Empire Room. Forceful, friendly, sixty-five-year-old James Leftwich, with his conservative suits and G.I. haircut, had been leading the company life as another former recruit to the bookkeeping department. The incentive scheme still operated: no executive from store manager to president was on salary but was rewarded by commission on profits earned by his individual sphere of authority. (A senior manager took home $75,000 a year.)

"We Woolworth men feel," Leftwich said, "as if we were spending from our own pockets." But spend they must, and borrow on the market, too, to stay in step. Damage done by Barbara's notoriety had been discounted long ago. Leftwich had bigger problems.

Labor was one of them. Annual turnover in the work force was a stultifying forty-three percent as salesgirls quit, complaining about lack of opportunity for women. Long-term leases on stores made it hard to pull up stakes and follow the customers' flight to suburbia. "There are two hundred stores that Woolworth would be happy to give you if you'd take these leases off their hands," one executive confided. And the vast bulk of sales came on items priced at $3 or less, which pared profits thin.

One change made by the new chief executive would have been dismissed by Frank without discussion. Woolworth's organized its first systematic advertising program, on radio, in magazines, and then in newspapers. Too many years of playing things Frank's way, leaving it to the goods to sell themselves, had reduced the company from its former place as fifth biggest among all American chains to a humbler place as number seven. The past could no longer dictate the terms of doing business. The order of the day was innovation.

There was long debate before "serve yourself" was introduced.

An echo of Frank's fears resounded in the words of one board member after clerks had been taken out from behind the counters and cashiers were relocated by the exit doors: "We are a temptation for every child to steal something. That is the price we pay for the privilege of displaying our merchandise."

Price-tag limits were abolished and tests started of a revolving credit plan, a clear necessity when customers were being tempted with television sets, carpeting and sporting equipment, cans of paint, shoes, clothing, diamond rings, caviar and mynah birds ($44.95).

Some sort of record for opulence was set when the Menlo Park, New Jersey, branch pulled in three thousand visitors a day to a two-week sale of five hundred Old Master paintings, valued at half a million dollars and staged in a basement gallery on easels watched over by a club-carrying guard. Artists represented included Renoir ($1,900 for one of his watercolors), Van Gogh (a pastel offered at $1,000), Cézanne (an $1,800 landscape) and Brueghel the Younger (his "Town Meeting" bore the top price—$150,000).

"I had imagined," the manager said, "that some people might think it inconceivable—or at any rate, presumptuous—for Woolworth's to be doing this, but we've had an amazingly generous reception." He reported the comment of a male customer who found to his amazement that a Renoir he was interested in had already been sold. "What kind of store is this?" he demanded. Said the manager: "You would have thought he was shopping for a can opener."

As a means of impressing readers—and investors—with the staggering heft of the corporation, the strewing of statistics like corn fed to a poultry flock continued without letup. Woolworth's, it was reported, was the world's largest server of food, dispensing 109,000,000 cups of coffee in 1958; sold more dolls (9,768,151 in 1961) than any other retailer anywhere, more brassieres (7,000,000 that same year), more pairs of panties (38,000,000).

Pressure from competitors increased, as if hungry wolves were closing in on an ailing moose. The leader of the pack was clearly Kresge's, whose founder old Sebastian the teetotaler, was still active in his nineties as honorary chairman. With its K-Mart department stores, Kresge would shortly claim to be the most successful

discounter on the world scene, pioneering in a field that
Woolworth's had left unexplored. When James Leftwich retired as
both president and chairman at the age of sixty-eight, there were
those in the board room who felt he had overstayed his welcome.

There was no change yet in the hallowed practice of filling the
two uppermost offices with men who had risen through the company's civil service, but the "start in the stockroom" regulation
was abandoned. Recruiting teams began to tour colleges and uni-
versities on the lookout for graduates to train in chain management. Woolworth's made a late entry into discounting in 1962 by
opening the first links in a new chain of low-margin department
stores—Woolco. The total reached 318 in 1980, but they operated
at a loss from the start. They also posed an unforeseen problem of
identity. The company was wearing two hats, one as a variety outlet, the other as a discounter—"the luxury of ambivalence," in one
critic's description.

Ambivalence was a luxury that Barbara regarded as part of
her rightful inheritance. "Ambivalent," was a polite description of
her relationship with the next man to impinge on her life. Lloyd
Franklin, English and able-bodied, was twenty years old and she
was forty-eight when she ran across him one night in a Tangier
bar, where he earned a meager living with his baritone voice and
his guitar. Dawn was tinting the sky as she asked him to go back
with her to her place in the Casbah.

A month later, her money had transformed him, like a mascu-
line version of Eliza Doolittle, into an amateur gentleman with an
acquired taste for polo. For almost four years, she took him with
her on the preordained rounds on which she existed—Paris, London, Venice, Mexico, Los Angeles. Then she heard that in Deauville he was acting like another Rubirosa, combining polo with an
affair with a maharani. She ordered her servants to bar him from
every house she owned and quickly found one more husband.

Doan Vinh Na Champassak, an artist by profession, had the
sturdy good looks of an Occidental athlete, though he had arrived
in Tangier from his native Laos. She referred to him as "prince"
and resumed the title of "princess," which did not deter the headline writers from continuing to call her "Babs," after a poolside
wedding at her Japanese hacienda in Cuernavaca. When they
parted two years later, he said with an air of dignity, "She gave
me more than four million dollars. She gave me love."

Soon afterward—on December 11, 1966—Jimmy Donahue, the only man who had given her undemanding love of a rarefied kind, died in his mother's Fifth Avenue apartment. His boyish good looks had long since been ravaged by years of alcoholism, augmented by the taking of barbiturates to ward off the depression that attacked him when he reviewed the emptiness of his existence.

He had attempted to disguise his sexual habits by escorting any number of pretty girls around the circuits of high-flying society. The pretense was abandoned at discreet gatherings where he was apt to kiss the men as well as the women. He was also a regular patron of clubs catering to the gay trade, notably the Manhattan hideaways of "Madame Fox" and "George."

His father had ended his life at the age of forty-four. Jimmy had hung on for seven years longer. Once again, the circumstances of death among the Woolworth's were obscured in the reporting. There were neither signs of violence nor visible evidence of poison. "Visceral congestion" was the explanation offered before the autopsy, whose results went unpublished. The medical examiner, in fact, attributed "acute alcohol and barbiturate poisoning, circumstances undetermined" as the cause. Jimmy had swallowed a massive overdose of Seconal.

Jessie from then on chose her own way of retreating from a world in which she had received little she had not paid for. She hid herself in the apartment, with the curtains permanently drawn in every room, to live in senility for five more years.

In 1972, Lance Reventlow was killed in a plane crash; in 1973 cancer took Woolworth Donahue. With no relative left or anyone else with whom she felt intimacy, Barbara holed up in the Beverly Wilshire Hotel in Los Angeles. She had the windows of her suite lined with foil to keep out the sunlight and the lamp shades dimmed with pink paper napkins. Her flirtation with alcohol and sleeping pills was overcome, but she insisted on her Coca-Cola being served with round ice cubes because square ones repelled her. She whispered that her telephones were bugged and her incoming mail examined before delivery. She spread the word that she was broke.

Although the business her grandfather had propagated nearly a century ago was safe from being caught in a similar predicament, it had to hurdle some financial obstacles. It had taken over

Kinney Shoes, the country's largest retailer of footwear, and Richmond Brothers, which was in the same enviable position in the manufacture and sale of ready-to-wear clothes for men. Yet Woolworth's ranked fourth in the 1973 retail stakes that gave Sears a mile-wide lead, trailed by J. C. Penney and Kresge's. Woolworth's profit margins of 1.8 percent were too small to generate capital for further expansion, so more borrowing had to be done.

The first generation of college-educated executives to work at headquarters measured the chain's efficiency with business-school yardsticks to find what a square foot of floor space earned in a year. "We'd love to get $100 per square foot in sales or even $75," one of them confided. "But we get $57.82."

Income from the British holdings was declining. The average American branch was overstaffed and the company so big that neither right nor left hand knew what the other was doing. "If I could pick my competition for myself," said a Wall Street scrutineer, "it would be Woolworth. They're the easiest."

Some drastic new move had to be made for the sake of self-preservation. It was done by scrapping promotion from within and appointing the first noncareer Woolworth man as president. When burly, bespectacled Edward Gibbons, who had served his time with United Brands, took up office in the Empire Room in 1975, Woolworth's was the only so-called five-and-ten surviving in America. He predicted a healthy future. The variety store, he insisted, "is alive, kicking and getting better all the time."

A few months afterward, he resigned, his weight down by forty-five pounds, a victim, according to his doctors' speculating, either of undetected heart attacks or cancer. They discovered, instead, that he had a hiatal hernia, which they treated, and he returned to work as chairman of the board. Feet up on the Napoleonic desk, he would joke over a cup of coffee that market analysts and the investing public were as wrong about the company as the medical profession had been about him.

"Any damn fool can destroy as he builds," he said. He had an unequivocal message to deliver: "Gibbons is here to save old Frank Woolworth's empire, not to liquidate it." It was an act of courage when brokers were claiming the whole company could probably be bought for a trifle more than half a billion dollars, whereas Kresge's K-Mart, with forty-three percent more in sales, had five times that market value. But Gibbons was reputed to be a good man with figures.

In 1978, during his first stretch as chairman, he chalked up earnings of $130,000,000 on sales of more than $6 billion, a better than fifty percent improvement over the previous twelve months. This, he knew, left company stock seriously undervalued. "That makes you a sitting duck," he said. A takeover bid was bound to be made by somebody. One question was *who?* and another *when?*

On May 11 in the centennial year of what had once been her grandfather's business, a heart attack killed Barbara. After the arrivals and departures of seven husbands, none of them American born, she had reconciled herself to solitude. "The biggest worry in a woman's life when she becomes sick and old is not loneliness," she concluded as she reflected on her condition. "The most pressing worry is lawyers. Lawyers suddenly don't want just a piece of cake but the whole cake. They are far more lethal than those greedy husbands I had."

The "strong genes and vigor" which she claimed to have inherited from Grandpa Woolworth were a myth. If there was any unusual genetic legacy, it resulted in an unbalanced mind. The symptoms in Frank's case were megalomania; Barbara in old age had grown paranoid, blaming a mysterious conspiracy of strangers for keeping her friends from the Beverly Wilshire Hotel. Her fame proved as fitful as her sanity. When her body was borne to a mortuary for embalming, the attendants were unaware of exactly who was sixty-six-year-old Mrs. Doan, as she was named on the death certificate.

The *New York Times*, observing the preferences of feminists, called her "the Woolworth heir" in its obituary. She was buried in the Woodlawn mausoleum built too late to receive her grandfather.

The expected assault on the chain had been launched from across the Canadian border a month earlier; it grew more intimidating as the days passed. The Toronto-based conglomerate Branscan Limited aimed to take Woolworth's at a conqueror's price of $35 paid in cash for every share of stock, for a total of well over a billion dollars.

The declaration of battle came in a telephone call from Brascan chairman John Moore to Gibbons, who sat slouched behind his desk in shirtsleeves. "Grossly inadequate," he retorted before he hung up. It was an audacious statement when, though the book value of a share was $38, its current quoted price was down to $20.

He had aged unbelievably since he assumed top command. He pushed the buttons to deploy his defenses. "We set the ground rules and arranged the division of labor. Some would do the worrying and work on the tender. That would be my job. The rest would dedicate themselves to keeping the sales and earnings up."

Branscan settled down to besiege its hoped-for prey, trusting to pick off so many stockholders eager to make a quick financial killing that control would slip from Gibbons's hands. But he stood tough, and after seven weeks victory was his, won by a counterattack from a different quarter, not on Woolworth's but on Branscan.

The Canadian firm had $400,000,000 in accumulated cash in readiness to pay out in a *coup de grâce*, which made the assailants more vulnerable than the defenders. Branscan became the takeover target of other acquisitors, Edper Equities, controlled by a Dutch mining company and two Bronfman brothers, Edward and Peter, members of a Canadian family synonymous with Seagram's international liquor interests. Edper struck hard to increase its stake in Branscan from five to thirty-one percent and, in the process, called off the advance against Woolworth.

"We believe," said a coolly impartial recommendation by a brokerage house in July 1980, "that F. W. Woolworth has reached a turning point in its performance and perception by investors." What Frank had spent his working lifetime assembling was still holding on to its independence.

* * *

No ghosts of the Woolworths of Jefferson County haunt a Woolco store today. Cars are parked on the deserts of asphalt outside, and customers make their way in through the enclosed mall where potted greenery struggles to survive and attendants scoop up discarded cigarette butts and candy wrappers. Doors as such have been done away with in a Woolco, replaced by walls of glass slid into place after closing time. Feet are cushioned by carpeting laid everywhere except on the approaches to the toilets, the telephones or the credit department. The layout of the floor, a single, unbroken shopping area that seems as big as a baseball field, is cunning. A labyrinth of racks and stacks and island displays slows down shoppers and entices them into looking around to surrender to the impulse to buy something, anything—a name-brand dress or an electronic game, a bicycle or a patio set, a tennis racket or a pair of spectacles. The only staff in sight are stockroom boys and the cashiers who finger the keyboards of the computerized registers. The lights are bright as the sun, the music soft; the announcements made over the sound system of fresh bargains going on sale throughout the day are gently persistent.

There will be at least thirty new Woolcos opened every year if company plans are realized, each of them scheduled to contribute to revenues an annual average of $77 from every square foot of floor space. Virtues worshipped by the founder before wealth blurred his vision—Yankee thrift, frugality, cash on the barrelhead—are as dead as he is. The five-and-ten has gone the way of the village pump, the zinc bathtub, Barbara's inheritance, and the flightless, lame-brained dodo bird.

Acknowledgments

While the conclusions, judgments of character and inter-
pretations of events are the author's alone except where they are
otherwise identified, invaluable help in research is most gratefully
acknowledged. The people who have contributed include F. M.
Kirby; Seymour H. Knox; John B. Johnson of the *Watertown Daily
Times*; and Evelyn H. Nunes, staff writer on that newspaper.

The most important single work of reference proved to be *Five
and Ten* by John K. Winkler (New York, Robert M. McBride &
Company, 1940). Also consulted were *McBrier Genealogy* by Edwin
Merton McBrier; *From Dimes to Millions* by Frank W. Woolworth
(an unfinished autobiography written in collaboration with Edward Mott Wooley); *The Woolworth Story* by Robert R. Kirkwood
and R. John Berridge, published in the *Christian Science Monitor,*
March 30 to April 4, 1959; numerous brochures and annual reports of F. W. Woolworth Co., including *Woolworth's First 75 Years*
and *100th Anniversary*; the July 7, 1980, analysis of that company
prepared by Kidder, Peabody & Co., Incorporated; *The Great Merchants* by Tom Mahoney and Leonard Sloane, (New York, Harper
& Row and Reader's Digest Association, 1951); *Chain Stores in
America* by Godfrey M. Lebhar (New York, Chain Store Publish-
ing Corporation, 1963); *Million Dollar Baby* by Philip van Rensse-
laer (New York, G. P. Putnam's Sons, 1979); *Barbara Hutton* by
Dean Jennings (New York, Frederick Fell, Inc., 1968); *Heiress* by
William Wright (Washington, D.C., New Republic Books, 1978);
Gone With the Windsors by Iles Brody (Philadelphia, the John C.
Winston Company, 1953); *Incredible New York* by Lloyd Morris
(New York, Random House, 1951); *This Was New York!* by Max-

well F. Marcuse (New York, LIM Press, 1969); *The Vanderbilts and Their Fortunes* by Edwin P. Hoyt (New York, Doubleday & Company, Inc., 1962); *The World's Tallest Building* by Spencer Klaw, published in *American Heritage,* February 1977; *Skyline Queen and the Merchant Prince* by John Peter Nichols (New York, Trident, 1974); *The Grand Emporiums* by Robert Hendrickson (New York, Stein & Day, 1979); *Encyclopaedia Britannica; Presidents of the United States* (American Heritage Publishing Co., Inc., 1968).

Source material was also culled from *The New York Times, Current Opinion, World's Work, Everybody's, American Magazine, McBride's, Literary Digest, Architectural Record, System, Magazine of Business, Business Week, The Nation, News Week* and *Newsweek, Time, Collier's, Fortune, Reader's Digest, The New Yorker, Dun's Review, Nation's Business, Forbes, Maclean's.* Much is owed, too, to a series of articles by Evelyn Nunes printed in the *Watertown Daily Times,* May 29 to June 12, 1979 and to the *Watertown Daily Times* for providing early photographs.

While it may be obvious that such detail went unrecorded, it is emphasized in the interests of accuracy that dialogue reported in some of the foregoing scenes has been extrapolated from firmly established fact.

About the Author

James Brough is the author of the bestseller *An Untold Story* (with Elliott Roosevelt), *The Prince and the Lily, Princess Alice, The Vixens,* and *Miss Lillian Russell.* He lives in Massachusetts.

☙ Index ☙